LABOUR PARTY PLC

LABOUR PARTY PLC

Party of Business

David Osler

MAINSTREAM
PUBLISHING

EDINBURGH AND LONDON

Copyright © David Osler, 2002
All rights reserved
The moral right of the author has been asserted

First published in Great Britain in 2002 by
MAINSTREAM PUBLISHING COMPANY (EDINBURGH) LTD
7 Albany Street
Edinburgh EH1 3UG

ISBN 1 84018 600 3

. A catalogue record for this book is available from the British Library

Typeset in Stone
Printed and bound in Great Britain by
Creative Print Design Wales

CONTENTS

ACKNOWLEDGEMENTS

THANKS for help in various ways is due to Paul Anderson, Janine Booth, John Booth, Anna Chen, John Connolly, Lawrie Coombes, Liz Davies, Henry Drucker, Mark Fischer, Paul Foot, Steve Godward, Tim Gopsill, Phil Hamilton, Will Hutton, Tim and Justine Finke, John Lister, Kevin Maguire, Nyta Mann, Mike Marqusee, Andy McSmith, Peter Oborne, Greg Palast, Dave Parks, Harry Paterson, Tim Pendry, Robin Ramsay, Tom Rigby, Gareth Robertson, Brian Reyes, Lee Rock, Charles Shaar Murray, Mark Seddon and all the team at *Tribune*, David Shaw, Martin Thomas, John Underwood, Pete and Deb Wieland, Roland Wood and a number of others who prefer not to be named. The Red Star Research website, the *Tribune* archives and *Labour Research* magazine were also godsends.

Julian Bray – editor of *Lloyd's List* – has surely cut hundreds of years off his time in purgatory by allowing me a sabbatical and subsequent virtual flexitime in order to get this book finished. My colleagues at the world's oldest daily newspaper are also due gratitude, especially fellow reporters forced to pick up my workload during my extended absences. Thanks also to my agent Robert Dudley, and to all at Mainstream, including Bill Campbell, Jessica Thompson, Ailsa Bathgate for a fantastic job of editing and Tina Hudson for a great cover.

As is traditional, the author dutifully acknowledges his other half Sarah Finke and daughter Rachel, victims respectively of partner and parent neglect during long months of book-writing. Thanks also to Trish and Tony Finke for babysitting above and beyond the call of duty. Responsibility for any errors or omissions rests with me and me alone, although Clissold Wines may be guilty of contributory negligence.

FOREWORD

Shortly before the 1997 general election I was chatting confidentially to a senior politician in the Labour Party, who told me the following story. Quite recently, he said, he had addressed a huge meeting of ecstatic Labour Party members. His theme was the scandal of corruption and patronage in the Tory government. To illustrate the extent of the scandal, he revealed that when Labour took office the Prime Minister and the leading Secretaries of State in the new government would have at least 10,000 jobs entirely at their disposal. He studied his audience as he spoke, expecting a deep sense of shock and outrage. To his horror, the chief reaction seemed to be one of eager anticipation and delight. Thousands of jobs for us! What a thrill!

The history of British politics over the last five years has been dominated by the excited and satisfied hopes of those thousands of Labour activists. The Labour Party came into existence to represent trade unionists and socialists in Parliament. In the various periods before 1997 when they have achieved office with a parliamentary majority, the influence of those socialists and trade unionists, though waning, has at least been detectable enough to worry big business and their media. All that worry has now gone. Systematically and with tremendous application and dedication, New Labour has striven to tear up the roots left by Old Labour and to turn itself into a business party every bit as credible and friendly to big business as the Tories had been. In the course of this endeavour, Labour's historic commitment to the trade unions and to socialists has been erased. Not a single one of the anti-union acts passed under Thatcher or Major has been repealed. As for socialism, the very word has effectively been banned from Labour circles.

The details of this process have not been highlighted in the media or by political commentators, most of whom come from the New Labour stable. Now and again there is a flurry of media interest in a political scandal. The million-pound donation to Labour from motor racing millionaire (and Tory) Bernie Ecclestone followed by a reversal of the party's policy on tobacco advertising was one example. Another was the strange story of the billionaire Hinduja brothers and their successful passport application after a hefty contribution to the Dome. Even these matters have not been properly run down or exposed in anything like as thorough or convincing a manner as they are in this book. But even that is not the book's main achievement. Dave Osler, a working journalist whose socialist commitment has grown more and more indignant, has traced the entire story of the transformation of the Labour Party from a social democracy into a party that has dropped every vestige of commitment to socialism or democracy. He turns over the individual heroes one by one: Maxwell, Robinson, Levy, Murdoch, Hollick, Mittal, Mandelson, Draper etc. etc., but he is far too perceptive for the usual 'rotten apples in the barrel' analysis. He takes the story on from a few glimpses of individual influence to a critique of what is happening to British society in general. His most illuminating passages take the story on from the vast web of Labour lobbyists and spin doctors to the effective privatisation of whole tracts of previously public enterprise such as transport and health by means of the sinister Private Finance Initiative (PFI). His conclusion is as devastating as it is justified by his prodigious research. The whole barrel is rotten. 'New Labour is institutionally corrupt' and has dragged the British party system down to the level of the United States. Where there is no difference between two big political machines paid for by big business, ordinary people's interests in and involvement in politics collapses. Less people vote and less people care. All politics becomes contemptible, and the way is open for the racialist and the dictator.

This book is a must not just for every political commentator but for everyone who wants to understand how and why the Labour Party has dropped so low.

Paul Foot
July 2002

INTRODUCTION

BUSINESS support for New Labour is now officially a morality-free zone. Questioned over whether the party should have accepted a £100,000 gift from the wealthy pornographer behind such doubtlessly wholesome magazines as *The Very Best of Mega Boobs* and *Spunk-Loving Sluts*, one cabinet minister retorted: 'If you are asking if we are going to sit in moral judgement and have a political judgement on those who contribute to the Labour Party, the answer is no.'[1]

Perhaps it would have been better if political judgement *had* been exercised. The decision to take the money and run must have cost at least 100,000 votes. But then, why single out pornomerchants as any worse than the tobacco advertising lobby, sundry union-bashers, arms manufacturers, or businesses accused of human rights abuses in the Third World?

Founded just over 100 years ago as the Labour Representation Committee, with the express aim of securing parliamentary representation for the working class and the unions, the Labour Party nowadays describes itself as many things. But among the definitions it habitually bestows upon itself, Labour is adamant that it is now 'the party of business'. This soundbite can be heard in numerous Blair speeches. And every time the Prime Minister boasts that Labour is the party of business, he is effectively saying that Labour is the party of the Private Finance Initiative (PFI), the party of the World Trade Organisation, and the party of Rupert Murdoch.

This ideological paradigm shift has been accompanied by important changes in Labour's sources of finance. The party has gone from almost total reliance on union donations to more than matching the Conservatives pound for pound when it comes to coaxing senior executives into writing seven-figure cheques.

In the crucial quarter leading up to the 2001 election, three fabulously rich men supplied more money than all trade unions put together, donating £6.1m between them. That marginally topped the £6m given by affiliated unions, with millions of members between them. In the event, union donations accounted for 35 per cent of New Labour's 2001 election spend, just half the corresponding figure for 1992. It all brings a whole new meaning to the old socialist slogan of 'make the rich pay'.

The corollary is that the political concerns of wealthy individuals now carry greater weight than those of organised labour. The talk is all of partnership with the private sector, with unions stigmatised as 'vested interests' and 'wreckers' leaving scars on the poor old Prime Minister's back.

It wasn't always this way. At some point during the 1970 election campaign, a small boy interrupted a political programme being broadcast on his family's black and white telly to ask his father what the difference was between Labour and the Tories. The late Johnny Osler, active in the National Union of Railwaymen, told me that the Conservatives were the party for people with money; Labour was the party for those who worked for a living. Millions of people will have similar childhood recollections. Further millions will remember being told that Labour represented the great unwashed and otherwise feckless, and that the Conservatives rightly stood up for shopkeepers, small businessmen, middle managers, company directors, or whatever the hell it is that kids unfortunate enough to be born into Tory families get told.

Of course, it was never that simple. Even under Wilson, a select coterie of businessmen – not all of them entirely upright – enjoyed close ties to the Labour Party. Nevertheless, the differences were there to see. By the time my own little bundle of joy gets round to asking me the question, Daddy is going to be hard pushed for an easy answer.

Never has the gap between Britain's two main political parties seemed so narrow. Primarily they differ in their emphases over how best to promote the agenda of the people with money. Inevitably, sentiment is growing that politicians are all the same. Partly as a result, public interest in politics is plummeting frighteningly fast. We are told, however, that such apathy doesn't particularly matter. Middle England is in the grip of an outbreak of mass contentment. All that 1970s retro-chic class politics nonsense went out with glam rock, didn't it? Every last Nicole Farhi sweatshirt-clad man jack of us is tippling from the same bottle of Oddbins New Zealand sauvignon blanc, sitting back as house price inflation boosts our net worth without us lifting a finger, so we are assured.

Politicians who believe that kind of nonsense really should get out more. Millions of the inner-city disaffected now do not vote at all. Such inaction is not tantamount to tacit backing for New Labour, whatever some Blairites would have us believe. This Government has the active support of just one in five of those of voting age. Thousands of working-class people across the North are backing fascists at the ballot box. Meanwhile, the Greens, the Scottish National Party, Plaid Cymru, the Scottish Socialist Party and even the Liberal Democrats are increasingly likely to collect the crosses of progressive voters.

Important differences between Labour and the Conservatives do remain, of course. Among other important reforms, Labour has introduced a minimal minimum wage and a limited right to union recognition. On the other side of the balance sheet, we have seen such utterly reactionary measures as the abolition of student grants, attacks on single parents and the disabled, and Britain's slavish acquiescence in US warmongering. Even so, I would still rather play six successive rounds of Russian roulette with the same revolver than ever vote Tory. Dad taught me that much.

But from the point of view of business, Labour and the Conservatives are now essentially interchangeable. In some respects, Labour is even preferable. With its transformation has come a whole new world of potential conflicts of interests. The party's relationship with business has been central to most of the political horror stories that have repeatedly rocked the Blair governments. Another week, another scandal. If this is Tuesday, it must be Lakshmi Mittal.

This Government's record is littered with private sector rip-offs, scams, dodgy deals, downright flops and sleaze. Think about the Dome, Railtrack, the air traffic control and London Underground privatisations, PFI hospitals, Education Action Zones, and the Enron affair. Consider the furores over 'cash for ash', 'cash for access', 'cash for passports', blind trusts and honours for donors.

So far, Labour is largely getting away with it. Many businessmen – including some of the most powerful ones – are largely anonymous to the general public. Most readers skip the City pages and head straight for the sport. And even in the broadsheet business sections, the activities of private companies are little reported. When news breaks that businessman X has given Labour £1m, people shrug their shoulders. So what? Never heard of the bloke. One of the tasks of this book is to explain who these people are, and why their financial support for Labour should be of vital concern for all democrats.

Despite the arguments advanced by some on the party's residual left, New Labour is not in the grip of a 1950s Sci-Fi-style invasion of the body snatchers. What we have witnessed over the last decade is the organic transformation of a major political party. If Blair fell under a privatised bus tomorrow, the changes would stay in place.

Where once even Conservative prime ministers were able to attack the unacceptable face of capitalism, today's Labour Party seems to find every last visage of the market perfectly agreeable. Mechanisms such as the policy forum have stripped ordinary party members of any real opportunities to influence Labour policy through its internal processes. Instead, unelected businessmen crop up again and again in quangos beyond count, giving rise to the horrible suspicion of clique government. Many of them are, of course, Labour donors. Not insignificant numbers go on to secure knighthoods or even peerages.

Even Labour supporters with no qualms about taking money from private companies as a point of principle will be forced to concede that there are real question marks over the ethical track records of several corporations that have made out cheques to New Labour.

There never was one unified 'Old Labour', of course. The party was always a coalition of Fabians and Marxists, social democrats and Christian socialists. But there were always common objectives and shared nostrums. Notions of social justice, redistribution of income, wealth and power, a universal welfare state financed by progressive taxation and full employment achieved through Keynesian macroeconomic management provided the cement that held together the disparate elements.

Adherence to such ideas is decidedly a minority stance within the Labour Party today. Many longstanding members, incorrigibly attached to these policies, have upped and outed. Meanwhile, many of the replacements to sign up in recent years are informed by values that would in the 1980s have widely been derided as Thatcherite.

Yet millions of Britons have decisively rejected Conservatism since the recession of the 1990s. Britain voted Labour in 1997 and again in 2001 because it wants to see our Third World National Heath Service and public transport infrastructure rebuilt, something done to tackle the shameful state of education in Britain today, and an end to child poverty and homelessness. Instead, Labour Party plc is offering them the full-on in-your-face business agenda. There may yet be a considerable political price attached.

NOTES
[1] John Reid, Secretary of State for Northern Ireland, in a BBC interview, quoted in *Daily Telegraph*, 13 May 2002

1. THE PREHISTORY OF PRAWN COCKTAILS

IRONICALLY, it was a parliamentary wisecrack from a leading Tory that ensured the phrase 'prawn cocktail offensive' a permanent place in the British political lexicon. During an opposition debate in February 1992, Michael Heseltine – playing it for laughs rather than bothering actually to respond to tough questioning from Labour leader John Smith – told the Commons: 'I hear wherever I go that the right honourable and learned gentleman has become a star attraction in the City. Lunch after lunch, dinner after dinner, the assurances flow. Not a discordant crumb falls on to the thick pile.'

Yet, Heseltine maintained, other senior Labour politicians had admitted that the City would probably be 100 per cent against even Labour's limited public spending plans. 'All those prawn cocktails for nothing. Never have so many crustaceans died in vain. With all the authority I can command as Secretary of State for the Environment, let me say to the right honourable and learned member of Monklands East, "save the prawns".'[1]

Very droll. But as the last decade shows, those shellfish went to seafood heaven for a purpose. They died in the name of the progressive delabourisation of Labour. Prawn cocktail offensive is now the stock phrase used to describe Labour's early efforts at rapprochement with business. Although the process reached its present apotheosis under Blair, it was already well in train when Hezza originally cracked his corny gag.

Even the prawn cocktail offensive represents only the culmination of a tendency that has long been a factor in Labour politics, dating back at least to the day Ramsay MacDonald accepted a car from a biscuit manufacturer. While never as prevalent as they are today, links between the Labour leadership and business are hardly a New Labour creation.

Historically speaking, the overwhelming majority of the business community has looked on the Conservatives as the natural party of business. But there have always been a handful of Labour backers with keys to the executive washroom. Many of them were working-class boys and girls made good, still feeling some kind of emotional pull from their upbringing. Others were intellectual converts to the logic of notions such as economic planning, Keynesian demand management or the mixed economy. Others still were undoubtedly motivated by the prospect of preferment or business advantage. None of these reasons for supporting Labour were necessarily mutually exclusive, of course.

Typifying Labour's links to the City in the Wilson and Callaghan years were men such as the late cabinet minister Harold Lever. Lever made a considerable fortune from share deals and company flotations, leaving him rich enough to waive his government salary. He was entrusted with a number of delicate missions to the US, where he talked Chrysler out of shutting down its British operations with 27,000 redundancies in 1975, and secured Washington's support for sterling in 1979. After retirement from politics, Lever took a number of directorships with banks and investment companies. Robert Maxwell – the spectacularly crooked publisher who features in chapter 11 – was also a Labour MP between 1964 and 1970. At this stage his business interests were centred on Pergamon Press.

Even at the time there were widespread suspicions that many of those Wilson nominated for honours – in particular those honoured on his retirement, with places on what came to be called the 'Lavender List' in 1976 – were being rewarded for their financial contributions to the party.

Wilson's former press secretary Joe Haines has recently confirmed the claims, singling out Lord Kagan, a raincoat manufacturer later jailed for corruption, and Sir Eric Miller, a businessman who committed suicide while under investigation by the fraud squad.

'They were the people who I know made contributions to the running of the office and were in my view wrongly honoured,' Haines opined. Wilson only gave the honours 'grudgingly', under pressure from party fundraisers, who sought money from business because trade unions were not meeting all of Labour's running costs, he went on. 'Wilson said to me about one man, "Why should I give him anything? I hardly know him".'

Haines turned down a Lavender List peerage, mainly because of his political opposition to the House of Lords but also because 'I did not wish to appear in the kind of list which had Joe Kagan and Eric Miller and others whom I regarded as undeserving.'[2]

That controversies over Labour's links with business weren't born with Blairism is evidenced by the T. Dan Smith affair. Smith was the leader of Newcastle Council in the 1960s, and head of the planning, finance and housing committees to boot. From this local power base, he oversaw the demolition of the slums of Scotswood, and pushed forward a bold £200m plan to turn the city into 'the Brasilia of the North'. Such efforts brought him national prominence, and by 1965 he had been appointed chairman of the Northern Economic Planning Council. He was even being talked up as potential cabinet material.

Then, in 1970, Smith was arrested on bribery charges. On this occasion, he got off. Two years later, he was not so lucky. Architecture firm Poulson went bust in 1972, and examination of its books found payments of

£155,000 to Smith-owned companies. There were also allegations of free holidays and kickbacks for contracts placed.[3]

This time Smith got six years, serving three of them before being released on parole. Other players in the scandal included Labour national executive committee member Andy Cunningham, father of Blair cabinet minister Jack Cunningham. The affair also claimed the scalp of Tory Home Secretary Reggie Maudling, who was forced to resign.

A miniature version of this imbroglio was more recently played out – the second time as farce, as Marx might have put it – in rock solid Labour Doncaster Council in the 1990s. Two former council leaders and two former mayors were among the 21 councillors subsequently convicted of fraud.

Another very real interface between government and business during the post-war period was the nationalised industries. Since the Attlee nationalisations of the late 1940s, Britain had operated a mixed economy. The Labour governments of 1974–9 pursued what would in today's terms be seen as a markedly interventionist industrial policy, spending large sums of money bailing out major companies that had got themselves into trouble. Labour was still constitutionally committed to common ownership of the means of production, distribution and exchange, and, during his stint as Secretary of State for Trade and Industry, Tony Benn undertook three major nationalisations, namely British Shipbuilders, British Aerospace and the British National Oil Corporation.

By the time the party left office, however, the ideological tide had turned in favour of the free market. Labour was replaced by a succession of Conservative administrations that, over the next 18 years, systematically set about returning every major nationalised industry to private control. By 1987, Britoil, British Telecom, British Aerospace, British Gas, British Airways and British Steel were all – in whole or part – back in private hands. Rover and most water and electric utilities had followed by 1992, and coal and the railways by 1997.

For its part, Labour swung sharply to the left. Ironically for a party nowadays committed to the Private Finance Initiative as a means of extending privatisation wider still, it opposed every single Tory sell-off. By the time of the miners' strike of 1984–5, hostility between Labour and business had reached its highest-ever pitch. In 1986, nine months before Margaret Thatcher's third election victory, the Confederation of British Industry (CBI) did not even allow John Smith – Trade and Industry spokesperson for Britain's main opposition party – to enter the main hall as an observer during its annual conference. This is all a far cry from today, with Blair and a bevy of senior cabinet ministers a fixture at the event.[4]

Yet even by this period, the heyday of the Bennite left was already over. Neil Kinnock, who had taken on the Labour leadership in 1983, started Labour's long march first towards the political centre and ultimately onto its current terrain. Attitudes toward public ownership were one of the first visible signs of this transformation. Outright expropriation was deemed politically inadmissible, while the cost of returning privatised industries to the public sector through buying out shareholders was seen as prohibitive. Talk of public ownership was dropped in favour of the cuddlier nomenclature of social ownership.

As late as the 1987 manifesto, Labour was still committed to seeing such basic utilities as gas and water socially owned. The residual 49 per cent state shareholding in British Telecom would be used to control the company, while a new state holding company called British Enterprise would be created to take stakes in high-technology businesses. But after that year's defeat, Kinnock instigated a review of all Labour policies. Smith became shadow Chancellor, with Gordon Brown effectively his number two as shadow Chief Secretary to the Treasury. Policy research was undertaken by an economic secretariat with considerable input from City economists. Among those involved were Neil MacKinnon of Yamaichi, Gerald Holtham of Shearson Lehman Hutton, and Gavyn Davies of Goldman Sachs. The story goes that Smith became frustrated with the group, because it could never agree a common line.

Davies – erstwhile economic adviser to the Callaghan government – went on to become an important New Labour player, and is today chairman of the BBC. Holtham did his bit as founder of the Institute for Public Policy Research, and is now back in the City as a fund manager, bitterly complaining about the way the government wound up Railtrack.

Among the most important policy decisions taken was one to support British membership of both the EEC and the exchange rate mechanism, the distant ancestor of today's euro. Both moves were openly designed to reassure City opinion that Labour was no longer committed to what was dubbed 'tax and spend' economics, and in government would instead conform to the disciplines the exchange rate mechanism would enforce. Long before Blair's leadership, Labour was doing its best to appear business-friendly.[5]

The policy review took Labour to the point where an ambiguous reference to 'public control' of the national grid and water supplies were all that was left of nationalisation in the 1992 manifesto. Gone too was a commitment to the post-war 'full employment consensus', now hardly a consensus given that the Tories had ditched the idea years ago. In its place came so-called 'supply-side socialism', a buzzword to describe minor reform measures in areas such as education, training and infrastructure.

As well as his pet economists, Kinnock was also able to count on a number of genuine Labour supporters in the business community, who were prepared to back the party before it was either fashionable or advantageous.

Closest to the Labour leader was Clive Hollick, multimillionaire managing director of financial services and advertising conglomerate the MAI Group, given a peerage at Kinnock's behest in 1991. Hollick – profiled in chapter 12 – was then active in fundraising for the party. It remains uncertain whether he put his hands in his own pockets, or restricted himself to soliciting donations from others.

One known benefactor was publisher Paul Hamlyn, who despite earlier support for the SDP provided a six-figure donation specifically to help Labour develop its arts and cultural policies in 1990. He went on to give millions of pounds to the party after Blair took over, and was eventually created a peer three years before his death in 2001.

Highly placed Labour insiders from this period believe that Maxwell money may have been going to the private offices of individual Labour politicians, but Labour was savvy enough to turn down his offers to donate to the party itself. 'Larry Whitty [then general secretary] spent quite a lot of time preventing Robert Maxwell giving money to the party. We didn't know then that he was a crook, but somehow we knew that if we accepted money it would rebound on us,' one source recollects. How vindicated that gut instinct proved.[6]

Others among the Labour business fraternity during the Kinnock years were Greg Dyke, at that point chief executive of London Weekend Television; steel magnate Swraj Paul; and Chris Haskins, chairman of Northern Foods. All were ultimately to experience preferment under Blair.

Central to many of the links between Labour and business since the Wilson era has been the Labour Finance and Industry Group (LFIG). The organisation was originally formed in 1972 by around a dozen Labour-supporting businessmen committed to the mixed economy, to offer informal advice to Wilson on industrial policy. It continued to play an important role under Callaghan.[7]

The LFIG could fairly be described as a crony group, in the dictionary sense that it was bound together largely by personal friendships. But most of those involved were motivated primarily by a desire to put their business experience at the service of the political party they supported. In the 1980s, Pro-Labour business people were so thin on the ground that LFIG would have looked like a crony group whatever it did, activists from the period maintain.

Others were very likely prospecting for gongs and peerages. But even then, the LFIG's defenders point out that such rewards could have been far more easily obtained through the Conservative Party, at a time when many political commentators felt there would never be another Labour government. Moreover, the LFIG's constitution specifically defined the group as socialist, and committed it to serve the entire labour movement. Its overall politics may not have been to the taste of the Bennite left, but then most Bennites distrusted anybody involved in business.

By the early 1980s, the group was seeing relative decline. Relationships between Labour and industry were anyway at a nadir, and Labour leader Michael Foot didn't particularly seem to want LFIG assistance. A number of leading members defected to the SDP. The remaining rump – led by Lord Haskel, a Lords frontbencher with interests in textiles and later a whip in the first Blair administration – was largely based on the Kagan network, many of whom were Jewish.

Few of this LFIG core group were actually active in business themselves, although several enjoyed links with the arms manufacture and intelligence sectors. One of them, Lord Gregson, even became president of the Defence Manufacturers' Association in 1984. John Gilbert, the MP who was vice-chairman of the LFIG from 1983 to 1992, enjoyed strong ties with the US embassy, and was later to serve as Defence minister in the first Blair government.

In 1982, the LFIG fused with another group, the Labour Economics, Finance and Taxation Association, giving it for the first time a grassroots business membership of around 500.

The LFIG's fortunes revived considerably under Kinnock, as it developed a system of study groups to support relevant shadow ministers. Its input was evident in the late 1980s policy review, particularly in policy areas such as company law, competition, monopolies and mergers. Later the group undertook much of the preparatory research that lay behind Labour's adoption of the Private Finance Initiative, and claims authorship of 'much of the work which went into developing systems for using private sector funding to deliver public sector capital projects and service provision.'[8]

Indeed, the party's conversion to Public–Private Partnerships was unveiled at an LFIG event at which Cook, Prescott and Brown all endorsed the idea, thereby undermining any real chance of a traditionalist revolt on the policy.

But what now gave the group weight within Labour's deliberations was the ability of its leadership to raise funds through the blind trust system, which will be explained in detail in chapter 4. John Smith's main funding conduit, the Industrial Research Trust, was founded by Haskel. Gregson served as chairman of the trustees. Just how much money was collected by this set-up – and even more importantly, who the donors were – may perhaps never be known.

It was under Smith that the LFIG reached the apex of its influence, being very close to the leader and, in shadow cabinet terms, closer to Brown than Blair. Such was its importance that the early 1990s saw a sustained factional attempt by a group around Gerald Frankel, chairman of British Office Technology Manufacturers' Alliance, to capture control. What exactly Frankel's agenda was is a subject on which veterans of the group are divided. It is apparent that he was working closely with Jack Cunningham, then trade and industry spokesperson, although Cunningham's role was passive. The real question is to what extent was Frankel acting at the ultimate behest of Tony Blair.

While the battle was ostensibly waged over the issues of internal democracy and accountability, there were deeper questions at stake. Those around Haskel and LFIG secretary Peter Slowe saw the LFIG as a quasi-civil service to the Labour leadership, while the Frankel group wanted closer links with business, and big business in particular. Frankel attracted few takers. The old guard suppressed the insurrection, with either 'no small degree of political ruthlessness', or just simple 'political clumsiness', according to conflicting accounts.[9] Defeated in his efforts, Frankel started up a rival concern, the Industry Forum, in 1993.

That wasn't the end of the disruption. A second struggle broke out in 1995 between the core group and a faction around SDP returner Dr Dickson Mason, who wanted the LFIG to take a more proactive role in making party policy. Haskel was properly insistent that this was the job of Labour's conference and national executive. He may also have been worried that overt LFIG influence would have exposed the low-profile outfit to greater media scrutiny. Unflattering articles were already starting to appear.[10]

The inevitable outcome of this ongoing petty feuding was the marginalisation of the LFIG. Moreover, the Blair camp did not see much point in conducting its relationship with business through an intermediary when links could be forged directly. By the time New Labour was in power, the LFIG had lost much of its *raison d'être*. Blair's office even let it be known that Haskel and Slowe did not command his full confidence.

The infighting was finally resolved when Brown supporters engineered a coup in 1998, ousting Slowe in May. Geraint Davies MP became chair, while his Blair babe colleague Yvette Cooper – wife of Brown speechwriter Ed Balls – won a place on the executive within days of joining as an ordinary member. While this was all done within the means of the group's constitution, the aftermath saw writs flying around and expensive legal opinions taken. Remarkably, once the fuss died down, Slowe was co-opted back onto the executive.[11]

'As for spats, there were so many of them,' recalls one former activist. 'One of the reasons the LFIG lost credibility was that it was constantly under siege from internal factions and constantly being neutered by internal splits. Sadly, most of these were not about substantive policy, but were about capturing access to shadow ministers, to whom there was often the most painful obsequiousness.' [12]

So we have the LFIG as it stands today, testimony to the durability of a Labour right network established decades ago. Meanwhile, Frankel's breakaway Industry Forum – nominally headed by Cunningham, and also formally backed by Cook – proved something of a success, at least in the first instance. After just two years in existence, the group was able to announce in 1995 that over 100 large companies had joined, including Thorn EMI, Glaxo Wellcome, Alfred McAlpine, the National Westminster Bank and venture capitalists 3i. International companies with UK interests, such as Nissan, AT&T and Nynex, also signed up. Greg Dyke, later director general of the BBC, provided financial backing. [13]

But probably the most surprising name on the membership list was Hambros Bank, then the largest corporate donor to the Tory party. As its director Sir David Hancock explained with supreme pragmatism: 'Hambros has traditionally supported the Conservatives and a Conservative government is in the best interests of the company. But we are professional bankers who will do business with anyone.' Thorn EMI viewed its participation as a means of getting advance access to policy thinking: 'It's our policy to become involved in a wide range of think tanks. We see our membership as an early warning system of what new regulations might be in the pipeline.'[14]

3i even claimed that members of the forum were shown early drafts of policy statements from Labour's front bench. Given that the party was in opposition at the time, commercial advantage would at best have been small, although the parallels with later developments will be obvious.

> One participant now recollects: 'Jack, of course, had more business experience than most. Cunningham certainly gave time to Industry Forum contacts, but I got the impression he was too canny a political operator to be seduced into letting business contacts influence his politics. It probably had some impact in building comfort between some sectors of big business and New Labour.
>
> 'In practice, it was rather a weak operation, attracting heads of corporate affairs rather than the higher levels of business. Industry Forum members who were corporate affairs directors were fully aware that the whole thing was just public relations.'[15]

Among those heavily involved in secretariat function of the Industry Forum in the early days was Cunningham's aide, a young woman named Cathy McGlynn, who will pop up again later in this book. After a subsequent career move to lobbyist Bell Pottinger, McGlynn is now head of a group called the PPP Forum, made up of law firms, banks and builders that favour Public–Private Partnerships. Her early business contacts may have stood her in good stead. With the subsequent decline of Cunningham's political career, the Industry Forum now seems to be more or less in abeyance.

Another, slightly later, offshoot of the LFIG was Common Campaign, a limited company set up in 1994. All of those involved were part of the LFIG nexus, including Haskel; former eurocommissioner Lord Clinton-Davies; City PR man Tim Pendry, a key Labour backroom fixer; and Roger Warren Evans, a former Bovis and Sainsbury executive.

While the company had no formal connection with the party, its express aim was to raise £100,000 to fund political advertising at the next general election. The idea was to tap the support of those business people disillusioned with the Tories but not prepared directly to contribute to Labour. Common Campaign's articles of association limited its objectives to purchasing advertising independently of the party itself, and specified that it was to be wound up three months after the next general election.[16]

The venture was hardly a success. As Warren Evans remembers it: 'We certainly did not have any donations in excess of £5,000. In fact my recollection is that we did not raise in excess of £5,000 in total and the failure was so comprehensive that we decided that the right course was to pay back the donations we had received and to wind up the whole operation.

'None of us claimed any expenses. The truth is that we were simply brushed aside in the overall official party fundraising drive, and we felt there was no point in continuing. It was a well-meaning, but totally unsuccessful political initiative, sidelined by events.'[17]

But this is to run ahead of the story slightly. The main point to grasp is that the efforts of the LFIG and the Kinnock business coterie provided Labour with the advance landing party for the prawn cocktail offensive of 1992, offering at least some embryonic connections to the private sector of a kind that simply had not existed even five years before.

Kinnock himself took a back seat in all of this. In retrospect, it seems plain that, while he undertook much of the groundwork that subsequently made Blairism possible, he could never himself have devised anything quite like New Labour.

'Kinnock was old school. Kinnock didn't need advisers, newspaper advertisements, or focus groups,' observes one Labour figure close to the front bench at this time. 'He was happy to rely on trade unions.'[18]

One LFIG source adds that, while Kinnock fully sanctioned the restoration of party ties with business, he took little personal or political interest: 'He was naive [and] inexperienced and . . . he was also not being briefed properly.'[19]

Against this unpromising backdrop, John Smith and his economics team hosted their now famous series of lunches, in an attempt to persuade the City that a Labour government would not constitute the red menace redux. Deemed to have little impact on the target audiences, considerable media coverage doubtlessly boosted Smith's standing with the wider public.

By the time Labour published its 1992 manifesto, the radical policies of the 1980s were long gone. Such spending commitments as were set down in Smith's shadow budget that year were relatively minor, including a small emergency job creation programme and increases in pensions and child benefit.

Following Labour's fourth defeat in succession, Kinnock quit and Smith, the candidate of the Labour right, took over. Within months came the day that wiped the grin of Heseltine's face and destroyed for ever the Tories' reputation for economic competence. After Black Wednesday in September 1992, Labour became a shoo-in for the next election. Business was only too cognisant of the fact. The party no longer had to go in search of business. Business would now come in search of Labour.

NOTES

[1] Hansard, 19 February 1992

[2] *Daily Telegraph*, 7 January 2001

[3] *Mail on Sunday* 'You' magazine, 10 May 1987

[4] *Guardian*, 25 March 1997

[5] Robin Ramsay, *The Rise of New Labour* (Harpenden, Pocket Essentials, 1992), p.52. This short book paints an excellent, succinct picture of the party in this period, and is highly recommended to anyone seeking more detail.

[6] Former party official, interview with author

[7] *Independent on Sunday*, 14 May 1995

[8] http://www.lfig.org/history.htm

[9] Two LFIG activists, interviews with author

[10] *Guardian*, 16 May 1995; for some of the press criticisms, see Peter Oborne's piece in *Evening Standard*, 9 June 1995

[11] *Socialist Campaign Group News*, June 1998; interviews with author

[12] Tim Pendry, interview with author

[13] *Daily Telegraph*, 14 August 1995

[14] Ibid.

[15] LFIG activists, interview with author

[16] *Financial Times*, 13 December 1994

[17] Roger Warren Evans, e-mail to author

[18] Former party official, interview with author

[19] LFIG activist, interview with author

2. LABOUR PARTY PLC

IT'S almost reassuring to see New Labour commemorate the colour of the people's flag in some small way. Despite clocking up an income of over £29m in 2000 – the highest figure in its entire history – the party is currently at least £5m, and by some estimates as much as £10m, in the red.[1]

Political parties are not businesses, of course. But given Labour's current propensity to measure all things by business yardsticks, it's worth noting that its own financial performance hardly qualifies it as an entrepreneurial success story. In light of serial highly publicised donations of £1m or more, and continued if now declining support from most major British unions, the massive deficit even seems surprising at first glance. Surely Labour should be a cash rich organisation by now? The answer seems to be that while big money goes in, big money goes out. Looking at the picture over the last decade or so, the party has come full circle.

In 1991 Labour was in such severe financial straits that bankruptcy was internally discussed as at least a theoretical possibility. A document written by director of finance Mike Watts warned the party's ruling national executive committee (NEC) that, while Labour's overdraft limit was £1.7m, its projected deficit after a general election the following year would rise to a then unimaginable £2.5m. That would likely prove unacceptable to the party's bankers, the Co-operative Bank, then facing financial problems of its own after recording its own first-ever loss.

'If the bank were to withdraw its support, we would be effectively bankrupt,' Watts pointed out. 'The NEC should therefore be aware of their own responsibility . . . which is that they are jointly and severally liable for the debts of the party.' For the 29 members of the executive, including Neil Kinnock, the potential bill worked out at an alarming £86,200 a head.[2]

It's not that the Co-op would ever have actually pulled the plug. But Britain's opposition had clearly dug itself into a deep financial hole. What had gone wrong?

The main factor was the sharp decline in trade union membership. Unions had always provided the bulk of Labour's cash – 96 per cent as late as 1983, for instance – and accordingly wielded 90 per cent of the vote on the conference floor. This arrangement had always served Labour well, guaranteeing financial support in good times and bad. Then came the

Thatcher decade, with a string of anti-union laws and a series of demoralising industrial defeats. Combined membership of TUC affiliates fell from twelve million in 1979 to just eight million by 1991.

Inevitably, that entailed a sharp drop in affiliation income for Labour. The share of its income provided by unions fell from 73 per cent to 53 per cent in the five years leading up to 1991. In 1990, affiliated unions came up with £263,000 less than had been expected.[3]

In its efforts to make up the money, the party sold many of its assets and was increasingly reliant on individual supporters and its bankers for survival. To exacerbate immediate difficulties, Labour had been gearing up for a 1991 election that never came, hiring extra staff who now had to be kept on until Conservative Prime Minister John Major named the day, which he was not to do until the following year. Panic belt-tightening measures were soon the order of the day. Regional and youth conferences and a number of consultative forums were summarily scrapped.

Final returns for 1991 showed that the Labour Party had overspent its £6.9m income by £1.3m, a bravura example of the deficit budgeting tactics adopted by left-wing Labour local authorities in the 1980s. Large sums were attributed to 'other expenses' on the part of Labour's organisation directorate. In 1991, this accounted for £776,000, rather more than the £523,000 available to the party's nationwide network of local organisers, and about 9 per cent of 1991 total expenditure. Since organisers' expenses, regional office expenses, and even car leasing expenses were listed separately, where the money had gone appeared something of a mystery to observers at the time.

Most of it was actually being used to fight by-elections, with spending far outstripping all statutory limits. Party officials of the period now confess that they booked costs under this heading in the full knowledge that such outlays were probably not legal. With Major's small majority slowly falling away seat by seat, anything went in this particular war of attrition.

Where there was a possibility of a constituency changing hands, all parties were routinely exceeding the permitted expenditure level, sometimes by a factor of ten or more. This is a serious offence, punishable by imprisonment. Yet all parties shared the tacit understanding that it was in nobody's interest to highlight their rivals' malpractices, being well aware that their own side was up to the same tricks.

As a response to its growing financial difficulties, Labour had since the late 1980s been trying to develop ways to tap its membership – apparently over 300,000 strong on paper – for cash. But the first problem was that it did not really know who its members were. Such records as did exist were compiled by volunteer constituency membership secretaries, and frequently left a lot to be desired. Dead people were still on the rolls, for instance. Moreover, constituencies had to affiliate on the basis of a minimum number of members that many of them didn't really have.

Unions such as the GMB and TGWU agreed to pay for the computer hardware needed to set up a centralised membership system. Once accurate statistics became available in 1991, the party suddenly realised that it had 80,000 fewer members than previously thought. Even that depressing statistic may have overstated the position. Comparison of the claimed 1991 membership of 260,000 with audited income from individual subscriptions indicates that the latter figure may have been inflated by around 60,000. If the party really did have the members claimed by the NEC, subscriptions should have totalled £1.1m rather than the £791,000 listed in the accounts. Even by the official reckoning, Labour now had only 60,000 more members than the Liberal Democrats. It was all a far cry from Kinnock's 1988 promise to increase membership to one million, a level of popular support the party last enjoyed in 1953.

The unions also bankrolled a business plan that used this membership data for telephone fundraising and the solicitation of high-value individual donations, with the express intention of reducing Labour's dependence on union cash. In so doing, they both set in train and paid for the start of a process that was to dramatically minimise their political influence. As with so many of the developments now credited to Blair, it all began under Kinnock.

All told, 'income generation' initiatives between 1986 and 1991 raised £2.4m, although they cost the party £1.5m. In other words, fundraising was costing Labour over 60p in the pound, a level of profligacy no reputable charity would countenance then or now.

Commercial exhibitors had for some years already been allowed at the party's annual conference, in an effort to offset the cost. Unlike today, there were strict political criteria for acceptability. Companies linked to South Africa or tobacco would not have got a stand at any price. Even the Royal College of Nursing was refused a place because it was not considered a bona fide union. In 1986, Mercury Communications – a private sector competitor to BT – informally approached a senior member of Labour's staff with a request to be allowed to sponsor telephone equipment at conference. But the company was at that time involved in a union recognition dispute, and the proposal was not even considered.

Labour lost its fourth successive election in 1992, and Kinnock resigned immediately afterwards. The contest to replace him was not so much a leadership battle as a stitch-up so tightly controlled that the erstwhile National Union of Tailors and Garment Workers should surely have called a demarcation dispute. The main union leaders instantly came out in favour of John Smith. With the weight of the block vote in the electoral college arrangement in place at the time, the result was a foregone conclusion, desultory challenge from Brian Gould notwithstanding.

Meanwhile, Watts' earlier projections proved pretty much on the money.

Labour's overdraft did indeed reach £2.5m in 1992, with the Co-op Bank demanding repayment at £50,000 a month. In May of that year, a confidential strategy paper by general secretary Larry Whitty warned that Labour would find itself with up to 40 per cent less cash than expected to spend over the coming three to four year period. The outlook was, to use Whitty's own adjective, 'bleak'.[4]

Servicing the overdraft would dominate Labour's budgeting priorities for the foreseeable future. Unions were in no position to mount a bail out. 'Affiliation levels have fallen by over £1m since 1987 and are likely to fall by a similar amount by the time of the next election,' Whitty noted.[5]

Many unions had already exhausted their political funds, providing around £5m of Labour's £7.5m general election budget. Legislation restricting automatic 'check-off' deduction of union dues from pay packets was about to hit the labour movement's income hard, while compulsory government-imposed ballots on the very principle of whether unions should have political funds at all would come into force in three years' time. Even if the ballots were won, the entire exercise would inevitably prove costly, Whitty warned.

The general secretary dutifully sounded out union leaders on the possibility of a major increase in affiliation payments over the next three years, and wanted the plan agreed at the party's October conference. This was simply asking the impossible.[6]

But on the very day in July that Smith was formally confirmed as leader, representatives of 30 affiliated unions committed themselves to a 6.25 per cent increase in affiliation fees. That came to 10p a head, or £1.70 for each of the 4.5 million union members paying the political levy. However, the unions still rejected the party's call for increases in future years to be implemented automatically.[7]

Finances were debated at the 1992 party conference. Losses the year before had been £1.3m, with a projected year-end deficit of £2.5m.[8] Spending had been slashed by one-third, while the membership figure for public consumption was put at 261,000. What the delegates weren't told was that less than 200,000 of these members were up to date with their subs, even though 45 per cent of them paid a reduced rate that did not even cover the cost of servicing membership.

John Evans, chairman of Labour's finance working party, urged delegates to accept an increase of £3 a head on individual subscriptions, bringing the cost to £18 a year. Despite vocal opposition by some delegates, the subs duly went up. Interestingly, Evans's speech revealed that the party's single largest source of income was now a relatively prosperous layer of 28,000 individual members giving the party £5 or more a week, so raising £2m a year.

The December 1992 meeting of Labour's national executive meeting considered the overdraft situation, backing proposals from Evans recommending that the number of regional offices be cut to six, further cost-cutting carried out at head office, distribution of *Labour Party News* magazine reduced, and many internal conferences turned into biennial rather than annual events. Projections suggested a fall in levy payers from 4.6 million in 1992 to 3.6 million in 1996. Despite the recently increased affiliation fee, actual yield would drop from £4.8m in 1993 to £4.2m in 1996.[9]

Surprisingly, when the party's audited 1992 accounts were finally published, election defeat was found to have provided a desperately needed financial boost. The general fund saw a surplus of £1.3m, its first for many years. This reduced the accumulated deficit to £1.57m and the overdraft requirement from £2.5m to £1.9m. One official explains: 'The general election fund was a fantastic success. The longer Major delayed, the more was raised. Such were the leftovers that, after 1992, the party was in the black, thanks to fivers and tenners from ordinary members.'[10]

Another aspect of the improvement was a dramatic decline in 'other expenses' at the organisation directorate, down from £776,000 to just £77,000, presumably reflecting a far smaller number of by-elections after the general election.

Nevertheless, the accounts warned that if the overdraft was to come down further, Labour would have to get used to operating in reduced circumstances, despite the attendant political implications: 'This has serious consequences in limiting campaigning and organisational resources.'[11]

Among the brainwaves hotly debated in Labour circles at this stage was 'levy-plus', a scheme whereby members of affiliated unions who paid the political levy could upgrade to full membership for a small top-up fee. Given Labour's subsequent reliance on top ups from Lord Levy, there is some retrospective irony in the name.

Smith's death in 1994 saw succession pass to Tony Blair. The young and charismatic new leader proved popular in the country, with recruitment running at around 2,000 a week. It was under Blair that the first ever publicly recorded corporate donations starting rolling in, attracting considerable publicity.

While over-optimistic press reports that Labour had somehow built up a pre-election war chest of £9m were swiftly denied, such a sum was considered a realistic target for two years' time, when membership was expected to have risen from 300,000 to 500,000. In the event, it was never to get anywhere near this level.[12]

Nevertheless, it was still the case that by autumn, Labour had cash in hand for the first time in a generation. While the overdraft remained at £1m, there were even hopes that it would be eliminated by the time of the next election, expected in 1996.

This was the year in which the party secured its first-ever £1m gift, in the form of a pledge from insurance broker Matthew Harding. It was at that time the largest-ever publicly declared personal donation to a British political party. Six weeks later, Harding, founder of reinsurance broker Benfield Group, was dead, victim of a helicopter crash on his way home from a football match in Bolton. Prescott attended his funeral, while Blair told his memorial meeting: 'I shall never forget the debt we owe him.' Rarely can a eulogy have been so utterly quantifiable.[13]

Harding had already handed over £500,000, and verbally promised the second instalment by January 1997. But there was no such provision in his will, and sorting out his £200m estate proved highly complex. New Labour was not to get the rest of the money for over a year.[14]

Thanks to an influx of similar major donations, Labour was by now in a position to take out a lease on 25,000 sq. ft of office space over two floors of Westminster's Millbank Tower, establishing a campaign centre modelled on the one used by Bill Clinton in the 1992 US presidential campaign. The move didn't come cheap. On top of a rental bill of £586,000 for the next two years, the conversion work cost £2m. Over the next two years, the party moved its entire headquarters away from a terrace surrounded by the council estates of South London's Walworth Road – how Old Labour can you get? – and shifted them to the new base. Where previously Labour had been happy to rent premises from the Confederation of Shipbuilding and Engineering Unions, it was now a tenant of the insurance giant Legal & General. Soon the very term 'Millbank' became synonymous with New Labourism.

Accounts for the year showed that, for the first time ever, trade union contributions amounted to less then half of Labour's income, totalling around 45 per cent. The remainder came from individual and corporate donations, and commercial activities. A spokesperson commented: 'It shows the huge change there has been within the party. It shows that we now have so many members, and also the professionalism of the party in terms of fundraising.'[15]

Income in 1996 was £17.1m – substantially up from the £12.5m seen in 1995 – largely because of the usual rush of pre-election donations. But with the cost of moving to Millbank, the overdraft still totalled £4.5m.

Labour's May 1997 victory was achieved at an outlay of £1.95 a vote. Campaign spending over the preceding three years had been £26m, with half of that in the year immediately before the election itself. Given that 13.5 million people voted Labour, that worked out at just under £2 a head. The figures compared favourably to the £20m the Tories spent over the same period, garnering just 9.6 million votes for their money.[16]

Unions paid £11m into the election fund, on top of what they gave year in, year out, through affiliation fees. The value of their support was in reality a lot more, if donations to constituencies, officials seconded to the party, and provision of offices and office services is taken into account.[17]

Even so, the campaign had taken its toll. By the beginning of August, there were reports that Labour was almost £8m in debt. This figure was dismissed as 'utter nonsense'. But it was confirmed that the overdraft had hit £4.75m, the general election fund was £1m overspent, and there was a £2.5m debt on the party's general fund.[18] The official accounts record an audited deficit of £4.5m.

Matters could have been made worse by the need to return £1m to motor racing boss Bernie Ecclestone, after a row over Formula One's temporary exemption from a ban on tobacco advertising in sport. Fortunately for the party, burger restaurateur Robert Earl stepped in with a replacement £1m donation. The sorry saga of cash for ash is considered in chapter 5.

The affair had at least one lasting outcome, in the form of the review of party funding led by Sir Patrick Neill, announced in October 1997. This was the start of the process that led to the Political Parties, Elections and Referendums Act 2000, which imposes restrictions on all parties' fundraising efforts and electoral spending.

Critics of the review immediately detected partisan intent. For years, the Tories had been the primary beneficiaries of the secrecy that had prevailed until this point. Massive political donations – not infrequently of dubious provenance – stayed anonymous, providing they were given by individuals or overseas companies rather than British businesses. Press revelations over the generosity of Hong Kong businessmen, military dictator-friendly Greek shipping tycoon John Latsis and fugitive businessman Asil Nadir all added to the climate of sleaze that so debilitated the Major administration.

Labour had already stolen a march on Major by voluntarily disclosing all donors giving £5,000 or more, albeit without specifying amounts given. That still provided ample scope for evasiveness. Without knowing whether a gift was £5,000 or £5m, it was difficult to know whether or not any given donor was attempting to buy influence.

But for many Labour modernisers, the subtext was clearly the chance to break links with the unions. One unnamed minister commented: 'This could be a very significant moment in Labour's history. If spending limits are set at reasonable levels, it makes if far easier for us to cut the umbilical cord.'[19]

Just five months after the spectacular election landslide, membership levels were falling once again. Cuts to lone parent benefits, tuition fees for students and confusion over disability benefits saw many activists decide to quit. Membership – projected to reach 450,000 by this stage – instead fell to 405,000. For the most part, people were not formally resigning, but simply not renewing their party cards. The rate of lapses had shot up from the normal 5 per cent a year to around 20–25 per cent.

Unable to turn to a mass constituency base, Labour sought commercial sponsorship for party campaigning activities. In January 1998, Blair and several cabinet ministers decided to tour the country in a party capacity, with nine meetings to sell the latest round of benefit cuts to an unconvinced public. The gathering in Dudley was sponsored by engineering union AEEU. So far, so Old Labour. But a second meeting in Luton was sponsored by cable television operator NTL. Further business backers were keenly sought, and a memo to this effect from Labour's head of commercial marketing Simon Pitkeathley to lobbyists with clients interested in welfare found its way into the press. But Labour chief spokesperson Dave Hill – shortly to depart for the lobbying industry himself – insisted: 'It is a good thing that business wants to sponsor bread and butter debates rather than glitzy occasions. This is balance.'[20] How exactly welfare recipients were supposed to make their case was not explained.

Labour's accounts were discussed in January 1998 at a meeting of the party's finance committee, addressed by director of finance David Pitt-Watson. A graduate of the Labour Finance and Industry Group, where his work had included disciplining dissidents, Pitt-Watson had joined the party apparatus just two months earlier. He had previously worked for Braxtons, the consulting arm of accountancy major Deloitte Touche, where he had been managing director. Explaining his motivation for the switch, he argued: 'As far as I am concerned it is a fantastic opportunity to do a job I like doing.'[21] That fantastic opportunity came at considerable cost. Overnight, his annual salary fell from £300,000 to just £38,500.

But there are possible explanations for this seemingly retrograde career move. Although he consistently denied the suggestion, those who worked with him are certain that Pitt-Watson fancied a political career. He had previously been shortlisted for the Northamptonshire constituency of Corby, although he was not selected. He may also have seen himself as a future general secretary. A Labour Party member for 13 years, Pitt-Watson had given his services for free during the 1997 election, running the membership system. He was immediately appalled at the way the party handled its finances, and believed its operations were in need of total overhaul.

Once in post, Pitt-Watson immediately instituted a cost-cutting package, which he believed could reduce the party's deficit to £700,000 by the end of the year. Under the plan, spending would be kept to about £15m, set against projected income of £15–20m. Around half of that money would come from small donations from individual members, a further 30 per cent from unions, and the remainder from commercial activity and large gifts.

Publicly Pitt-Watson was optimistic, arguing: 'We are at the bottom of the Grand Canyon but we can still see our way out.'[22] In the event, Labour did even better than he hoped and all but wiped out its accumulated deficit.

By the end of 1998 it stood at just £6,000, with the party recording an operating surplus of £4.5m. Nevertheless, party documents freely admitted: 'Our financial position remains fragile.'[23]

Labour published its submission to the Neill inquiry in February 1998, demanding sweeping reforms to the whole culture of political funding. Under the blueprint, companies would have to obtain majority shareholder approval before making a political donation, while shareholders opposed to it would be entitled to a rebate in proportion to their shareholding.[24] Such technicalities would have made corporate political donations all but impossible. This now appears to have been so much grandstanding, safe in the knowledge that such measures would never be implemented.

In October, Neill finally published his findings, calling for a cap on overall spending and a requirement that parties disclose the value and sources of donations and sponsorship deals. By the time the Political Parties, Elections and Referendums Act 2000 came into force in February 2001, the restraints on corporate largesse that had formed the centrepiece of Labour's submission were nowhere to be seen.

Even by 1998, public concern over Labour's business links was already growing. One opinion poll found a two to one majority for the proposition that Blair paid too much attention to company bosses, and not enough to ordinary people. Some 54 per cent agreed that 'some rich people are buying political influence with this government by giving Labour large amounts of money'.[25]

Much of the concern was directed at the readily proffered chequebook of just one man. Lord Sainsbury of Turville – whose family owned the supermarket chain at one time much mocked by Labour supporters for its supposedly middle-class customer base – was revealed to have given Labour a donation of £2m. The financial support of Lord Sainsbury will be a recurring theme throughout this book. His backing for New Labour had at the time of writing exceeded a staggering £9m, equivalent to more than two years' worth of the entire party's membership dues. Never mind Labour's wider business support. Without this one man alone, the party simply would not be a going concern.

One of the most obvious external manifestations of Labour's commercialisation was on view at its annual conference. This was once a lively affair, dominated numerically by huge delegations from the manual unions, and politically by left-wing constituency activists. Every so often the leadership got a pasting in a card vote, although somehow this never made much difference to what the party actually did, especially when in government. But even the symbolism inherent in the spectacle of working-class organisations presuming to tell Labour what to do was too much for the Blairites.

Exit the protest T-shirt, enter the business suit. Of the 20,000 or so people who now attend the event, typically only 1,500 are actually delegates. The remainder are exhibitors, lobbyists or journalists. Proceedings are carefully stage-managed, with opportunities to make money by no means the least consideration. Not for nothing has Labour's conference been dubbed 'Western Europe's biggest commercial exhibition'.

The 1998 conference saw 189 firms pay up to £10,000 each for stands, generating revenue of £1.1m. Some 200 companies sent an average of six executives to the event, at a cost of £253-a-head for a two-day pass, bringing in a further £303,000. By contrast, the going rate to attend the conference of the once mighty Conservatives was just £155.

Sponsorship – from high-profile businesses such as Thomas Cook and Somerfield, and soon-to-be casualties Enron and Railtrack alike – amounted to at least £52,000. Why hand over the cash? For some, it was a straight marketing opportunity. Japanese toy manufacturer Tomy paid for the crèche, possibly hoping to secure many television shots of happy kiddies playing with its products. For others, there may have been more direct political considerations. Enron's attendance came just weeks after trade secretary Peter Mandelson gave the go-ahead for its £1.4bn takeover of Wessex Water, its biggest step yet into the UK business arena.

Meanwhile, Pitt-Watson's enthusiasm for party work was evidently fading. In September 1999 – after less than two years in post – he upped sticks to become commercial director at fund manager Hermes.[26] Labour officials privately cite personality clashes with general secretary Margaret McDonagh, whose job he coveted, as one factor in the departure. Pitt-Watson has since risen to become Hermes' managing director, responsible for £44bn of funds, including the BT and Post Office pension funds.

To be sure, Pitt-Watson left the Labour Party in far better financial fettle than he found it. However, he himself argued that its political condition deteriorated during his tenure. After his departure, he penned a document setting out fears that Labour was being transformed into a British version of the US Democrats, which was clearly the work of a disillusioned man. The gap between party machine and party membership had grown to the point where activism was on the point of collapse, he warned.

> The culture which underpins Millbank's speed, dedication and professionalism can have a cost. This is because its professionalism stands in contrast to the way the party is organised on the ground . . . Labour on the ground is a voluntary organisation. It will not, cannot, and arguably should not be able to respond in the way that a professional organisation can. As a result the culture of Millbank grates with that of the larger party.
>
> Because Millbank and the party in the country operate in these

two different political cultures, party members can think of Millbank
as distant, arrogant and controlling when it has no intention to be so.
And to the professionals, the party on the ground looks like a bunch
of amateurs and it treats them accordingly.[27]

Such concerns were clearly reflected in reality. Membership figures were
still, as the City jargon puts it, heading south. Labour's 1999 annual report
showed a drop from 405,000 to 360,000. As in the past, the official count
was probably too high, including many people six months or more behind
in subscriptions, but not yet formally lapsed. Labour insiders put the true
membership figure at something like 330,000.[28] This precipitous decline
had financial implications. The disappearance of 75,000 members at £17.50
a head implies a loss of £1.3m in revenue. Even though an unquantifiable
number of them would have been on the reduced rate of £6, lost income
was still considerable.

None of this stopped private companies doing everything they could to
market their services to Labour's membership base. Just before the
conference, the party announced a new project in collaboration with
Freeserve, then owned by Tory blowhard Sir Stanley Kalms. The Internet
service provider (ISP) agreed to host the www.labour.org.uk website, which
included a database enabling the party to target voters in key seats. The
database also allowed local parties to store detailed information about their
electorates, and to access campaign materials.

Two years later, Labour switched ISP to another company that promised
to split the revenues generated 50/50. Announcing the change in an e-mail
to party members, Labour seemingly hinted that Freeserve might not
remain in business for much longer. 'We strongly advise you to switch to
the new Labour ISP, as we are not able to guarantee that Freeserve will
continue their service,' the e-mail read. Freeserve was not best pleased at
such ingratitude, and secured a retraction after a stiff letter from its
lawyers.[29]

Another technology deal from 1999 saw IBM offer to hire computer
hardware to constituencies for £1 a day, under a 42-month leasing deal with
an option to buy at the end. The terms hardly seemed unduly generous.[30]

To cap everything, the year also saw Labour's membership department
outsourced to Anglo-French computer services company Sema. The ten-year
contract, reportedly worth more than £10m, was brokered by a
management consultant on secondment to Labour from KPMG. Labour
Party plc was now privatising itself.

Sema, which also handles membership services for the Royal Society for
the Protection of Birds and claims for disability living allowance made
through the Benefits Agency Medical Service, was charged with persuading
more members to pay party subs by direct debit, keeping track of address

changes, and cracking down on non-payment of dues. Its system is also capable of storing the times members prefer to be phoned, and even noting their particular political interests.

Twelve Labour Party employees saw their performance market tested against people in similar positions in the private sector. They were eventually given the choice between taking a job with Sema and taking voluntary redundancy.[31]

General secretary Margaret McDonagh made plain that only such core competences as the elections unit and the press office were certain to stay in-house. Those aside, the entire party machine was effectively up for grabs. 'It is a waste of Labour staff if they are trying to deliver services that can be done more effectively by an outside agency,' McDonagh maintained. 'The only benchmark for our services at present is the Conservative Party. I want to match our services to the best organisations in the commercial sector . . . Our current system is not fast enough, efficient enough and it is not accurate enough.'[32]

This outburst was to backfire on McDonagh and the party itself, after the new system – branded Labour.people – immediately met technical difficulties. Much information transferred from the old system was corrupted or lost, leading to long delays in sending out membership cards and confusion over who was entitled to vote in party ballots. Sema's services are currently costing Labour £1.8m a year, compared to the 1998 bill of £800,000 for an in-house membership department.

In other areas, Labour decided to embark on something of a spending spree. The '1999 Objectives' document tabled to the national executive, while travelling light on detailed figures, called for 'a considerable increase in party spending on key strategic objectives from £150,000 in 1998 to over £7m in 1999'. The bulk of this – some £4m – was expenditure on the Scottish and Welsh assembly and European parliamentary elections.[33]

The money was indeed spent. After having almost eliminated its deficit at the end of 1998, Labour's accounts for the for year ending 31 December 1999 show the party £2.1m in the red.[34] Income was up marginally to £22.6m, from £21m in 1998. This figure included £9m from donations, £4m from membership fees and £3m from commercial activity.[35]

Unions were still expected to carry a major share of the cost of the next election. A meeting in Millbank in November saw McDonagh ask leaders of the main affiliated unions for a cool £13m. The sum requested was the largest Labour had ever sought from the unions at election time, representing about half the projected cost of the forthcoming campaign, and a substantial increase on a 1997 contribution estimated at between £9 and £11m. Despite New Labour's continued talk of breaking the party–union link, the unions were still being asked to foot the bulk of the bill for returning it to office. Some of the participants were cheeky enough to mention policy disagreements, particularly over privatisation. But no policy concessions were promised in return for the money.[36]

The year 2000 was a lucrative year for New Labour. Its accounts for the period – the most recent available at the time of writing – reveal an all-time record income of £29.1m. More than half of that money, some £15.9m, came in the shape of donations.

But this financial performance was not achieved on the back of an enthusiastic and expanding membership. The total number of party card holders fell by 50,000, with membership down to 311,000. Embarrassingly, that figure is 7,000 less than the one claimed by the Tories. According to a spokesperson, the reason for the decline was largely technical, resulting from the new policy of lapsing those behind with their dues after six months rather than 15 months. Why those members were lapsing, he did not seem to ask.[37]

In line with the dictates of supply and demand, the top price for a stall at that year's Labour Party conference had risen to as much as £25,000. Takers included Nestlé, Camelot, British Nuclear Fuels, Arriva, Pfizer, Connex, Virgin Trains, Railtrack, the British Bankers' Association, Merck, Severn Trent Water, Biffa Waste, the Police Federation and the Countryside Alliance. Some 80 companies opted for a two-day corporate visitor package at £1,351. Briefings by aides to Chancellor Gordon Brown – not, note, the great man himself, just his bag carriers – were included in this bargain deal.

Manufacturers and retailers of pharmaceuticals were particularly prominent on the fringe. Health minister John Denham spoke on the New Health Networks platform sponsored by Superdrug. Another Health minister, John Hutton, addressed the Zito Trust, at a meeting sponsored by Prozac manufacturers Eli Lilly.

Pfizer – of Viagra fame – ran the most extensive programme. Speaking from a platform liberally decorated with Pfizer's corporate logo, to an audience tucking into Pfizer-provided wine and suitably phallic asparagus in prosciutto, Secretary of State for Health Alan Milburn was particularly fulsome in his praise for the company, citing it as 'an extremely important investor' that was vital 'not just for the health but also the wealth' of the nation.[38]

Cherie Booth, wife of the Prime Minister, posed for a photo opportunity with executives from Railtrack and First Group, two firms closely involved with the Paddington rail disaster. Transport minister Keith Hill spoke on a Railtrack-sponsored platform alongside Railtrack chief executive Gerald Corbett.

Private health insurer PPP sponsored a meeting under the title 'Can we Afford Long-Term Care?', with speakers including Financial Secretary to the Treasury Stephen Timms and Labour peer Lord Lipsey. Lipsey had earlier tabled a one-man minority report to a royal commission on the issue, arguing that the state most certainly couldn't afford it. Old people should instead sell their homes to pay for long-term care, he maintained.

After the conference, it was fundraising as usual. Right at the start of the following new year, the press discovered that Labour had received yet another one-off £2m donation. At first Labour refused to identify its provenance. For three days, the benefactor remained a mystery. Speculation – and protests from backbenchers – mounted steadily. Legislation forcing parties to identify major backers was due to come into force in mid-February. What was the government being so cagey about?

Finally, publisher Lord Hamlyn confirmed he had given the gift. While proud to be a Labour supporter, he proclaimed, he had kept the gift secret because he was abroad recovering from pneumonia. This was surely something of a non sequitur.[39]

The story didn't end there. Two further £2m apiece donors rapidly came to light. Science minister Lord Sainsbury was one of the usual suspects. A rather more surprising name was that of retired financier Christopher Ondaatje, a former Conservative in the process of joining the Labour Party, who came clean in the knowledge that he was about to named in *The Economist* anyway.

Ondaatje had already won a reputation for philanthropy, after endowing a wing of the National Portrait Gallery. He met Blair as a result and ultimately picked up a CBE for his generosity. Nor was this his only donation to the arts. As the gag had it, Ondaatje had endowed so many wings he would surely soon be starting his own airline.

Explaining his conversion, he made it clear that New Labour's love-in with business had been a major factor: 'My hesitation about Labour in the past has been a fear that they would not have been able to manage the economy. But I have been very impressed by their handling of the economy and their understanding and appreciation of business.'[40]

In an interesting Freudian slip on *Newsnight*, Clive Soley – chairman of the Parliamentary Labour Party – inadvertently referred to Labour's latest benefactor as 'Lord Ondaatje'. Even though he remained a commoner, Ondaatje shortly afterwards topped up his donation with a further £100,000 gift.

Blair was unrepentant at accepting the support of former Conservatives, arguing: 'I am absolutely proud of the fact that we have got successful entrepreneurs and disaffected Conservatives who look at the state of the Conservative Party and say, "it is hopeless, it is incapable of governing the country properly" and support the Labour Party.'[41]

The only snag is, successful entrepreneurs and disaffected Conservatives are not available in sufficient numbers to outweigh the patent disaffection of rank-and-file Labour Party members. On the eve of Labour's second successive election victory, internal party correspondence put membership at 280,000. That averaged out at 437 members per constituency party, of which only a minority are activists in any meaningful sense of the word. True membership had by now fallen below the level Tony Blair inherited when he took over seven years previously, and was over 100,000 down on that seen after the first election win.[42]

February finally saw the Neill inquiry recommendations on party finances become law. The first-ever quarterly accounts filed with the new Electoral Commission – not published until after the election – showed that in the three months leading up to polling day Labour raised £5.3m in donations, of which £3.8m came from unions. In addition, the unions provided a further £64,000 in kind, in the form of staff salaries, transport and office space. Yet even such impressive backing was dwarfed by the spate of big-business donations that came to light in January. Incidentally, in the same period the Tories accumulated donations worth twice those received by Labour, raking in £12.4m.

Labour confirmed its grip on power in June 2001, spending £11,140,019 on the campaign. Yet within a fortnight of the election win, the axe fell yet again on hapless party staff. Left-wing weekly *Tribune* obtained a copy of plans to reorganise Labour's regional structures, under which the number of full-time organisers in England outside the capital was to fall from 84 to just 60, and possibly as low even as 45. Four regional fundraisers were to be sacked after failing to raise at least four times their salary every year.

Millbank's grip on constituency Labour parties, which were to be offered a one-tenth contribution to the salary costs of a local organiser in return for a Millbank input into their appointment and their activities, was to increase. 'In return for this 10 per cent we expect to have certain rights, such as attendance on the interview panel, all disciplinary issues to be carried out either by or under instruction from head office, the organiser attending training events and helping in by-elections etc.,' announced the leaked document.[43]

Proving that even union patience does have its limits, the normally loyal general workers' union GMB shortly afterwards revealed plans to slash support for Labour from £650,000 a year to £400,000 for the next four years in protest at Blair's concerted drive to privatise public services. GMB financial backing for up to 100 MPs, whose constituencies received donations averaging around £5,000 each, was also to be reviewed, with the implication that slavish supporters of Blair's plans would suffer financially. Instead, the money will be spent campaigning against some aspects of New Labourism, including rallies and advertising against the Private Finance Initiative.[44]

By mid-2002, the transport union RMT decided that only MPs who sympathise with its core concerns will get any cash in future, and it has withdrawn payments to the constituency parties of Robin Cook and John

Prescott, among others. Prescott has quit the RMT as a result. Other unions are in the process of similar rethinks. There is even a realistic chance that some may decide to disaffiliate altogether. Even now this would be a financial blow to Labour. The extent to which it still needs union cash can be seen after the unions in 2001 refused to agree a 50 per cent increase in affiliation fees, from £2 to £3 a head. Labour was forced to seek a £2m extension in its overdraft limit, taking it to perhaps £6m.[45]

Labour has also had to quit Millbank for new offices just half the size, taking out a £5.5m mortgage on 11,325 sq. ft of open-plan space in Old Queen Street, Westminster. These premises are for the use of the latest general secretary David Triesman and his team, press officers and policy staff. Back office operations have been shifted out of London altogether, to North Shields, where costs – not least wages – are considerably lower. Several regional office positions were also axed in the latest austerity drive.

Labour's 2001 conference – the hundredth such gathering – was artificially truncated after the terrorist outrages in New York and Washington the previous month. But given the serious dust-up with the unions over PFI that had been shaping up, that was hardly an inconvenience to the party leadership. In other respects, the event would have had Kier Hardie spinning in his grave, and we aren't talking media manipulation here.

Even some die-hard New Labourites were shocked to learn that McDonald's was sponsoring a reception. The virulently anti-union junk food kings are a particular *bête noire* of the anti-capitalist movement after the famous McLibel trial. McDonald's agreed to foot the £15,000 cost of food and drink for 450 guests at a gathering in Brighton, but only if it could be guaranteed that the Prime Minister himself would attend. Speakers included a McDonald's director, and a McFilm crew was on hand to video the occasion. Cheekily, the company even asked if Blair would be willing to don a McDonald's hat. That was a request too far, even by the New Labour photo opportunity standards.[46] Incidentally, the Brighton burger bash was set up by top lobbyist Shandwick, where McDonald's £100,000-a-year account is looked after by key New Labour insider Colin Byrne.

Virtually every activity and every space at the conference was up for sale, making it a perfect microcosm of PFI Britain. Firms were invited to sponsor official fringe meetings involving cabinet ministers. The conference relaxation zone, video screens, recycling bins, and even the flower arrangements at the gala dinner were all open to sponsorship. So too was the conference ambulance service. A brochure attempted to entice potential backers with the words: 'NEW! Enjoy a positive profile through an association with the vital emergency service provided by the local ambulance service.'[47]

Two cabinet ministers – Stephen Byers and Robin Cook – joined Scottish Assembly minister Wendy Alexander at a fringe meeting on the topic of

'The Good State', organised by the Institute for Public Policy Research think tank. The gathering was sponsored by courier company DHL, owned by the German post office and not previously noted for its interest in the finer points of political sociology. It is, however, a potential buyer for a privatised Post Office. Ms Alexander's brother Douglas is the Trade minister with responsibility for postal services.

The IPPR also organised a fringe meeting on 'The Good Society', this time paid for by Provident Financial, a company that specialises in lending money to people who can't get credit from regular sources, at annual interest rates of up to 160 per cent APR. Access to credit at reasonable terms presumably did not form part of the definition arrived at by the meeting.

A gathering of the New Local Government Network, which brings together Blairite councillors with service providers, saw Education minister Stephen Timms share a platform with David McGahey, the former director of education at Buckinghamshire County Council. McGahey is now education managing director with Amey, one of the main beneficiaries of Public–Private Partnerships in education, discussed in chapter 8.[48]

Milburn again did the rounds of the fringe. A meeting titled 'Towards Stakeholder Healthcare' was sponsored by insurer Norwich Union, which has a commercial interest in private health insurance. Peter Hain, Minister for Europe, spoke on 'Making a Success of EU Enlargement' for the Centre for European Reform. The meeting was sponsored by United Utilities, which runs the privatised water system in Bulgaria and is naturally keen to see the country join the EU. On a similarly European theme, lobbyist and Labour donor Adamson BSMG backed a fringe meeting starring former foreign secretary Robin Cook under the title 'Europe – Winning the Argument'. Adamson BSMG is currently hoping to win the arguments with Brussels on behalf of chemical firms anxious to avoid tighter EU standards. And just months before its parent firm went bust, Enron subsidiary Wessex Water managed to line up Cook, *Guardian* columnist and SDP diva Polly Toynbee, and Blair adviser Charlie Leadbeater to address the topic 'A Radical Second Term'.[49]

Labour ended 2001 with a financial tonic, as Lord Sainsbury handed over his second £2m cheque of the year, taking his cumulative donations to New Labour to £9m.[50] But, despite the handout, problems were still evident.

Membership figures announced in January 2002 officially confirmed the earlier leaked total of 280,000, a reduction of 10 per cent. Once again, the old old story of changed administrative policy was held to be to blame. Members were being lapsed after falling five months in arrears, thus cutting the total by 13,000 at one stroke. Real membership figures may have been lower still. Only 254,000 ballot papers were sent out to paid up members in the 2001 national executive committee elections, for instance.[51]

By the following month, there were reports that Labour's overdraft had reached £10m. Party chairman Charles Clarke refused to confirm or deny the suggestion, but did admit: 'The general thrust is right. We have a significant overdraft position.' He added that Labour had introduced a business plan centred around a recruitment drive. Meanwhile, all 409 Labour MPs are to be forced to donate 2 per cent of their salaries to help make ends meet. The scheme will raise a £392,640 a year, hardly enough to make the 'significant overdraft position' notably less significant.[52]

The true state of Labour's finances finally emerged in July 2002, when a leaked national executive document confirmed that the party owed £6m in the current financial year, as well as further debts of another £2m. Membership dues would have to be hiked from £18.50 to £24 a year.[53]

Labour was, the report remarked, 'in the worst financial position it has ever been'. Those words are frighteningly reminiscent of what Mike Watts had to say a decade previously. Despite everything that has happened since 1992, Labour's finances are seemingly back to square one.

NOTES

[1] Labour Party annual report 2001; *Tribune*, 1 February 2002; *Financial Times*, 3 April 2002
[2] *Sunday Times*, 28 July 1991
[3] Ibid.
[4] *Guardian*, 23 May 1992
[5] Ibid.
[6] *Sunday Times*, 10 May 1992
[7] *Independent*, 19 July 1992
[8] *Guardian*, 30 September 1992
[9] *Guardian*, 12 December 1992
[10] *Guardian*, 2 August 1993; former party official, interview with author
[11] *Guardian*, 6 August 1993
[12] *Guardian*, 27 December 1994
[13] *Observer*, 4 January 1998
[14] Ibid.
[15] *Financial Times*, 13 August 1997
[16] *Observer*, 27 July 1997
[17] *Guardian*, 1 August 1997
[18] Ibid.
[19] *Financial Times*, 17 October 1997
[20] *Guardian*, 28 January 1998
[21] *Guardian*, 15 December 1997
[22] *Guardian*, 6 January 1998
[23] Labour Party Annual Report, 1999; 'Strategy and Budgeting for 1999', Labour document GS 28/7/99
[24] *Financial Times*, 27 February 1998

[25] *Observer*, 27 September 1998

[26] *Financial Times*, 6 September 1999

[27] *Guardian*, 8 May 2000

[28] *Daily Telegraph*, 3 September 1999

[29] *Daily Telegraph*, 5 October 2001

[30] *Financial Times*, 25 September 1999

[31] *Observer*, 29 November 1999

[32] Ibid.

[33] '1999 Objectives – Priorities and Budget', Labour document GS 7/1/99

[34] *Daily Telegraph*, 5 September 2000

[35] *Financial Times*, 7 December 2000

[36] *Sunday Times*, 28 November 1999

[37] http://news.bbc.co.uk/hi/english/uk_politics/newsid_1531000/1531932.stm

[38] *Private Eye*, 6 October 2000

[39] *Daily Telegraph*, 3 January 2001

[40] *Daily Telegraph*, 5 January 2001

[41] *Financial Times*, 8 January 2001

[42] *Guardian*, 6 June 2001

[43] *Tribune*, cited in *Guardian*, 22 June 2001

[44] *Guardian*, 18 July 2001

[45] *Guardian*, 1 August 2001

[46] *Guardian*, 30 August 2001

[47] Ibid.

[48] For details of these fringe meetings see *Private Eye*, 7 September 2001

[49] *Private Eye*, 18 October 2001

[50] *Guardian*, 14 December 2001

[51] *Guardian*, 29 January 2002; *Tribune*, 1 February 2002

[52] *Daily Telegraph*, 4 February 2002

[53] *Daily Telegraph*, 22 July 2002; *Yorkshire Post*, 22 July 2002

3. ENTREPRENEURS' CHAMPION:
THE BIRTH OF BLAIRISM

WHERE John Smith confined himself to prawn cocktails, Tony Blair was to prove the waiter who brought on the 14-ounce sirloin steak and chips. One theme dominated Labour politics in the three years between Blair winning the leadership and winning the election, and that was the party's increasing political accommodation of the private sector.

The aim was not just to neutralise business opposition, but to bring business fully on board. On offer was not merely vague consultation but direct input into policy-making. From the cornershop proprietor to the denizen of multiple multinational boardrooms, opinions were canvassed from businesses of all shapes and sizes. Endorsements from major business figures were hailed as triumphs. If they had previously been known Conservatives, so much the better.

The effect of these changes was all the more unsettling because the birth of Blairism was so unexpected. Until John Smith's sudden death on 12 May 1994, it seemed that nothing could conceivably stop him from forming an old-school Labour right government at some point in the next few years. After his death the question of succession was settled even more rapidly than it had been in 1992. Within hours, it was already obvious who the next leader was going to be, as Blair was relentlessly talked up by the media.

Initially, both Gordon Brown and Robin Cook saw themselves as potential candidates. Cook rapidly came to terms with his no-hoper status. But for Brown, who has nurtured a lifelong ambition to lead the Labour Party, the realisation that Blair had effortlessly attained an unassailable lead was a devastating setback. Brown's dinner with Blair at Islington's Granita restaurant on 31 May – at which he agreed to give his dining companion a clear run as the sole moderniser leadership candidate, in exchange for a price that has been much speculated upon ever since – has now passed into political folklore. One popular version is that the two struck a pact under which Blair would step down halfway through a second term and hand the reins to Brown. The more both men deny this story, the more widely it is believed.

In the event, Blair walked home in Labour's first ever one member one vote leadership election, pushing also-rans John Prescott and Margaret Beckett into second and third place respectively. The new regime wanted to force change through fast. One senior party staffer recalls: 'When Blair took over, it was like Pol Pot. It was like the year zero. Smith was airbrushed out of history, Kinnock was airbrushed out of history. If you bought the New Labour ideology, there was a degree of work that was necessary.'[1]

The Blairites already knew that attracting active support from business was central to what they were trying to do. But at this point they had little idea of where to start. Blair, still just 41, was a career lawyer with no first-hand experience of the business world and few connections either. Among his personal friends, only a layer of media executives – a group hardly typical of private sector management as a whole – could properly be described as businessmen.

Chief among them was Barry Cox, deputy chairman of Channel 4, who had known Blair for over a decade since the two were neighbours in Hackney. Cox had become a millionaire in 1991 thanks to the share option scheme in place at London Weekend Television. So enthused was he by the Blair leadership bid that he even took time off work to help organise the campaign, and convened a meeting for wealthy Labour supporters at his home. A whipround produced £88,000, not inconsiderable given an attendance of just ten people. Two of those present were Greg Dyke and Melvyn Bragg, both also LWT share options millionaires.

Other financial support for Blair in this internal party race included £5,000 from David Sainsbury, then chairman of the family supermarket, and music mogul Michael Levy. Blair was later to give both men peerages and political office.

Once installed, Labour's new leader was able to tap into both the Kinnock business network and the Labour Finance and Industry Group milieu. Yet even at this stage, Labour was formally opposed to large political donations from business, on point of principle. Brown told a television programme that August: 'In a democracy, the vast bulk of money [funding political parties] must come from individuals, either giving money as donations or as members.'[2] Big business involvement in politics was at this time one-way traffic. There were no known examples of any major company ever giving a serious donation to Labour. All that was about to change.

Within months of Blair taking over the leadership, a Bangladeshi businessman offered Labour a staggering £5m. Such a sum would have constituted the largest political donation ever given in Britain, and, indeed, it has only recently been matched by the generosity of IG Index betting tycoon Stuart Wheeler, who gave £5m to the Tories in 2001.

Labour officially confirmed that it had been approached by intermediaries apparently acting for a man named Dr Moosa bin Shamsher, chairman of Datco Group. The company specialised in supplying labour from his home country to the Middle East.

The offer probably was genuine. The trouble was, the party had consistently attacked the Tories for accepting gifts from foreign businessmen. Moreover, there were questions over Bin Shamsher's business record. Malaysia was then seeking his extradition from Bangladesh on fraud charges. Bin Shamsher's money was rejected.[3]

But Blair's much-repeated message that New Labour had dropped past hostility to the private sector was clearly having an impact. By the time preparations were in hand for the October 1994 Labour conference, there was already a noticeable thaw in business attitudes, as the realisation grew that this was Britain's next party of government.

So many companies wanted to take out exhibition space that a waiting list had to be opened up, eventually stretching to 27 businesses, including such big names as Sega and Securicor. There were even press reports that traditional Tory supporters like Marks & Spencer and United Biscuits were considering donations to Labour, although there is no record that either ever did give money.[4]

Business was also invited to participate in Labour's first ever conference corporate day. Coverage in the *Financial Times* was notable for its wry sarcasm:

> It had all the hallmarks of a Conservative fundraising event. Chief executives and directors of some of Britain's biggest companies lunching on Chablis and canapés, sponsored by Philip Morris the tobacco company, which hired Baroness Thatcher as a consultant. But there wasn't a Tory in sight – at least none willing to admit it.[5]

The function was carefully planned as a set piece. Although the participants would not have known in advance, the £350-a-head they paid to attend entitled them to witness a small piece of history. Corporate day coincided with Blair's first leader's speech to conference. He planned to use the occasion to announce the scrapping of Labour's formal commitment to common ownership, then enshrined in the famous Clause Four of the party's constitution:

> To secure for the workers by hand or by brain the full fruits of their industry and the most equitable distribution thereof that may be possible on the basis of the common ownership of the means of production, distribution and exchange and the best possible obtainable system of administration of each industry or service.

The new leader was well aware of the significance of what he was doing. Clumsy though the formulation was, for many old-school Labour activists, Clause Four was the very definition of socialism. The party faithful were being asked to stop worrying and learn to love the market. Historical precedents underlined that this was a high-risk strategy. Labour leader Hugh Gaitskell had tried a similar move in 1959, but had been unable to secure acceptance. Given the ideological impact of the collapse of Communism, Blair was now convinced that he could succeed where his predecessor had failed.

The decision to drop Clause Four was motivated largely by symbolism. Labour had already been in retreat from commitments to common ownership for over a decade, and no serious commentator saw the slightest likelihood of a Blair administration emulating Atlee in this respect. Now no more than a dead letter, it might just as well have remained a harmless ornament in the constitution.

But the Blairites spied a marketing opportunity. What better way to reassure business that there was zero chance of a Blair government taking the Tory privatisations back into state hands? And, just to make sure that the move hit home with the target market, Labour's corporate day ensured that some top business people were there to get that reassurance in person.

Lunch was held in a hotel room. Nicki Lewis, Labour's corporate relations manager, played the hostess with the mostest. Boosting the occasion's rather paltry glamour quotient, the party had even drafted in two early signings to the Luvvies for Labour brigade, author Ken Follett and film director David Puttnam. Labour supporter Richard Faulkner of lobbyist Westminster Communications, a future peer, was also present.

But why did the businessmen come along? John Moores, director of Littlewoods football pools and a Westminster Communications client, had no doubt about why he was there: pragmatism, rather than sudden conversion to the party's aim and values. 'Since Labour is going to form the next government, it's worth getting to know them,' he announced.[6]

Other guests included Sir John Egan, chief executive of airports group BAA, already engaged in its marathon, but ultimately successful, campaign to secure a fifth terminal at Heathrow; Michael Cassidy, chairman of the Corporation of London's policy committee; and Hanson director Peter Harper. Although Harper's company was still one of the biggest financial supporters of the Tories, he had been given Labour as a watching brief and had also participated in Jack Cunningham's Industry Forum. Lesser lights from Tesco and Motorola were also in the room.

After the meal, guests were transported to Blackpool's Winter Gardens in time to hear Blair's pronouncement. Covering the proceedings as a journalist for the Labour left weekly *Tribune*, I was present for the speech and saw how genuinely shocked many were on the conference floor. Leaving the venue by the back door afterwards, I bumped into Robin Cook, who asked me what I made of the development. Knowing Blair's ideological underpinnings, I replied, nobody should be particularly surprised. Cook vowed to lead the campaign against the move. His subsequent opposition proved less than earth-moving. Even as this conversation was taking place, Blair left the stage to host a drinks party for the business brigade. This was followed by dinner, with Prescott joining in the repast.

Despite the *coup de théâtre*, most guests concluded that the jury was still out. Cassidy professed disappointment that Brown did not set out his policies for business, and warned against punitive taxes. Harper maintained that Labour had yet to grasp that high dividends did not restrict investment, and that the threat of takeover actually worked to enhance rather than diminish corporate efficiency. Best pleased was Egan, who modestly affected: 'As a privatised company we have a case to prove that we are able to continue to generate wealth and it is encouraging that Labour want to listen to it.'[7]

After an internal contest Blair never looked like losing, the Clause Four campaign culminated in a special conference in April 1995, where Labour adopted a new version calling for the party 'to work for a dynamic economy serving the public interest, in which the enterprise of the market and the rigours of competition are joined with the forces of partnership and cooperation'. Whatever that means.

The rewards for embracing the enterprise of the market were quick to flow. Even as the debate was being had, out came the first documented instance of a public company making a five-figure donation. Business-friendliness clearly paid. Media group Pearson – publishers of the *Financial Times*, the newspaper that had gently mocked corporate day – handed over £25,000. Just to be even-handed, it also gave the same amount to the Conservatives.

Pearson chairman Lord Blakenham, a crossbencher, explicitly explained that the cheque was designed as an incentive to political moderation: 'The Labour Party has moved much more towards the centre and are the leading opposition party, so it is logical to help them.'[8]

Wags in the National Union of Journalists – not affiliated to Labour – joked that newspapers were now the only industry where the employees gave money to Labour, but the unions didn't.

Even at this stage, Labour was starting to discover some of the difficulties that were bound to arise from courting business. As part of her campaign to popularise plans for a minimum wage, employment spokesperson Harriet Harman in March released a dossier listing five major businesses guilty of holding down wages while donating substantial sums to the Tories. The suggestion was that these businesses benefited from the Conservatives' abolition of wages councils, previously the only legal protection on offer to the lowest paid.

Harman singled out the Comet chain of electrical stores as the worst offenders, and pointed to the £25,000 parent company Kingfisher had recently given the Tories, challenging the Conservatives to repay the money. She was quite clearly caught on the hop when Kingfisher retorted that it had provided Labour with £17,000 in sponsorship, dinner tickets and services in kind the year before.[9]

But on the whole, business opinion was now clearly warming, and Labour began to work on new ways to warm it further. One decision was to launch the Commission on Public Policy and British Business in April 1995, charged with drawing up a report that asked not what business could do for politics, but what politics could do for business. Agenda items included ways to increase investment, possibly through tax reform; training, including the idea of a compulsory training levy; and the minimum wage.

Technically the commission came under the auspices of the Institute of Public Policy Research, a New Labour-oriented think tank that was not formally a party unit. The organisation had been established by Gerald Holtham, the Lehman Brothers economist and Kinnock secretariat alumnus, later to return to the City.

Because the commission's findings would have no official standing, the leadership would be able to dismiss tiresome objections that policy should be formulated only through the party's democratic structures. But IPPR was at the same time close enough to Blair for participants to be certain that their deliberations would carry real clout.

Some suitably heavyweight players were lined up. Professor George Bain, principal of the London Business School, agreed to act as chairman. Bain would go on to serve on the Low Pay Commission – the body that puts a figure on the minimum wage – once Blair was in office.

Also signing up was Sir Christopher Harding, chairman of British Nuclear Fuels. Harding had for two decades been a director of Hanson, and was in addition chairman of insurance group Legal & General and services conglomerate BET. Other participants included the ever-dependable Lord Hollick, Kinnock's key business ally; Bob Bauman, chairman of arms manufacturer British Aerospace; George Simpson of another weapons maker, General Electric Company; Bob Bischoff, chairman of fork-lift truck makers Boss Group; James Hall, managing partner of Andersen Consulting; Janice Hall, European chief executive of advertising and marketing services group GGT; and the ubiquitous David Sainsbury.

To further enhance the commission's business street cred, trade spokesperson Jack Cunningham sounded out the CBI in advance, extracting a promise that, come the formal launch, the CBI would welcome the idea and pledge a written submission.

'Balance', such as it was, came from the input of John Monks, general secretary of the TUC; Lucy Heller of radical publishing house Verso; and Professor John Kay, a Labour-leaning academic. As one of those involved later commented: 'Our members range from those who think of themselves as middle-of-the-road Tories to soft-left Labour supporters.'[10] As detailed below, the commission's report – finally published in the run-up to the next election – came as a major boost to Labour's business credentials.

Meanwhile, whole sections of business were by now openly supporting some New Labour policies. Often those policies were of direct commercial benefit to the companies concerned. A striking example came at the 1995 Labour conference. Following negotiations with British Telecom, Blair was able to announce that the company had agreed to hook every school in the country up to cable, in return for permission to enter the cable entertainment sector.

Just weeks later, Blair got one of his first major opportunities to woo a business audience. He was invited to give the keynote address at the CBI conference, an event which only nine years earlier had banned Smith from even sitting in the audience. Britain needed successful business people, Blair told the assembled crowd of successful business people. Labour, he reassured the CBI, no longer saw fiscal policy as a means of wealth redistribution: 'Penal rates of taxation do not make economic or political sense. They are gone for good. I want a tax regime where, through hard work, risk and success, people can become wealthy.' He did add that he was opposed to greed, although this vice was apparently displayed only by privatised utility bosses, a soft target at the time.[11]

Fuelled by such speeches, business backing for Labour reached hitherto unimagined heights. An Institute of Management poll of 380 members found that support for the Conservatives among managers and senior executives had fallen from 64 per cent in 1992 to 43 per cent. Support for Labour had doubled, from 12 per cent to 25 per cent.[12]

But trust was not yet complete. For instance, three-quarters believed that direct taxation was more likely to rise under a Labour government, and half expected indirect tax increases as well. Only 22 per cent expressed confidence in Labour's policies for business, while 47 per cent said the party was not in tune with the real needs of business.

By now, many remaining vestiges of identifiably social democratic policy were rapidly being hurled overboard. In his early search for a defining big idea, Blair had toyed with the concept of a 'stakeholder economy', a concept developed by *Observer* editor Will Hutton in his bestselling book *The State We're In*. The phrase was interpreted to imply that the state should seek to ensure that business took the interests of employees, customers and the wider public into account when taking major decisions that ultimately shape everyone's lives. The Tories did their best to portray it as code for union rights. After featuring in several Blair speeches, the concept suddenly disappeared without trace.

One contemporary account contended:

> One minute the then-editor of *The Observer* was sitting in Blair's
> kitchen, watching Tony push down the plunger on the cafetière, as he
> said, 'Will, stakeholding is going to be our Bible' . . . Just six weeks
> later a perplexed Hutton found his idea had been dropped, after
> Blair's adoption of it had been greeted with suspicion by the business
> world.[13]

To this day, Hutton finds himself unable to blame Blair personally for the
way that stakeholding was discarded, and instead accuses an unholy
alliance of camp followers and unreconstructed leftists of the crime.

> Stakeholding was killed in the first three months of 1996 by a
> combination of ultra-Blairites around the Prime Minister taking the
> view that you cannot allow New Labour to be defined by one book,
> and Old Labour, which was very suspicious of a creed that had no
> overt socialist content. Tony Blair found no supporters on the right
> and no supporters on the left.

He adds that while 'some people' have pointed a finger in Peter
Mandelson's direction, he himself has 'no evidence' to that effect.[14]

Even as stakeholding was on its way out, moves were afoot to give
business greater direct input into Labour policy-making. Trade and industry
spokesperson Margaret Beckett announced in February the creation of six
taskforces under the auspices of Cunningham's Industry Forum.[15]

Publicity for the launch of the initiative centred on retailer and
restaurateur Sir Terence Conran, who announced that he would now be
voting Labour. But the significance was far greater than one man's ballot
paper. Here was a string of major companies – Hanson, Powergen, British
Gas – being offered and then accepting the chance to draw up the industrial
policies of a party that none of them supported. Hard-headed business
people all, they could hardly be expected to press the interests of employees
or consumers over their own bottom lines.

Chris Strutt, director of pharmaceuticals major SmithKline Beecham,
argued:

> Our involvement is not an expression of support for Labour and
> neither does it reflect expectations about the likelihood of a Labour
> government . . . It is a sensible approach intended to ensure Labour
> develops sound policies in areas crucial to our company. If we don't
> take part we may end up with unhelpful policies.

Bradley Herrmann, company secretary of cable television operator
Videotron, was even more explicit; 'Some of those involved are clearly

dedicated Labour supporters. But most, like us, simply want to influence policy.' [16]

Another participant was David Allen, marketing director of computer group Digital Equipment. He had never voted Labour in his life, he cheerfully confessed. Now he was helping the party formulate its policy on science and technology. Other participants included Hambros, Nissan, Tesco and Glaxo Wellcome.

Even small businesses, historically a core social base for Conservatism, could hardly fail to notice there was a charm offensive going on. Blair made a point of addressing the British Chambers of Commerce and Federation of Small Businesses annual conferences. The *Financial Times* was moved to comment: 'At present, the Federation of Small Businesses seems to be exercising more influence over Labour's employment policy than do the trade unions.'[17] Quite a surprising claim, considering that the organisation was still seeking to have smaller firms excluded from paying a minimum wage, no matter how low.

MP Barbara Roche was appointed spokesperson for small businesses, touring the country to put across the New Labour message. Attractive policies included action against late payment, a particular bugbear for small firms, and better access to venture capital funds. Labour's opposition to a government decision to transfer the cost of statutory sick pay from the state to employers also went down well.

In April 1996, it was revealed that Mirror Group Newspapers had given Northern Ireland spokesperson Mo Mowlam £21,000 to pay for a research assistant. Even before Maxwell, the Mirror Group had traditionally been a Labour supporter. But chief executive David Montgomery was a long-term Ulster Unionist and the paymaster's views on Irish politics were, therefore, somewhat well entrenched.

Moreover, Mowlam had previously been Labour's spokesperson for heritage, a brief that had included media ownership. MGN was, out of self-interest, lobbying against a bill that would stop any company with a 20 per cent or greater share of the national newspaper market from holding a television franchise. Labour, which previously broadly supported such a stance, was now arguing that the threshold should be raised to 25 per cent, just enough to let MGN into the market. MGN denied that this was a factor in the donation, arguing that the money was made available for 'the sole purpose of supporting the peace process in Northern Ireland'.[18]

Throughout the rest of the year, Labour continued to come up with pro-business policies and bask in the resultant business praise. In July, the party called for a £60-a-week tax rebate for six months, payable to companies that took on long-term unemployed youth. Small businesses would get £1,560 up front. GEC's George Simpson welcomed the proposals as 'an innovative project which deserves support'. Unilever's

Sir Michael Perry and Jaguar chairman Nick Scheele also proffered backing.[19]

In September, Labour published for the first time a list of large donors, albeit a list of large donors for the previous year. In an attempt to highlight Tory secrecy on such matters, it even gave the size of the donations. This gesture has yet to be repeated. All subsequent annual reports have simply listed such gifts as '£5,000 plus', a very understated way of describing cheques that sometimes reach seven figures.

Attention centred on a £1m donation from a hitherto little-known group, the Political Animal Lobby, which sought only a free vote on fox hunting. Arguably more significant are the first-ever known sizeable cheques from major companies. As well as the already publicised cash from Pearson, Tate & Lyle handed over £7,500, while reducing support to the Tories from £25,000 to £15,000. The sugar firm has a long record of support for the political right, from the use of its Mr Cube cartoon character in campaigns against nationalisation in the late 1940s, to subsequent support for the Economic League, a right-wing outfit that maintained a blacklist of trade union activists well into the 1990s.

There was also £30,000 from GLC, a City firm managing investment futures, and £20,000 from TU Fund Management, a trade union-based unit trust business. In all, donations in 1996 exceeded £6m.

The 1996 conference leader's speech saw Blair namecheck two businesses. Both J.C. Bamford (JCB) and Raytheon – a US-owned arms multinational – had recently played host to Blair visits, and had both obligingly provided him with a lift in their corporate aircraft.[20]

JCB is Britain's largest manufacturer of construction equipment and, indeed, one of the biggest privately owned manufacturing concerns of any kind. It employs around 3,000 people, clocking up annual sales of around £700m. Chairman Sir Anthony Bamford – proud owner of a £10m home in Gloucestershire – is well known as a Conservative supporter. Only months before, he had warned that Labour plans to implement the EU social chapter could jeopardise the company's investment plans.

Nevertheless, he had clearly been charmed by Blair's visit. A company spokesperson commented: 'Sir Anthony was impressed with Mr Blair as an individual and would have liked to have had more time with him.'[21]

Raytheon's best-known products are the Patriot and Sidewinder missiles, making it the kind of business not many ethical investment trusts would knowingly buy into. More peaceably, it also manufactures electronics systems and corporate jets. Blair had visited Raytheon's site at Hawarden, near Chester, where the company was scaling down its workforce from 500 to 150.

Another initiative of the period was the 'Road to the Manifesto' document, a combination of policy statement and marketing exercise that cost the party around £1m. The outlay included sending a potted version to every household in the country, producing two million copies of a 12-page tabloid extolling its virtues for distribution in key marginals, and a plebiscite of all party members to endorse its contents. The expenditure was only possible through the backing of publisher Paul Hamlyn, who provided £500,000–£600,000 towards the project. He could well afford it, having made £20m from the sale of his interests in Reed International the year before.

Then came word of the largest personal donation to the Labour Party yet. Following a number of meetings with Blair, Matthew Harding – a self-made insurance millionaire – pledged to give £1m. The money was earmarked for funding a poster campaign. Harding had a 27 per cent stake in Chelsea FC and was vice-chairman of the club. Accordingly, public confirmation of the donation in September proved a mild embarrassment for Prime Minister John Major, a Chelsea fan. Harding justified the gift on the grounds that Labour had 'a greater understanding of enterprise' than the Tories.[22]

The closer it came to election time, the more business chiefs bought into Labour. Alec Reed, chairman of the eponymous employment group, argued it would be 'a tragedy' if Blair did not become prime minister, while Cob Stenham, chairman of Arjo Wiggins Appleton, insisted that 'serious and forward-looking business people should back New Labour'.[23]

Even the big league were by now coming on-side. By January 1997, a group of top businessmen were regularly meeting Blair at a series of private Monday-evening dinners, there to be sounded out on economic and industrial policy. Invitations came courtesy of Hollick, with members of the Federation of Small Businesses decidedly not on the guest list. Known attendees at this particular Monday club included British Airways chief executive Robert Ayling, Pearson chairman designate Dennis Stevenson, new Unilever chairman Niall FitzGerald and David Sainsbury, yet again. The presence of these senior figures did not imply personal or corporate backing for Labour, it was stressed. But Labour sources briefed journalists that they considered the gatherings to constitute a network of informal advisers.[24]

More publicly, three business figures were appointed to advise on competition issues. These were named as Lord Borrie, former director general of fair trading; Brian Sanderson, chief executive of BP Chemicals; and Professor John Vickers, erstwhile Shell financial analyst and by now professor of political economy at Oxford University.[25]

Labour even managed to neutralise the CBI and the Institute of Directors (IoD), which both pledged not to take sides in the forthcoming election. Even the IoD's uncompromising Thatcherite director general Tim Melville-Ross admitted that Labour had been transformed, although he was sceptical over the durability of the changes: 'The question remains, if Blair does not win a large majority, whether it will be sustained.'[26]

After two years of deliberation, the IPPR was finally ready to publish the report of its Commission on Public Policy and British Business. The timing – January 1997 – resulted in a spectacular propaganda victory for New Labour, just months before the election. The word 'Labour' appeared just once in the document's 270 pages. Yet a swathe of influential business people were willing to put their names to a document echoing many New Labour criticisms of the Tory years. Conservative embarrassment was compounded by Deputy Prime Minister Michael Heseltine gatecrashing the launch meeting, infuriated as a string of senior executives criticised his government's failure to promote competition.[27]

What condign revenge on the man who dared mock the prawn cocktail offensive! Efforts to present New Labour as the red menace incarnate were due to form a key plank of the Tory election campaign. Here were top brass from British Aerospace, GEC, Sainsbury and Legal & General arguing otherwise.

They explicitly backed many Labour policies, including a minimum wage – providing it wasn't set at a level they considered too high, such as, say, enough to live on – as well as improvements in education, training and transport infrastructure and tax incentives for long-term investment. Other points of the report included a call for restrictive practices or abuse of dominant market position to be made illegal. Companies guilty of anti-competitive behaviour should be fined up to 10 per cent of turnover, it argued.

However, the document rejected Labour's policy of merging the Monopolies and Mergers Commission and the Office of Fair Trading into one super-watchdog, and also the idea that all takeovers or mergers should be justified on public interest grounds.

'Eighty per cent of businessmen would accept most of the report,' a commission member told the *Financial Times*. 'How Labour reacts will, therefore, be a test of whether it has really changed enough to embrace a pro-business agenda.'[28]

Labour *had* really changed enough to embrace a pro-business agenda. Blair's speech to the launch – against a conspicuous Union Jack backdrop – all but ruled out a new top rate of income tax and even backed the report's recommendations on takeovers, simply ignoring party policy. The Tories had not done enough to promote market competition, Blair insisted, while stressing that Labour's support for the limited employment rights contained in the EU's social chapter did not mean any dilution of its commitment to flexible labour markets.

'Over the past two years, I have addressed over 10,000 individual business people. It has not just been about collecting endorsements and support. It is about building a genuine new partnership with business for the future,' Blair pronounced. 'Today I offer business a new deal for the future. The deal is this: we leave intact the main changes of the eighties in industrial relations and enterprise.'

To top off this explicitly Thatcherite settlement, the leader of the Labour Party went on to promise the unions the worst deal in Europe: 'Our proposals for change, including the minimum wage, would amount to less labour market regulation than in the USA . . . In the USA it would never occur to question the commitment of the Democrats to business. It should be the same here with New Labour.'[29]

For the first time in its history, Labour entered an election with both a main manifesto and a separate 'business manifesto', mailed out to executives in an effort to attract their backing. The 20-page document was drawn up with the help of CBI leader Adair Turner, a one-time SDP supporter. It reiterated an earlier promise to stick to Conservative government spending limits for the first two years of a New Labour administration, and argued that 'tax and spend is being replaced by save and invest'. Labour, it added, will 'ask the question any manager in a company would ask: not how much more to spend but how to spend existing resources more effectively to meet our priorities'. There would be personal contact with business; no repeal of most anti-union legislation; no increases in tax; a tough inflation target; and increased spending on education and skills.[30]

Launching the business manifesto, Blair promised: 'A New Labour government will work in partnership with business. We want Britain to be a great place to do business. Labour is now the party for business, the entrepreneurs' champion.'[31]

A party election broadcast aired on 10 April opened with a montage of shots of the City taken from unusual camera angles. The voiceover featured four powerful business leaders. The Body Shop's Anita Roddick started by observing: 'Business is more powerful than government. It is quicker, more creative.'[32] Such an observation is more acute than Roddick herself probably realises. Business is indeed now more powerful than government, and that is a worrying state of affairs for democracy. She was followed by Labour neophyte Terence Conran, who argued: 'Business is the lifeblood of the country.'

Then came Jonathan Charkham of retailers Great Universal Stores, who maintained: 'From business come all the benefits that society needs: employment, investment, revenue for social programmes.'[33] The converse argument that from those who make up society come all the benefits top businessmen get – salaries, bonuses, share options, pensions – was not on offer this particular evening. Finally viewers heard from lifelong Tory Gerry Robinson of Granada, who had recently switched camps: 'I think, frankly, there's only one party that can represent Britain best, getting business right, and that's New Labour.'[34]

The first two weeks of the six-week campaign were dominated by the scandal over claims that Tory MPs were tabling parliamentary questions in return for money. For the final four, the Conservatives busied themselves in internecine conflict rather than electoral work. Meanwhile, Labour was greedily seizing last-minute business photo opportunities. Five days before polling, Tony and Cherie Blair caught a Virgin train from Euston heading for the north-west. On board with them was Virgin supremo Richard Branson.

At no stage was the result of the 1997 general election ever in any more doubt than the 1994 leadership contest. Britain had a new Prime Minister.

NOTES

[1] Former party official, interview with author

[2] *Guardian*, 22 August 1994

[3] *Guardian*, 29 August 1994

[4] *Daily Express*, 11 August 1994

[5] *Financial Times*, 5 October 1994

[6] Ibid.

[7] Ibid.

[8] *Guardian*, 8 February 1995

[9] *Daily Mail*, 18 March 1995

[10] *Financial Times*, 9 January 1997

[11] *Guardian*, 14 November 1995

[12] *Financial Times*, 20 February 1996

[13] *Independent*, 4 July 2000

[14] Will Hutton, interview with author

[15] *Financial Times*, 6 February 1996

[16] Ibid.

[17] *Financial Times*, 9 July 1996

[18] *Mail on Sunday*, 21 April 1996

[19] *Financial Times*, 13 July 1996

[20] *Financial Times*, 1 October 1996

[21] Ibid.

[22] *Daily Telegraph*, 7 September 1996

[23] Anderson and Mann, *Safety First* (London, Granta, 1997), p.41

[24] *Observer*, 19 January 1997

[25] Ibid.

[26] Ibid.

[27] *Financial Times*, 9 January 1997

[28] Ibid.

[29] Anderson and Mann, *Safety First* pp.40–1

[30] *Guardian*, 24 March 1997

[31] Press Association, 11 April 1997

[32] www.psr.keele.ac.uk/area/uk/pebs/pblab97.htm as of 16 November 2001

[33] Ibid.

[34] Ibid.

4. TAKING IT ON TRUST

ALVIN Stardust, Bad Manners and The Darts are just a few of the naff 1970s pop acts that get walk-on parts in the New Labour story, courtesy of former record boss Michael Levy. Close friend Pete Waterman once remarked: 'People say he is a schlock merchant, he likes twee rock 'n' roll.'[1] Given the roster of bands Levy signed during his music biz days, even that description grossly overestimates the man's musical tastes.

That was an earlier life, of course. These days Levy has reinvented himself as a world statesman, a Foreign Office minister in all but name, as the Prime Minister's special envoy to the Middle East. This is an astonishing appointment for a man whose open espousal of Zionism and ties to the Israeli establishment automatically compromise him in Arab eyes. Yet there is nothing on his curriculum vitae that indicates any experience relevant to this delicate diplomatic role in a perpetually crisis-ridden region.

One only has to hope that Blair's appointment was not based solely on Levy's activities between these two careers, as the Prime Minister's special envoy to the extremely rich. Levy has raised around £10m for the New Labour cause. 'He knows how to shake down the fat cats,' one Labour insider remarked disapprovingly. 'He takes them to meet Blair for 20 minutes and then marches them off to the nearest cash point.'[2]

Much of this money bypassed the party proper and went straight to Blair's private office, increasing the leader's financial – and thus political – independence from both the membership and the trade unions. Among the posts the funds helped pay for while Labour was still in opposition were those of chief press officer Alastair Campbell and chief of staff Jonathan Powell.

Levy's importance to Blair can hardly be overstressed. The two first met at a dinner party in 1994, given by senior Israeli diplomat Gideon Meir, and Levy soon became the politician's tennis partner. After financially backing Blair's leadership bid from his own pocket, the following year he was entrusted with setting up the so-called Labour Leader's Office Fund blind trust to finance the Leader of the Opposition's private office. Equally importantly, he also revolutionised the Labour Party's already established efforts to find high-value donors.

The phrase 'blind trust' refers to a funding conduit that allowed people to make donations to politicians via independent trustees, without the politicians themselves knowing who their backers were. Theoretically, this ruled out the possibility of donors buying influence. There was an added bonus for businesses, as, unlike gifts to a party, support for a blind trust did not have to be declared in company annual reports. Throughout the mid-1990s, Labour made full use of such mechanisms. Neither the money nor the benefactors were listed in the party's voluntary annual round-up of £5,000-plus donors, as donations to Labour frontbenchers through blind trusts were not deemed donations to the Labour Party itself. The trusts themselves were not bound to make their accounts public. The common missing link here is accountability.

The problem with blind trusts is that they are not so much blind as just a little bit short-sighted. Not only did the beneficiaries regularly find out who their supporters were, but sometimes the world and her cohabiting partner did so as well. Such was the public disquiet that such arrangements are now banned under the Political Parties, Elections and Referendums Act 2000.

But Levy took full advantage of the system while the going was good. His adept blind trust fundraising enabled Blair to run the biggest opposition leader's office in history, employing some 20 full-time staff on appreciable salaries. Although figures remain confidential, the best guess is that in just three years the Labour leader received around £2.5m in this manner before becoming Prime Minister.[3]

Most of this came from an unknown number of wealthy individuals. To this day, only four of Blair's benefactors have been identified for certain, while there are fingers pointing to a few other names. But of the known donors, two subsequently received peerages. While it does not necessarily follow that the scheme was anything other than the model of probity, there is at least an argument that Lloyd George knew its father. With full details unlikely ever to emerge, we will probably never be in a position to make an informed judgement.

Blair was not the only Labour politician on the blind trust bandwagon. John Prescott, Gordon Brown, Margaret Beckett and some lesser lights were also in on the act. David Shaw – the Conservative backbencher who led the charge on the issue for the Tories – claimed in 1997 to have identified a constellation of six or possibly seven New Labour blind trusts. These he named, under parliamentary privilege, as the Leader of the Opposition's Fund; the Deputy Leader's Fund; the Shadow Chancellor Fund; the Industrial Research Trust; the Westminster Objectors' Trust; the Front Bench Research Fund; and the Soho Fund, linked to Mandelson. In a none-too-subtle dig at Mandelson's sexuality, Shaw added: 'I shall not say anything more about the honourable gentleman and his connections with Soho.'[4]

Shaw now freely admits he milked the issue for party purposes and has little in the way of documentation. The Westminster Objectors' Trust, for example, was primarily a local vehicle for opponents of the activities of Westminster's Tory council leader Shirley Porter, and thus hardly in the same political league. He also appears to have missed out the Marjorie Mowlam Research Fund. In 1999, Mowlam was rebuked by the Commons Committee on Standards and Privileges for failing to declare a donation of £5,000 made five years previously by Greg Dyke, the media chief now in charge of the BBC.

Who else paid into the blind trusts? How did their interests subsequently fare under New Labour? Details are sketchy at best. But one point is both clear and extremely important to grasp. Big business was the provenance of most of the money that flowed in. That, of course, dovetailed nicely with Blair's political project. Financial independence from union funding was seen as a good in itself. Conversely, the willingness of a layer of business people to put their hands in their pockets represented one of the first concrete manifestations of rapprochement with the private sector. In short, the rise of the blind trusts marked an important staging post in the party's transformation.

Yet the first Labour politician to take advantage of such arrangements was the rather more traditionalist John Smith, the main beneficiary of the Industrial Research Trust, established in April 1993. Prime mover in its foundation was Smith's close friend Lord Haskel, a key player in the Labour Finance and Industry Group. The Leeds-based textile manufacturer, born in Lithuania, was ennobled as one of Smith's first batch of working peers. Haskel himself will neither confirm nor deny being one of the actual trustees.[5]

Less reticent about involvement in the Industrial Research Trust, although not exactly forthcoming, are Lord Gregson, industrialist and president of the Defence Manufacturers Association, and Baroness Lockwood, the one-time chair of the Equal Opportunities Commission, who have admitted their role as trustees.[6]

Some 20–30 parties made donations to the trust, the trustees confirmed. These included the Caparo Group, owned by Indian-born industrialist Dr Swraj Paul, which has gone on the record as giving £130,000 over a number of years. Dr Paul was upgraded to Lord Paul in 1996.[7]

Smith didn't keep all the cash to himself. Money from the Industrial Research Trust was also paid to other senior Labour politicians including Brown and Cook, as their entries in the register of members' interests reveal.

Senior frontbenchers quickly cottoned on and set up blind trusts of their own. Prescott's office, with a staff of seven, established the John Prescott Campaign/Research Trust. Cook was backed by the World Affairs Research Trust, and Beckett by the Margaret Beckett Research and Administration

Trust. Yet another fund, the Labour Front Bench Research Fund, helped meet the costs of other frontbenchers.[8]

On taking over the party leadership in 1994, Blair found himself entitled to more than £1m in so-called Short Money, as state handouts enabling parties with seats in parliament to fulfil their duties are called. Blair could also claim a cut – presumably the lion's share – from the old Industrial Research Trust.

But he evidently found such backing insufficient. So in 1995 the Labour Leader's Office Fund was born. Trustees in this instance included Lord Merlyn-Rees, home secretary under Callaghan; Baroness Jay, Callaghan's daughter; and Baroness Dean, the erstwhile print union leader. Although not a trustee, Levy had the job of bagman.[9]

No press release was issued proclaiming the fund's establishment. Its existence only became public knowledge with an article in *The Sunday Times* in November 1996. The Blair camp was quick to defend its integrity. One unnamed spokesperson argued: 'It is not a secret fund, it is a blind trust, which means that no one in the office knows who the donors are. Certainly not Tony.'[10]

Certainly not Tony? Given that details of four prominent businessmen backers were published in the newspaper, that argument hardly passed muster. Among those named were the late Sir Emmanuel Kaye and Sir Trevor Chinn.

Kaye had sold his industrial vehicles business Lansing Bagnall to Linde of Germany for an undisclosed sum, reportedly £100m, in 1989. Getting him on board was a particular coup for Levy. Kaye, who died in 1999, had a history of mobilising business for the Conservatives. In 1968, he founded the Unquoted Companies Group, an alliance of major private firms. It waged political campaigns against Labour industrial relations reforms, and later lobbied Thatcher for tax breaks for entrepreneurs.

He was also a member of the CBI council from 1976 to 1989, and its financial policy committee from 1985 to 1992. As befits a staunch eurosceptic, he had given substantial cash backing to the Conservatives. Yet, somehow, Levy managed to bring him into the Labour funding milieu. Kaye went on to become an important financial backer for the Labour Party, with at least one six-figure donation under his belt.

Chinn joined the board at Lex Service in 1959, building a small group of garages into a self-described 'broad-based provider of motoring and business solutions'. Lex acquired the Royal Automobile Club in 1999, and the following year severed all ties with the motor retail sector on which it was once based.

Like Levy, Chinn had long been involved in charity work, including such causes as the Variety Club and the Great Ormond Street Hospital Wishing Well appeal. Indeed, his charitable activities were the official reason for the award of a knighthood from Margaret Thatcher in 1990.

The other two persons named by *The Sunday Times* as Labour Leader's Office Fund donors – printing millionaire Bob Gavron and Granada Television's Alex Bernstein – both subsequently secured peerages. That all four of the backers, as well as Levy himself, were Jewish was a point picked up on by commentators as diverse as the *Jerusalem Post* and the British National Party.

There are further Jewish connections. The trust's books were handled by London accountants Blick Rothenberg, which also looks after many major Israeli companies operating in Britain. The Conservatives allege that Maurice Hatter, chairman of IMO Precision Controls, also gave to the trust.[11] Hatter is known for certain to have given £1m to government education initiatives, £10,000 to Labour election funds and £25,000 towards Frank Dobson's abortive London mayor campaign.

Late publisher Paul Hamlyn was already a substantial Labour donor and is also likely to have given to Blair's blind trust. He was friend of both Gavron and Levy, who later extracted from Hamlyn a £2m donation to the party proper in 2000.

But in this case there is no need to resort to anti-Semitic conspiracy theory to explain all this. First, there is a longstanding layer of Labour-leaning Jewish business people, which formed the core of the Labour Finance and Industry Group. Second, in the early days Levy was quite obviously working his own contacts. As one Labour source put it:

> The nexus is not sinister. It is probably the social relations that surround a particular reform synagogue in North London. If you crack that congregational network, you have probably cracked much of the cross-linkage. It may explain some of the anomalies in the fundraising and the unexpected sources of funds traditionally associated with the Tories.[12]

What of the other blind trusts? MP Alan Meale, trustee of the John Prescott Campaign/Research Trust, argues that most of the money that came in was generated by Prescott's outside earnings, such as fees for speeches and articles.[13] But at least £10,000 was given by Haris Sophoclides, a British-based Greek-Cypriot property developer. Prescott has holidayed on several occasions at Sophoclides' villa in Cyprus, after getting a taste for the country during his days as a steward on cruise ships in the eastern Mediterranean.

Sophoclides owns J&P Ltd, one of the Middle East's largest property and construction firms, building hotels, airports, hospitals and military bases worldwide. He also plays an influential role in the Greek diaspora as president of the Greek Cypriot Brotherhood, an organisation which is in its own right a corporate donor to the Labour Party, and is vice-president of the

World Council of Hellenes Abroad, described as a non-governmental organisation, albeit one 'created by a 1995 presidential decree'.[14]

His son Tony Sophoclides spent four years as a Prescott aide before becoming a lobbyist. While working for the Deputy Prime Minister in 1997, Tony led a delegation of Labour MPs – including Meale, Rudy Vis, Stephen Twigg and Joan Ryan – to the island, where they met top Cypriot politicians. Sophoclides senior has been officially accredited as a parliamentary researcher too, with privileged access to the Commons courtesy of a pass provided by Meale.

Gordon Brown received a £50,000 cheque from Kaye through the Industrial Research Trust. The donation followed a meeting between the two men at a function organised by the Labour Friends of Israel group in 1996. A spokesperson insisted: 'Gordon had no idea, neither had any of his staff, who funded the blind trust.'[15]

But some of those who saw the blind trust system up close and personal are not so sure just how blind it was. Henry Drucker, briefly a key player in Labour's search for big donations, has described the set-up as essentially 'evil'. This is criticism from a surprising quarter. The US-born academic, who now holds dual nationality, is a longstanding Labour Party member. In 1979 he co-edited a book with Brown, and was later chairman of Cook's constituency party.[16]

Drucker founded the Oxford Philanthropic fundraising consultancy, known as Oxphil, which specialises in finding backers for good causes. Clients include Nottingham University and the Welsh National Opera. He successfully raised £340m for Oxford University, Alma Mater of many a leading politician. Little wonder Labour wanted him on board.

In March 1996, Drucker was hired until after the next election to work on ways of extracting sums of £25,000 or more from companies and wealthy individuals. This was a time when Labour still considered a £5,000 donation a relatively big gift. But, as Drucker points out, the super-rich are happy enough to hand over £100,000, or even £1m, for causes they truly support.

Right from the start, press coverage pointed to probable tension between Drucker and Levy. But no matter. The appointment was obviously personally sanctioned by the party leader himself. Drucker recalls being recruited by Blair's chief of staff Powell, after Blair had just returned from a trip to Hong Kong. 'People told Blair the Tories came to Hong Kong with a bag and left with it full of cheques. Basically he wanted to know how to do the same thing.'[17]

Oxphil agreed to assess the market, its standard methodology, and was given a tight deadline. Powell supplied a list of people he thought would give sizeable sums, and Drucker set about interviewing them. That didn't prove too difficult. 'This was a period of maximum charisma for Blair and

New Labour,' Drucker recalls. 'They were clearly going to win the next election, and all sorts of people wanted to be on Blair's good side.'[18]

The object of market assessment is to tell clients what they have to change about themselves to get the money rolling in. What Drucker found was enormous resentment of blind trusts, and widespread disbelief that they were indeed anonymous. Additionally, people were fed up with being approached by multiple competing blind trusts. The whole shooting match was also considered hypocritical on the part of a party pledged to openness in matters of political funding. No message could have been more guaranteed to infuriate Levy.

Drucker made his findings clear through progress reports fed to Powell, who by now realised blind funds were a big issue. 'What I, in retrospect foolishly, didn't appreciate is that there was no way Michael Levy was going to live with the recommendation of no blind funds, and no way Blair was going to live with recommendations Michael Levy would not live with.'[19]

After just seven weeks later Drucker and Labour parted company. The official line was that the party had decided to keep fundraising in-house rather than relying on a paid outsider. But the main reason for the rapid divorce was Drucker's moral concerns.

A showdown between Levy, Drucker and fellow Oxphil consultant Rebecca Rendel took place at Levy's home in the spring of 1996. Drucker recalls the gathering vividly.

> I think I was set up by Levy. He knew perfectly well what we were saying because Jonathan told Tony and Tony told him. As soon as we got to the house we were subject to a verbal assault. He was shouting and unpleasant . . . It was obviously an authority issue. Who the hell did we think we were? He was running this. What the hell were we doing making recommendations?
>
> I knew he was running Tony's blind fund so I didn't anticipate a very pleasant meeting. It was basically, 'this is what I am doing and therefore you will accommodate it'.[20]

Shortly afterwards, Drucker formally presented his findings to a Labour delegation at Pall Mall's Reform Club that included general secretary Tom Sawyer, finance director Paul Blagbrough and two or three others. The meeting made no difference. Drucker was thrown off the case. His views found sympathy in some quarters, however. He recalls a one-and-half-hour telephone consolation chat with Donald Dewar – later First Minister of the Scottish assembly – who advised him not to take things personally.[21]

Despite parting on bad terms, Drucker is still unwilling to disclose the names of the donors he canvassed. 'You would be able to guess two-thirds of them,' he maintains. 'The other third is too obscure.' Nevertheless, he does recollect some pretty in-your-face approaches from honours-seekers. One British-based businessman with foreign connections came right out and asked how much the going rate was for a peerage. He was willing to pay several million pounds for the privilege, Drucker believes.

He also offers an interesting insight on one of the ways that blind trust donors could be sure that Tony knew of their kindness.

> If Michael Levy thought you would give a lot of money to the party, he would invite you to play tennis at his house and say 'there's a fair chance Tony will turn up'. Tony turned up, of course. When Tony left, Levy asked for money. I'm sure Levy, being the sort of guy he is, would ring Blair up ten minutes later and say, 'we got two £500,000 cheques today'.[22]

Just when the blind trust issue was all but forgotten, the Labour Leader's Office Fund hit the headlines again with the publication of Geoffrey Robinson's memoirs in 1999. The former Paymaster General insisted that he had been 'happy' to give a substantial donation to support Blair's work as leader of the opposition. Controversy revolved around both the size of the gift – as much as £250,000, according to press reports – and the channel through which it was made. Labour went to some lengths to quash any suggestion that the money was paid into the Labour Leader's Office Fund.

Parallel to the blind trusts, but rather less secretive, Labour has, with initial trade union encouragement, maintained a high-value donors' unit since the early 1990s. After a shaky start, its efforts have met considerable success. Levy has played a major role in the unit's work. For instance, he was directly involved in soliciting the £1m donation from Formula One chief Bernie Ecclestone through the unit.[23] But much of the graft was undertaken by his protégé Amanda Delew, whom he had met through the charity Jewish Care. Delew took the job of fundraising consultant to Blair in 1996. Together, Levy and Delew are reported to have raised £12m before the 1997 election.

The following year Delew, whose CV also includes stints at the Imperial Cancer Research Fund and Scope, transferred from Blair's staff to the head office payroll, running the high-value donor unit until her departure in 2001. Not for nothing did Millbank insiders refer to her as 'Amanda the Loot'. Her approach to fundraising appears openly to have been based on the maxim 'flattery will get you everywhere'. As Delew explained in a memo written just after the 1997 election win, but only leaked the following year: 'Major donors expect to be invited to Number 10. If this cannot take place then income levels may be affected.'

What she appears to be saying is that she considered it her job to sell the rich the chance to rub shoulders with the powerful. The document set down her strategy to bring in £12.5m over the following four years.

> The support of Tony Blair and Jonathan Powell is critical to the success of the programme. Major donors need to feel they are at the centre of things . . . Jonathan offers an opportunity for them to meet someone at the focus of all activity, who will answer their questions, while providing a reason for them to visit Number 10. He offers authority and integrity and has proved his ability at charming and impressing . . . donors.[24]

Her ideas on the subject didn't stop there. She called on the Prime Minister to hold 'private meetings with some of the more interested supporters . . . These meetings should never address the subject of money and wherever possible Michael Levy should be in attendance. The meetings should simply be for Tony to meet people who are supportive of the party.'[25]

When the text of the memo hit the press, Labour spokesperson Dave Hill was at pains to dismiss the document as naive, and, what is more, one that was quashed before it even reached the party leadership. 'No one who gives money to the party is given preferential treatment and no one can buy access to Downing Street,' he indignantly insisted. Secretary of State for Culture Chris Smith insisted it was merely 'a paper that was prepared by a middle-ranking official'. That was hardly an accurate description of a woman who played a central role in the party's drive to attract six-figure donations.[26]

For instance, it was Delew who organised the event dubbed 'the most expensive cheese and wine party in British political history', held in January 1997. Business and celebrity guests included Greg Dyke, Jeremy Irons, Melvyn Bragg and David Puttnam. The keynote speech was made by Peter Mandelson, who – only half-jokingly – suggested that no one should leave before they had donated £25,000. Moreover, such subsequent £2m Labour donors as Christopher Ondaatje and Lord Hamlyn have been regular guests at Delew bashes.[27]

A second leaked Delew memo made it to the press in September 1999, when the *Sunday Telegraph* revealed a list of high-value donations and pledges to Labour totalling over £5m. The 31 names mentioned formed an eclectic mix of people from the worlds of business, media and the arts.[28] Showbiz names were prominent, including Creation Records chief Alan McGee and Simply Red singer Mick Hucknall. But business people were also to the fore. These included such usual suspects as Lord Haskins, Gavron and Bernstein. Some names were slightly more surprising. Previously unsuspected Labour supporters included property tycoon John Ritblat and publishing boss Felix Dennis.

Ritblat – chairman of British Land, Britain's second largest property company – had been an outspoken Thatcher enthusiast. He was a reported past donor to the Millennium Club, a Tory fundraising group that requires a minimum payment of £2,500, although Ritblat denies this is the case. After publication of the Delew list, he also denied having given any money to Labour, causing the *Sunday Telegraph* to retract the suggestion.[29]

Dennis first hit the headlines as a defendant in the Oz obscenity trial in 1971, before making good as the lad-mag entrepreneur behind *Maxim* magazine. In the process, he has accumulated a £200m fortune, and any residual hippy idealism has gone out the window. Dennis has pointedly failed to deny the suggestion that he keeps ten girlfriends on the go at any one time, owns countless cars including five Rollers and a Bentley, and has 23 kitchens spread across several homes.

Pledges, however, are a different matter from money in the piggy bank. The memo acknowledges that only £1m was actually in hand. Much of the remaining £4.38m may have been more by way of Delew's wish list than hard cash.

Three of those named – Hatter, Haris Sophoclides and David Goldman – were listed as having pledged £1m each. Labour admitted that Goldman, chairman of BATM Advanced Communications, had not actually made such a commitment, despite five-figure donations to Labour in the past. Hatter also denied having promised £1m in this instance, past generosity notwithstanding. Whatever the case, within months of the alleged pledge, he received a knighthood for public services. Sophoclides' largest known donation to Labour is £5,000-plus worth of dinner tickets in 1999, although his support for Prescott as an individual politician has been at least twice that.

The largest subsequently confirmed donation on the Delew list came from Gavron, then chairman of the Guardian Media Group, owner of *The Guardian* newspaper. He had in the past both expressed his admiration for Thatcher and been courted by the SDP. Gavron gave Labour a reported £500,000, handed over in the same month he became a peer.

Another subsequent donor was Gulam Noon, founder of Noon Products, which makes frozen curries for Sainsbury, Waitrose and Marks & Spencer. The company was involved in a bitter strike in 1998, when it refused to recognise the GMB union at its plant in Southall, even though 90 per cent of the 300-strong workforce had joined. There were allegations of low pay, oppressive management and favouritism at the factory. Noon – one of Britain's wealthiest Asians, worth some £10m – gave Labour £100,000. He picked up a knighthood in 2002.[30]

Jeremy Mogford, founder of the Brown's restaurant chain, pledged £100,000, while Derek Johnson, chairman of shipping agents JSA, admitted that he had indeed promised £100,000 but had not yet paid up.

Delew has now moved on to become campaign director at the Giving Campaign, a government-backed initiative to increase support for charities, where her job will once again be to encourage the corporate sector to put its hands in its pockets. Giving Campaign backers include Blair peer and Labour donor Lord Joffe, former chairman of Allied Dunbar.

Further down the food chain from the high-value donor unit is the 1000 Club, Labour's organisation for those in a position to contribute a comparatively modest annual £1,000 or so, which has existed since the early 1990s. The symbolism is all important here. While its activities may make middle-class participants feel like big shots, it has few links with the real centres of power in the Labour Party.

Early efforts were headed by Jack Cunningham, with a steering committee including Lord Graham of Edmonton, Labour right fixer Mary Goudie, MEP Pauline Green, and Sarah Macaulay of Hobsbawm Macaulay Communications, later to marry Gordon Brown. Great and good involvement in the early period also included European commissioner Bruce Millan, novelist Ruth Rendell, Jonathan Powell and Tom Sawyer. Three of the steering committee have since been awarded peerages, and are now known as Baroness Goudie, Baroness Rendell and Lord Sawyer respectively.

The covering letter accompanying the club's promotional literature in March 1996 – laden with such Blair cliches as 'young country' and 'new economy' – promised invitations to special summer and Christmas receptions, an annual conference dinner, campaign briefings and chances to meet members of the Shadow Cabinet. The reply-paid envelope was addressed to Hobsbawm Macaulay Communications in Soho's Poland Street.

The 1000 Club organises Labour's £500-a-plate fundraising dinners, an annual event that raises around £500,000 while spreading warm fuzzy feelings among those well-heeled enough to attend. For what was once a workers' party, this event is probably the ultimate in post-modern irony.

The first of these dinners took place in 1991, with speeches from Kinnock and barrister-playwright John Mortimer, and a celebrity auction featuring actor Stephen Fry as master of ceremonies. Items up for grabs included the script of television drama *A Very British Coup*, an early 1980s fantasy about the election of a working-class left-winger as Labour prime minister.

While the attendees obviously didn't miss the price of admission, few could properly have been described as front-rank business people. VIP guests included Sir Kenneth Berrill, former chairman of the Securities and Investments Board, and head of the Central Policy Review Staff at the Cabinet Office between 1974 and 1980 and Gerald Frankel, chairman of the British Office Technology Manufacturers' Alliance, later a leading light in the Industry Forum. Merchant banker Jon Norton, later Mo Mowlam's partner, was there with his then-wife.

Within five years, the event had grown considerably in stature. The 1996 dinner saw 450 tickets sold out a month before it was held in July. Hobsbawm Macaulay refused to release the guest list. 'This is a private function,' an employee explained. 'People who have bought tickets have asked not to have their names disclosed.'[31] Names that did slip out included Bruce Shepherd, managing director of Shepherd Offshore; Caparo's Swraj Paul; Ulster Unionist David Montgomery, chief executive of the Mirror Group; and Hanson director Peter Harper, the company's linkman to Labour.

The Cable Communications Association booked a table for ten, the magic number guaranteeing that a Shadow Cabinet member would be seated with them. Meanwhile, an array of enticing corporate sponsorship options were available. Full-page advertisements in the souvenir programme came at £12,000, while sponsors were sought for the champagne reception, the wine, the after-dinner whiskey or cognac and the chocolates. The obligatory auction gave MP Tony Banks the chance to shell out £17,500 for Eric Cantona's football shirt.

On the celebrity front, Richard Attenborough, Ruth Rendell, Richard Wilson, Simon Mayo and Claire Rayner – later to switch political preference to the Liberal Democrats – tucked in to mixed leaf salad with asparagus and chicken, salmon in watercress sauce, and lemon brulée on a raspberry coulis. Not a prawn cocktail in sight. Lesser-known individuals were there too. Lobbyist Neil Lawson – two years later famous for 15 minutes in the cash for access affair – commented: 'Well, I'm a Labour man. So £500? I don't care. I can afford it.'[32]

Once Labour was in office, the big business A-list started suddenly coming to the fore. At the 1998 dinner, held at the Park Lane Hilton, spin doctors made much of the presence of Richard Handover, chief executive of WH Smith; John Rose, chief executive of Rolls-Royce; and party donor Gerry Robinson, chairman of Granada. Companies with an estimated combined stock market value of a cool £250bn were represented at the event. Yet not one important trade union leader is known to have been on the guest list.[33]

Attendees were divided into two categories: the rich and the very rich. The hoi polloi were taken to a general reception, there to be plied with cheap champagne. The elite were whisked away to the Curzon Room, there to mingle with the Cabinet. This upper echelon included Elizabeth Murdoch, who was personally consoled by Cherie Blair over the break-up of her parents' marriage. Yet not even the media mogul's daughter qualified for one of the prized seats at Table 24. This privilege was for serious money backers only. Those dining with the Prime Minister and his wife included Levy, Sainsbury, Hamlyn, Gavron and Goldman.

In retrospect, 1998 marked the high point in the history of the annual dinner. Attendance was down the following year, with not even such dependables as Hollick and Puttnam showing up. Nevertheless, business guests included Creation Record's McGee and Tim Waterstone, founder of the eponymous bookshop chain. Enron, riding high at the time, took a table for ten.[34]

The 2001 bash, held at the Hilton Metropole, further underlines just how far the calibre of attendees has gone downhill. The 600 guests, who feasted on grilled artichokes, best end of lamb and bread-and-butter pudding, were led by Big Brother star Dean Sullivan, Jenny Seagrove, Lord Attenborough and thriller writer James Herbert, none of them exactly business movers and shakers.

New Labour fundraising dinners of this type are now replicated on a miniature scale across the country. For instance, just before the last election, Chief Secretary to the Treasury and Oxford East MP Andrew Smith sent personal invitations to a £65-a-head dinner to hundreds of business leaders in the Oxford area. Speakers included e-commerce minister Patricia Hewitt, addressing the topic 'the new economy and business success', and Smith himself, although even his friends would admit that he is hardly a great orator. What was not made clear in the letter – which did not even mention the Labour Party – was that proceeds were destined for constituency funds.[35]

What, then, of the ultimate architect of Labour's funding revolution? What manner of man is Michael Levy? Acquaintances routinely describe him as bad-tempered, even prone to tantrums. Guitarist Chris Rea, one of the many Levy launched to stardom, remarks: 'He is extremely tough, one of the hardest bastards I have ever met, but I would leave my children with him rather than anyone else.' Drucker weighs in with the observation: 'People hated him, for all the reasons Labour people hate people. He'd only joined the party three weeks ago. He is vulgar, which surprisingly matters in the Labour Party.'[36]

Whatever his personality traits, Levy's career success has made him extremely rich. Together with his wife Gilda, he maintains luxury homes in both North London and Israel. Such is his standing in the Jewish community that the *Jerusalem Post* has hailed him as 'undoubtedly the notional leader of British Jewry', a standing that must come as news to the Chief Rabbi.[37]

Yet for all his current status, Britain's envoy to the Middle East hails from modest East End origins, growing up in a house without a bathroom. After leaving Hackney Downs Grammar School at the age of 16, he trained to be an accountant. His ability to audit the books of record producers gave him entry into the music business. Levy founded Magnet Records, which at one stage enjoyed 8 per cent of the entire UK singles market, and sold it to Warner Brothers for £10m in 1988. Afterwards he founded M&G records – the initials stand for Michael and Gilda – which did not meet the same success. By the 1990s, Levy was devoting much of his energies to his role as chairman of Jewish Care, raising an estimated £60m for the charity.[38]

Although a lifelong Labour supporter, Levy had never been an active grassroots member. Nevertheless, by this point he had personal access to the party leadership. Smith regularly visited the Levy's huge Totteridge abode to enjoy Gilda's impeccable *heimisch* cuisine.

Blair became another regular guest, and a strong friendship has clearly developed between the two men. Indeed, during my one brief meeting with Levy, the fundraiser informed me that he and the Prime Minister are 'like brothers'.

A life peerage followed within months of Labour taking office. This, according to record producer pal Pete Waterman, is incredibly important to Levy: 'This peerage possibly means more to him than anybody else. Being brought up where he was . . . that would have been the greatest accolade anyone could have achieved. Working-class people like accolades. He is still working class. He personifies what people call working-class millionaires.'[39]

The following year Levy was even appointed to Panel 2000, the government body charged with selling the idea of 'Cool Britannia' to a sceptical Britain. Just how cool can an erstwhile rock 'n' roll schlock merchant pretend to be? Yet there are suggestions that he may not be paying his way as one of Cool Britannia's citizens, after Benjamin Pell – a Londoner who makes a living selling documents found in law and accountancy firm waste bins to the press – uncovered details of his tax affairs. Levy unsuccessfully sought a high court injunction to prevent publication of Pell's findings.

Levy paid only £10,000 in the 1997–8 tax year, and just £5,000 in 1998–9. At less than the cost of a table at a New Labour gala dinner, £5,000 is a remarkably low tax bill for a man worth an estimated £10m, being the equivalent to what a basic-rate taxpayer pays on a salary of around £21,000. *The Sunday Times* later suggested that during the 1998–9 period, Levy drew £50,000 in business expenses from his company Wireart Ltd, including a £31,000 mileage allowance.

Levy insisted he had done nothing untoward. He stressed he had not resorted to offshore arrangements, despite earlier involvement with a Guernsey trust and his previous part-ownership of a firm of tax avoidance advisers. Levy maintains that in 1998–9, the bulk of his money was tied up in property and a pension, and he lived off his capital, in order to devote himself to political and charitable activities. His tax bills over the preceding 12 years had totalled £3.5m, he added.

The latest controversy to engulf Levy involves claims that he set up meetings between ministers and an Australian property group called Westfield, which hired him as a consultant to assist the company in expanding its chain of shopping centres in the UK. The contract, worth somewhere between £100,000 and £250,000, was terminated four months sooner than planned, allowing Levy to avoid declaring the consultancy in the House of Lords register of interests. There have also been reports that Levy has been paid a six-figure sum by Universal Music, a subsidiary of France's Vivendi, and around £100,000 by BEA Systems, an American company. Levy strongly denies any impropriety.[40]

After his peerage came the job of special envoy to the Middle East, an appointment that seems to derive purely from his sway with Blair. Never having run for political office in his life, Levy effectively bought his way into international diplomacy. In 1999 alone, he visited Syria, Jordan, Oman, Qatar, Israel, Egypt and Lebanon, usually staying in British embassies in the process. Since the launch of the US war against terrorism, the post is suddenly even more crucial then it was before.

But is Levy the right man for the job? As Foreign Secretary, Robin Cook was barely on speaking terms with the Prime Minister's appointee. Businessmen closely involved in the Middle East add that Levy is widely distrusted by Arab nations and British diplomats in the region alike. Given that he has personal and family ties to the Israeli Labour Party, even Ariel Sharon has grounds to consider him partisan. The Tories have also suggested that he may be engaging in Labour fundraising during his regular visits to the country.

Nevertheless, Levy has been able to act as broker in talks between Palestinian leader Yasser Arafat and Israeli foreign minister Shimon Peres, that may not have taken place if he had not been on hand to facilitate them.[41] In a region perpetually on the brink of war, we need to hope that the man who brought Alvin Stardust to the nation's youth can now save us all from Armageddon.

NOTES

[1] *Guardian,* 18 August 1997
[2] *Jerusalem Post,* 24 September 1999
[3] *Daily Telegraph,*18 October 2000
[4] Hansard, 12 February 1997
[5] *Independent on Sunday,* 14 May 1995
[6] *Guardian,* 16 May 1995
[7] *Observer,* 8 October 1996
[8] *Daily Telegraph,* 12 March 1997
[9] *Observer,* 17 November 1996
[10] Ibid.
[11] *Daily Mail,* 17 November 1997

[12] Labour insider, interview with author
[13] *Financial Times,* 23 November 1996
[14] *Sunday Telegraph,* 5 September 1999; World Council of Hellenes Abroad website as of 4 December 2001
[15] *Sunday Times,* 10 May 1998
[16] *Guardian,* 19 March 1996
[17] Henry Drucker, interview with author
[18] Ibid.
[19] Ibid.
[20] *Guardian,* 18 August 1997
[21] Henry Drucker, interview with author
[22] Ibid.
[23] *Sunday Times,* 10 May 1998
[24] *Observer,* 30 March 1998
[25] Ibid.
[26] *Daily Telegraph,* 30 March 1998; *Observer,* 7 January 2001
[27] *Daily Telegraph,* 30 March 1998; *Sunday Telegraph,* 5 September 1999
[28] *Sunday Telegraph,* 5 September 1999
[29] *Private Eye* (recent retraction)
[30] *Guardian,* 14 February 1998
[31] *Financial Times,* 15 June 1996
[32] *Observer,* 14 July 1996. Lawson was working for Lowe Bell at this time.
[33] *Daily Express,* 26 April 1998
[34] *Observer,* 11 April 1999
[35] *Guardian,* 22 February 2001
[36] *Guardian,* 18 August 1997; Henry Drucker, interview with author
[37] *Guardian,* 18 August 1997
[38] Ibid.
[39] Ibid.
[40] *Financial Times,* 8 April 2002; *Financial Times,* 15 April 2002
[41] *Daily Telegraph,* 4 October 2001

5. FORMULA ONE MILLION:
THE ECCLESTONE AFFAIR

'I said to him, "If you wanted to be a Conservative, I think you'd still get the same votes as you're going to get for Labour" . . . I could see that he was probably more Conservative than Major. He was just doing what Mrs Thatcher started a long time ago.' When Bernie Ecclestone first met Tony Blair at the British Grand Prix in 1996, he obviously didn't mistake the leader of the opposition for a dangerous radical.[1]

So began the events that culminated in a watershed for many New Labour enthusiasts, who sincerely believed that whatever other failings their government might develop, there was no way it could stoop to quite the depths that had characterised the Major administration. The way in which details of the 'cash for ash' saga had to be dragged out of New Labour – confession by torturous confession – in retrospect marks the exact moment that particular illusion evaporated in a cloud of cigarette smoke.

We now know that, just four months before New Labour took office, Bernie Ecclestone – the former second-hand car salesman who had risen to become unarguably the most powerful man in Formula One, and almost certainly the richest in all of sport – gave the party a cheque for £1m. We now also know that shortly after the election victory, Ecclestone and his aides met Blair in Downing Street. The Government, which had not made public Ecclestone's six-figure donation, almost immediately exempted Formula One from its proposed ban on tobacco industry sponsorship of sporting events.

Labour has maintained ever since that the donation did not influence its thinking. But in some ways, the admission that the Government did not act on a specific request is even more damaging than the suggestion that it did. The Ecclestone affair smells of something far worse than obscure Conservative backbenchers pocketing payments for tabling parliamentary questions. If Labour's version of the story is taken at face value, it seems we have a Prime Minister who acts in the interests of the rich while on auto-pilot.

Labour's U-turn on the advertising ban surprised many. During its extended term in opposition, the party had often pointed to the links between the Conservatives and the big tobacco firms. One incident in particular stands out in Labour folk memory. Imperial Tobacco booked up hundreds of prominent billboard sites in the first part of 1992, at a time when it was uncertain whether or not an election would be called. Once Major named the day, it turned over rights to use them to the Conservatives. Such blatant acts of partisanship added greatly to Labour's dislike of the industry in general, and Imperial in particular.

Tobacco companies were also a major source of income for the Conservatives. In 1996, Kevin Barron pointed out that the Tories had received at least £500,000 from the tobacco sector since 1991. Labour's health spokesperson went so far as to write a letter to the Tories, asking rhetorically: 'Can you explain why your party continues to oppose a ban on tobacco advertising and to block the EU directive [restricting tobacco advertising]? Is the Conservative position influenced by the fact that tobacco companies are among your major donors?'[2] Little could Barron have known that hardly one year later, similar accusations could – with more than ample justification – be levelled at Labour. Also in 1996, Blair made his first speech devoted entirely to health since becoming party leader. Proposals for a tobacco advertising ban formed part of a five-point plan to revive the NHS.

The industry was well aware of the likelihood of a Labour election win. Philip Morris, the biggest manufacturer and a major Formula One advertiser, had already begun lobbying Labour opinion formers. A copy of the strategy document drawn up by Morris's public relations firm was leaked to Barron. Efforts were to be concentrated on senior Labour politicians, trade unionists and Labour-aligned think tanks. Even fairly lowly party members were to be wined and dined.

By contrast, Ecclestone's philosophy was to go straight to the top. Labour's tobacco-tainted benefactor was born in Suffolk in October 1930. Just before the Second World War, the family moved to the London suburbs. Ecclestone left school at 16 and worked for a gas company, before taking a degree in chemical engineering from Woolwich Polytechnic and then moving into the second-hand car and motorcycle trade. By now his hobby was Formula Three racing. One notable contemporary claims that Ecclestone even showed a modicum of ability. The legendary Stirling Moss recalls: 'He was not a great driver, but not bad either.'[3]

Ecclestone's *métier* was indeed not racing, but business. While still in his 20s, he built up the second-largest motorcycle business in the country, as well as a significant car auction operation. Such was his success that, by 1957, he was able to indulge his passion for motorsport by buying a Grand Prix team, but pulled out after a friend was killed in the following year's Moroccan Grand Prix. By the late 1960s, he was back, managing Austrian driver Jochen Rindt. Rindt tragically suffered a fatal accident at Monza in 1970, already having stacked up enough points to win that year's world championship. This time Ecclestone did not give up, and he went on to buy the Brabham team, which won two world championships under Brazil's Nelson Piquet.

Ecclestone was the first to realise the financial potential of his chosen sport, at that time largely the preserve of gentleman amateurs. By the early 1970s, team owners were already allowing him to negotiate with television companies on their behalf. After Formula One's governing body, the Federation Internationale de l'Automobile, agreed in 1981 that television rights should be held by the teams for a 14-year period, the teams appointed Ecclestone to market them worldwide on a commission basis. Advertising proved an essential part of an extremely lucrative mix. And the most generous advertisers were cigarette manufacturers, desperate to circumvent restrictions on television exposure for their lethal product, and willing to pay accordingly.

The teams were initially happy enough with the results, as was Ecclestone, who became extremely rich. It wasn't until the contract came up for renewal in 1995 that the two sides clashed, after Ecclestone secured exclusive television rights for himself. Litigation looked a distinct prospect. But eventually the matter was settled out of court, with the teams getting something like a satisfactory cut.

Ecclestone was by this stage officially the FIA's vice-president for marketing. But few were in any doubt that Ecclestone was the man really in charge of this extremely secretive organisation. Even the FIA's titular president Max Mosley, was none other than Ecclestone's lawyer. Mosley, incidentally, is the son of Sir Oswald Mosley, the pre-war Tory-turned-Labour MP who went on to establish the British Union of Fascists. Mosley junior has publicly supported Labour and reportedly contributed to party funds.

By this stage, the FIA was going out of its way to cultivate politicians with both donations and hospitality. It made a series of annual £25,000 gifts to the Automobile Users' Group of Euro-MPs, headed by Labour's European parliament leader Alan Donnelly. Donnelly travelled to Monaco, France and the US at the FIA's expense, and some of the money funded his private office. Morris also picked up Donnelly's tab for club class flights and luxury hotels.[4]

Ecclestone's first meeting with Blair was part of the same public relations strategy. The leader of the opposition and his children were invited to attend the 1996 British Grand Prix as Ecclestone's guests. What father would have refused? Seats for five in the grandstand would have set back a normal family £725, although Blair failed to declare this hospitality in the register of members' interests. The day clearly went well, with the Formula One boss later remarking that he found the politician both enthusiastic and sincere, as well as pretty much to his right-leaning political liking.

The trip had been arranged by David Ward, European director-general of the Formula One Association. Ward enjoys impeccable Labour connections, thanks to past jobs as campaigns officer for the Parliamentary Labour Party and special advisor to John Smith, with a far higher standing than might be inferred from the job title. He was an important party figure under the late leader. Ward also set up Ecclestone's later Downing Street get-together with Blair, which he also attended, as well as meetings over the tobacco ban question with both Health minister Tessa Jowell and Sports minister Tony Banks.[5]

Ward sought to influence other parties too, most notably the Liberal Democrats, who have consistently campaigned against tobacco advertising in motor racing. He made a series of phone calls to the office of Lib Dem leader Paddy Ashdown. An Ashdown spokesperson confirmed: '[Ward] told one of our health researchers that he was going to get Paddy to sack him . . . He was arrogant and his tone was bullying. He told us that the Liberal Democrats would be in all sorts of trouble if we went ahead.'[6]

Ecclestone by now enjoyed all the trappings of billionaire status, including the obligatory trophy second wife. Croatian-born Slavica, a former Armani model, is 30 years his junior and, at six foot two, a good ten inches taller than her husband. Meanwhile, he was gearing up for greater things yet. Plans were announced at the start of 1997 to float Formula One on the London Stock Exchange, with investment bankers Salomon Smith Barney advising on the deal. It was around this time that Ecclestone was successfully tapped for the then-secret £1m donation. It is unclear who actually solicited the money. A number of newspaper reports subsequently named Levy, although more recently Formula One figures have pointed the finger at Jonathan Powell, Blair's chief of staff.

Labour won that year's general election, on a manifesto explicitly promising an outright ban on tobacco advertising, in line with EU policy. Within weeks of taking office, Secretary of State for Health Frank Dobson reiterated the policy in a speech to the Royal College of Nursing: 'We will ban tobacco advertising. It will cover all forms, including sponsorship.'[7] It would have been impossible to make things any clearer.

The tobacco industry was predictably outraged, and pledged an immediate fightback. Gallagher – the people behind Benson & Hedges and Silk Cut – put it bluntly enough: 'Our aim is to do as much as we can for as long as we can to defeat the ban and justify sports sponsorship.'[8]

The case for an advertising ban is clear cut. Tobacco is indisputably Britain's number one avoidable killer, causing 120,000 deaths a year. On the Government's own calculations, an advertising ban would save the NHS around £40m on the treatment of smoking-related diseases.

But human lives are obviously a secondary consideration for Formula One, which rakes in a considerable proportion of the tobacco industry's ad spend because it provides such a glamorous means of promoting lung cancer. Just to get some idea of the stakes here, even Ecclestone's massive donation to Labour represented only 1 per cent of the estimated £100m a year that Formula One motor racing teams such as McLaren, Williams and Jordan raked in from tobacco advertising in the year the gift was given.

It was against this backdrop that on 16 October 1997 – just four months after Blair was installed at Downing Street – the Prime Minister held a meeting with the man who had previously left £1m as his calling card. As Ecclestone tells it, the event was little more than a fireside chat over a cosy cuppa. 'No, I wasn't asking for anything when I was invited to go and see [Blair]. We had a general discussion about life. I don't remember because I didn't record the conversation, and I don't remember things that are of little, if any, importance to me,' he relates.

> I went with Mosley and he did most of the speaking. It was nothing
> to do with asking for anything for anybody. It was him being polite,
> that's all. I think the meeting was set up after Silverstone, when they
> said it would be nice just to catch up and have a cup of tea.[9]

What actually was said is known only to those present. Jonathan Powell ordered civil servants from the room, so that the conversation could proceed without an official record. If Ecclestone's account is to be believed, the Government's subsequent actions, which so clearly coincided with the commercial interests of Formula One, were the most fortuitous of coincidences. Only a fortnight later, the Department of Health circulated proposals to European ministers, setting out the case for the exemption of Formula One from the advertising ban. Jowell was able to secure a stay of execution, hardly the most appropriate action from a woman charged with the role of Public Health minister. Two months later, an EU compromise was struck, under which tobacco sponsorship of sports could continue until October 2006.

Labour was either oblivious to the idea that Ecclestone's donation would generate the impression of a serious conflict of interest if it became public knowledge, or simply hopeful that it would not become public knowledge. Given that Levy was by this stage attempting to solicit a second contribution from the Formula One supremo, again asking for £1m, the latter appears the most likely option.

The *Sunday Telegraph* was soon to get word of the initial donation, publishing a story in early November that also noted the subsequent policy reversal. Yet for five long days, the Government refused to confirm the facts of the matter. Throughout this period, the controversy dominated the headlines.

By way of a decoy tactic, Labour's general secretary Tom Sawyer wrote to

Sir Patrick Neill – about to succeed Lord Nolan as chairman of the Committee on Standards in Public Life – to ask whether the second donation should be accepted. The ploy was to backfire. Not only should a second donation *not* be accepted, Neill argued, but the first should be returned, to avoid the appearance that it had improperly influenced policy. This can hardly have been the result cash-strapped New Labour was seeking. Now it was forced to admit that the *Sunday Telegraph* was, quite literally, on the money.

Yet the Government still denied that the £1m gift had in any way influenced its judgement on the advertising ban. The argument inevitably met widespread scepticism, reinforced when it subsequently emerged that Jowell's husband David Mills had previously been both legal adviser and non-executive director of Benetton Formula, a Formula One racing team.[10]

By the end of the week, Blair publicly apologised . . . but only for the way in which the Government had handled the affair. This was far from an admission of guilt. There had been no wrongdoing, the Prime Minister persisted. Ecclestone was indignant at the very suggestion that he had been throwing his cash around in a bid to influence government policy. He insisted: 'I have never sought any favour from New Labour or any member of the Government, nor has any been given.'[11]

Labour complied with Neill's advice and returned the Ecclestone money, £4.5m overdraft notwithstanding. It must have been cursing its luck. Had the press not been on the case, word of the donation would have been delayed for almost a full year until the 1998 annual report, where it would simply have been listed as a run-of-the-mill '£5,000-plus' gift.

Still the affair would not lay down, with Ecclestone attempting to reinforce his protestations of innocence by refusing to cash the cheque. Labour indicated that if he did not do so within the six-month deadline set down by the banks, it would give the money to a cancer charity instead. Eventually Ecclestone decided £1m was worth having after all, finally presenting the cheque to his bankers in late February or early March 1998.

Ecclestone wrote to Neill setting down his reasons for the gift, which he explicitly linked to Blair's decision as leader of the opposition to keep top-rate income tax at 40 per cent, despite calls from with the party for this to be increased to 50 per cent or even 60 per cent. 'As a substantial contributor to the Inland Revenue, I have clearly benefited from his decision,' Ecclestone wrote. 'I want to reinforce his independence in a party substantially dependent on finance from trade unions.'[12] On this official account, then, the donation was purposely designed to help Labour break the union link, an explanation that can hardly have gone down well with the Old Labour camp.

Financial pressures on Labour were eased when a burger king saved its bacon and came up with a matching £1m donation to replace Ecclestone's.

This time the money came from Robert Earl, the man behind the Planet Hollywood chain of movie-themed burger joints, who offered diners rather plainer fare than that served at New Labour's £500-a-plate events. Earl insisted that his generosity came with no strings attached. 'I have no hidden agenda, no policy I wish to influence, no favour to curry on my own behalf or to benefit my company. I believe this Government to be dynamic, honest and absolutely committed to creating a new and better society for Britain. I am proud to be able to contribute to their efforts,' he maintained.[13]

Earl, 46 at the time, was based in Orlando, Florida, although he was born in London and is a graduate of Surrey University. He launched the first Planet Hollywood – backed by movie stars Bruce Willis, Arnold Schwarzenegger and Sylvestor Stallone – in New York in 1991, and built it up to the point where it had 87 outlets worldwide, including London, Hong Kong and Moscow. He also owned a string of hotels, casinos and cinemas, making him worth around £800m. Such was his success that only a few months earlier *Time* magazine had voted him one of the 25 most influential people in America, an extremely high ranking for a glorified fast food merchant.

Planet Hollywood has since fallen on hard times, twice having to file for bankruptcy. After its first collapse in October 1999, attributed to over-expansion, it was resurrected by Earl and Prince al Waleed of Saudi Arabia, the world's sixth-richest man. Eventually it was able to relist on Nasdaq in May 2000. It collapsed again in October 2001, with the blame laid this time on a fall in custom following the terrorist attacks of 11 September.

Meanwhile, Ecclestone's flotation plans were forced into the pitstop, after the EU objected to the terms of the Formula One television agreement on competition grounds. It also pointed to a potential conflict between Ecclestone's role in charge of marketing at the FIA and his private business interests. Despite the opposition emanating from Brussels, Ecclestone has still been able to cash in. His Luxembourg-listed Formula 1 Finance BV has undertaken a $1.4bn eurobond issue, a massive loan secured against profits from future TV rights.

He also managed to effectively sell the television rights anyway. After a series of complicated transactions thought to have netted Ecclestone $2.3bn, a 58 per cent stake in his master company SLEC – the name derives from the initials of Slavica Ecclestone – passed into the hands of German pay-TV giant Kirch, which has since gone bust. There has been speculation that Ecclestone could buy back the stake for as little as $800m. Meanwhile, SLEC is poised to secure a 100-year extension of commercial rights to the sport, taking it up to 2110, for a relatively nominal amount.

Ever since the cash for ash scandal first broke, it has continued to display an uncanny ability to haunt New Labour. Publication of *Observer* journalist Andrew Rawnsley's book *Servants of the People* in 2000 – serialised in the

Daily Mail – reignited the issue at a time that could hardly have been worse from the Government's point of view, coinciding with Blair's opinion poll nadir resulting from that year's fuel crisis.

The well-informed Rawnsley contended that Gordon Brown had knowingly lied to Radio 4's *Today* programme when asked whether Labour had received any money from Ecclestone. Brown replied: 'You'll have to wait and see, like I'll have to wait and see when the list [of donors giving more than £5,000] is published because I've not been told and I certainly don't know what the true position is.'[14] But Brown had been told. The author quotes one witness who saw the Chancellor shortly after the broadcast. 'Gordon went mental,' according to Rawnsley's anonymous source. Brown shouted at his staff: 'I lied. I lied. My credibility will be in shreds. I lied. If this gets out, I'll be destroyed.'[15]

Brown denied this account. Rawnsley stuck to it. However, Brown was forced to issue a statement admitting that he had discussed the donation with Blair three days before the interview, thereby confirming the substance of the allegation against him. The confession inevitably sparked Conservative calls for the Chancellor's resignation.

Even now, the controversy refuses to die. Cash for ash lit up again in April 2002, when Mosley and Ward appeared before the legal committee of the European Parliament. Mosley claimed that it was in fact Powell, and not Levy, who had initiated the donation.

Labour introduced a Tobacco Advertising and Promotion Bill in 2001, but failed to find parliamentary time for the legislation before the election. After Blair's second victory, the measure conspicuously failed to make it into the 2001 Queen's speech, despite pressure from Secretary of State for Health Alan Milburn for its inclusion.

At the time of writing, the Department of Health was informally advising Liberal Democrat peer Lord Clement-Jones on a private members' bill introduced in the Lords, an exact copy of the earlier Labour bill. While it is expected to carry, Formula One will still be able to carry tobacco advertising until 2006. It looks like Ecclestone's donation was money well spent.

NOTES

[1] The following section draws on a revealing 1997 profile by Robert Chesshyre originally published in the *Daily Telegraph* and now available online at http://ukmotorsport.com/misc/ecclestone.html

[2] *Independent on Sunday*, 16 August 1996

[3] http://ukmotorsport.com/misc/ecclestone.html

[4] *Sunday Times*, 6 June 1999

[5] *Daily Telegraph*, 8 November 1997

[6] *Financial Times*, 10 July 1998

[7] *Daily Mirror*, 20 May 1997

[8] Ibid.
[9] http://ukmotorsport.com/misc/ecclestone.html
[10] *Daily Mail*, 11 November 1997
[11] Ibid.
[12] *Guardian*, 13 May 1998
[13] *Guardian*, 24 November 1997
[14] *Guardian*, 20 September 2000
[15] Ibid.

6. SIMONY AND SECONDMENTS

REWARDING donors was once a commonplace part of the British way of political life. Gladstone was happy enough to sell honours to boost Liberal Party funds, while Lloyd George was a past master at dishing out peerages to cronies, often the profiteers of the First World War. There was a baronetcy for a convicted food racketeer, and another for a South African diamond merchant found guilty of serious fraud.

Such practices could not possibly persist in this day and age. So it could only have been happenstance that between 1979 and 1992, industrialists were ten times more likely to pick up knighthoods or peerages if their firms had donated to the Conservative Party.[1]

Handing over a sizeable cheque doesn't damage anyone's chances of preferment under New Labour, either. One in three big Labour donors in 1997 got peerages, ministerships or roles advising Labour on policy within little more than a year of the party taking office.[2]

Since then Blair has systematically set about creating peers at a faster rate than any other prime minister in British history. The total stood at 206 in April 2001, compared to just 201 peerages granted by Thatcher during her entire 11 years in office.[3]

Labour announced its first list of 31 working peers shortly after taking office. Four of the people given permanent seats in Britain's legislature – Lords Montague, Puttnam and Sainsbury and Baroness Rendell – were high-value donors, while a fifth, Lord Levy, had been a key fundraiser.

Charles Falconer, one of Blair's closest personal friends, was given a peerage to allow him to serve as Attorney General, after attempts to find him a safe Labour seat proved unsuccessful. In the New Year Honours List that followed, publisher Paul Hamlyn, another major donor, was also made a Lord. Alexander Bernstein, chairman of Granada Group from 1979 to 1996, was made a life peer in 2000, after three unspecified high-value donations to Labour and a gift to Blair's blind trust.

As well as Lord Sainsbury, two other leading businessmen – Lord Simon and Lord Macdonald – have been ennobled specifically to enable them to take ministerial office without having to win a democratic mandate at the ballot box.

This Government is not the first to adopt such tactics, of course. Edward

Heath recruited John Davies from the Confederation of British Industry straight into the cabinet, while Margaret Thatcher similarly promoted Lords Levene and Young. But no past prime minister has gone as far as Blair in recruiting industrialists and entrepreneurs to other public positions. Over 2,000 people, the majority of them businessmen and women, have been given places on review groups and taskforces.

This chapter looks at the stories of some of the top businessmen and leading lawyers who have been granted peerages, knighthoods and posts on public bodies by New Labour, and examines the secondment of private sector staff to the civil service.

Robert Ayling was one of the leading players in Labour's opposition efforts to rehabilitate itself with business, and such a close friend of Jack Straw's that the two men held a joint fiftieth birthday party. Soon after taking office, Blair asked him to quit his job as chief executive at British Airways and head the policy unit at 10 Downing Street instead, an offer Ayling turned down.[4]

The former solicitor and Department of Trade and Industry civil servant seems to have expected the peerage that the top job at BA won for his predecessors Lord King and Lord Marshall as a matter of right. This failed to materialise after he badly mishandled an industrial dispute in 1997, threatening mass sackings of cabin crew for participation in entirely legal strike action, with disastrous publicity. The aftermath saw him frozen out of the New Labour inner circle, leaving him feeling 'snubbed and humiliated', according to friends.[5]

He did everything he could to get back into the party's good books. Ayling pumped BA money into the Millennium Dome and became chairman of the New Millennium Experience Company. He even hosted a BA champagne reception at the 1999 Labour conference. But investors demanded his head after watching the value of their shares halve, and BA dismissed him in March 2000. Fortunately for Ayling, the airline saw him all right with a £2m pay-off, and a pension worth £260,000 a year.

Within months, he was also forced to step down at the Dome, as a condition of a £29m cash lifeline from the Millennium Commission. Although his star has since remained in decline, Ayling was subsequently retained as a consultant by Serco, who felt his aviation expertise and political contacts would be invaluable in its so far unsuccessful bid to buy Britain's privatised air traffic control system.

Sir Malcolm Bates, chairman of insurer Pearl Group, was awarded a knighthood by Blair in 1998 and became chairman of London Regional Transport the following year. In this capacity he has an important say in the tube sell-off, and has awarded one of the infrastructure contracts to a consortium including Balfour Beatty. This is a business he should know rather well, as a past director of its parent company BICC. Bates first got the taste for public appointments under the last Tory government, when as deputy managing director of GEC he sat on the energy deregulation task force and Private Finance Initiative panel. Under New Labour, he has also acted as a special adviser to Paymaster General Geoffrey Robinson.

Lord Bragg enjoys unparalleled contacts in the worlds of art and entertainment, thanks to his longstanding role as controller of arts at London Weekend Television. One of a clutch of LWT figures who became multimillionaires in a 1991 share options deal, he was one of three beneficiaries of that scheme to fund Blair's leadership bid three years later. Best known to the public as presenter of *The South Bank Show* and *Start the Week*, Bragg was given a peerage in 1998.

Sainsbury chief executive **Sir Peter Davis** – currently filling the job vacated by Lord Sainsbury, now otherwise engaged as science minister – started working life as a jukebox salesman. His earlier career also includes a spell as chief executive at Reed International. Almost his first act at Reed was to sack 600 employees and derecognise the National Union of Journalists, despite a 97 per cent 'yes' vote for union representation. Labour leader John Smith took up the NUJ case, but Davis, then a staunch Conservative, rejected Smith's request for a meeting on the question.

After leaving Reed with a £2m pay-off in 1994, he became chief executive of the Prudential, a company so deeply embroiled in the 1980s pensions mis-selling scandal that it had to spend £1bn cleaning up the mess.

But times change, and so do political attitudes. Davis has since 1997 served as chairman of the New Deal Welfare to Work taskforce, seeking to 'mobilise the business world' on behalf of David Blunkett and Gordon Brown.[6]

In 2001 he was offered the job of heading a government inquiry into the role of non-executive directors, but turned it down, apparently worried about taking his eye off the ball at the troubled supermarket chain.

Lord Evans of Watford has worked as chairman of the Rickmansworth-based Centurion Press since 1971, a company that undertakes regular printing work for the Labour Party. Accumulated donations to the party have reportedly been of the order of £30,000. But none are known to have exceeded £5,000. He was made a peer in 1998.

Public relations man **Lord Faulkner** started his career as a journalist and research assistant for the Labour Party in 1967. He stood unsuccessfully in all four 1970s general elections, and acted as unpaid communications advisor to the party in 1987, 1992 and 1997. Then known as Richard Faulkner, he made a high-value donation to Labour in 1996, and was awarded a peerage three years later.

He is best known in political circles as managing director of Westminster Communications from 1989 to 1997, and then deputy chairman of Citigate

Westminster until 1999. Commercial clients of his lobbying outfits have included Barclays de Zoete Wedd, Standard Life and Littlewoods. Interests these days include a directorship at Cardiff Millennium Stadium Ltd and a job as strategy adviser to Incepta Group. He has also served on the Government's football taskforce.

Like Lord Evans and Robert Maxwell, **Lord Gavron** made his fortune in the printing industry, and was chairman of printer St Ives plc from 1964 to 1993, remaining a director for a further five years. While he reportedly expressed admiration for Thatcher and was courted by the SDP, he is nevertheless thought to have given Labour a six-figure donation under Kinnock, before becoming unhappy with the party's commitments of the day to repeal Conservative anti-union legislation. He came back into the fold under Blair, donating around £35,000 to the new leader's blind trust.

A peerage came in 1999, in the same month as Gavron had announced a £500,000 gift to Labour. At that time, he was chairman of the Guardian Media Group – publisher of *The Guardian* and *Observer* – but has since stood down from the post.

Baroness Goudie organised Labour Solidarity, the secretive early 1980s right-wing caucus in the Labour Party dedicated to fighting Bennite insurgency, from 1980 to 1984. Later she served on the steering committee of the 1000 Club for high-value donors. After jobs as public affairs director for the World Wildlife Fund and as a public affairs consultant, Mary Goudie became a peer in 1998. She is another listed high-value donor.

One of the most important financial backers of New Labour was the late **Lord Hamlyn**, a refugee who arrived from Nazi Germany at the age of six. After a wartime stint as a 'Bevan Boy' conscript miner, he launched his first business selling cheap books off the back of a barrow in Camden market.

The venture was a success, enabling him to found publisher Paul Hamlyn Group, specialising in high production value books at bargain prices. Like Maxwell, Hamlyn's efforts were facilitated considerably by deals with Eastern Europe. Many of the company's books were printed at low cost on state-owned presses in Czechoslovakia, on credit terms that made them virtually self-financing. Hamlyn sold the group for £2.2m in 1964, a considerable sum at the time.

After a spell in newspaper publishing for Murdoch interests, he founded the Octopus Group on capital of £10,000 in 1971. Sixteen years later it was sold to Reed International for £530m, in a deal that gave him a stake in Reed worth around £275m. Hamlyn acquired the obligatory corporate jet and French chateau, and became an active philanthropist. Large sums were handed over to the arts, charities, and eventually to politicians as well.

Hamlyn had originally supported the SDP but, after its collapse, gradually moved closer to Labour. His first known Labour donation was made in 1990, on the express condition that the £100,000 be used to develop policies on arts and culture. Six years later, Hamlyn handed over a further £500,000 to support the 'Road to the Manifesto' exercise. A peerage followed in 1998.

Following an approach from Levy, Hamlyn made a £2m donation in secret towards the end of 2000. Word of the huge gift – although not the donor's identity – reached the press on New Year's Eve. Labour refused to name its latest backer, leading to several days of media controversy and disquiet among backbenchers, at a time when the aftermath of the Ecclestone affair still loomed large. Legislation making it mandatory for parties to name every important financial backer was due to come onto the statute book in February. While anonymity was still within the letter of the law, this surely breached its spirit.

Within 48 hours, Hamlyn confessed all, in a statement issued on Labour Party letterhead. In it, he declared himself a longstanding Labour supporter. 'I have said nothing until now because I am overseas recovering from [a] serious illness,' he explained. 'For that reason I will be making no further comment.' He died in September that year.[7]

Lord Haskins is one of Labour's business old stagers, first joining the party in 1962, although it is unclear whether his membership is uninterrupted. As a young man he was even branded a troublemaker by Hugh Gaitskell, after helping to organise the Campaign for Nuclear Disarmament's famous Aldermaston marches.

It was also in 1962 that Christopher Haskins joined Northern Dairies, the company owned by his father-in-law, after unsuccessful spells at De La Rue and Ford. As if to confirm the old jokes about marrying the boss's daughter, he rose up the ladder, and until his recent retirement was chief executive of the business, which supplies around a quarter of food sold at Marks & Spencer, as well as Ski yoghurt and Bowyers sausages.

For a long time he kept his political sympathies quiet, but by the early 1990s he publicly supported Labour and served on a party Commission on Social Justice under Smith. Since then he has made donations of £5,000 a year for at least seven years, with further lump sums at elections.

Given a peerage in 1998, Haskins began to work two days a week in the Cabinet Office, as chairman of the Government's Better Regulation taskforce. Now free from his full-time job, Haskins denies seeking greater political involvement, although not everyone believes him.

Haskins has more recently been charged with helping those parts of the countryside devastated by the foot-and-mouth epidemic, under the job title of 'rural recovery coordinator'. His wide-ranging brief includes the entire rural economy, from tourism to small business and farming.

Lord Haskins' business interests naturally align him with the big supermarket chains as opposed to the small farmer. Unsurprisingly, he has outspokenly argued that when it comes to agriculture, bigger is simply better, and that while organic farming will remain 'a niche market for the well-to-do', only genetically modified crops can feed the world.

Farmers have been 'mollycoddled' for far too long, he believes, and there should be massive cuts to farm subsidies, which he believes encourage fraud. 'A lot of agricultural reformers, like the Prince of Wales, want farmers to stand around being subsidised and making thatched roofs,' he opined. 'Well, that's for the birds. Agriculture has got to strive to be more competitive and more productive.'[8]

Former Ford UK chairman **Ian McAllister**, variously described as 'a forceful operator with little tolerance for dissent' and even 'a bit of a bully',[9] is the man the Government has chosen as chairman of Network Rail, the company that will replace Railtrack. It is not immediately clear what someone who has spent 37 years with a motor manufacturer, mostly in sales and marketing, will bring to the job.

Previous public appointments include jobs as co-chairman of the Government's Cleaner Vehicles taskforce and chairman of the Carbon Trust, a company set up by the Government to persuade business to reduce carbon dioxide emissions. The idea of letting the boss of a company that sells 500,000 vehicles a year in the UK, and which is therefore responsible for a large tranche of exhaust fumes, head major initiatives against pollution may indicate that New Labour does have a sense of humour after all. McAllister's other quango slots include the Welfare to Work taskforce and the board of the Qualifications and Curriculum Authority.

Until recently, **Christopher Ondaatje** was overshadowed in the public eye by his younger brother. Novelist Michael Ondaatje wrote the blockbuster novel *The English Patient*, later adapted into an overlong – although multiple Oscar-winning – movie. Now Christopher's generosity to New Labour has made him famous too.

Ondaatje is another converted 1980s Conservative. The multimillionaire financier hails from a privileged colonial background, born on a tea plantation in what was then Ceylon in 1933 and educated at an English public school and the London School of Economics. But after his father drank away his inheritance he emigrated to Canada in 1956, arriving, or so legend has it, with just £10 in his pocket. A decade later he was a millionaire, finding time along the way to represent Canada in the 1964 winter Olympics, finishing 14th in a bobsleigh event.

Ondaatje's business interests included brokerage firm Loewen, Ondaatje, McCutcheon & Co. and publishing company Pagurian Corporation, which he sold in 1988. Now very rich, he suddenly realised there was more to life than money. 'I don't want to die with financier written on my gravestone . . . I have the fear of dying with the wrong acclaim,' he once revealingly commented.[10]

His wealth gave him the opportunity to indulge his other interests, which include history, writing and exploration. After reading a biography of Sir Richard Burton, he recreated many of the Victorian explorer's adventures, taking six journeys through Africa and India following in his footsteps. The cash also meant the chance to pursue what Ondaatje presumably sees as the right kind of acclaim as a patron of the arts. He endowed the Ondaatje wing of London's National Portrait Gallery with a £2.75m donation in 1995. It was this gift that bought him into contact with New Labour's Chris Smith. A number of lunches followed, as did a CBE in 2000.

Levy decided that Ondaatje was well worth wooing, and, three months after the gong award, got in touch. The erstwhile Tory decided to sign a serious cheque, giving Labour £2m. There have been further donations since, one of them for a six-figure sum. Ondaatje explained: 'I have been very impressed by Labour's handling of the economy and their appreciation of business, but in particular, I have been very impressed by the changes the Government made to boost charitable giving.'[11]

Chai Patel, who qualified as a doctor, but afterwards decided to work in the City for Merrill Lynch and Lehman Brothers instead, is managing director of Westminster Health Care. As well as being one of Britain's largest chains of nursing homes, the company owns the famous Priory Clinic, providers of detox services to the likes of Kate Moss and Robbie Williams.

Patel is a leading proponent of greater private sector input into the health service. He serves as chairman of the NHS Bed Use working group, a body which has recommended freeing NHS beds by transferring older patients to private nursing homes . . . such as those owned by Westminster Health Care, for instance.

But not all of Westminster's homes are pensioner paradises. A special unit for the mentally ill at one of its home in Knaresborough was ordered to close after critical reports from the North Yorkshire health authority. Problems included the level of skill of the staff, health and safety, lack of supervision and medication issues.[12]

Indian-born industrialist **Lord Paul** came to Britain in 1966, and now has wide-ranging interests in steel and engineering, holding 60 per cent of the market for nuts, bolts and screws. He has political connections in the old country too, and was Indira Ghandi's de facto high commissioner in London.

Paul's main company, the Caparo Group, has given money to both Labour and the Tories, with donations including substantial sums to John Smith's blind trust.[13] Swraj Paul was created a peer in 1996, although of late he has been sharply critical of the Government for its neglect of manufacturing.

Call **Lord Puttnam** – producer of *Midnight Express*, *Chariots of Fire*, *Local Hero* and *The Killing Fields* – a crony at your peril. The former SDP supporter has circulated in Labour business circles around Lord Levy since the mid-1990s. In 1996, he used a speech at a lunch organised by Levy's Jewish Care charity to give an overtly pro-Labour address, offending many in the audience.

As David Puttnam, he gave Labour donations reportedly totalling £25,000 before becoming a peer in 1997, and has served as chairman of six public bodies and member of nineteen. His positions include heading the National Endowment for Science, Technology and the Arts and chairing the General Teaching Council, ostensibly the voice of Britain's teachers.

But Puttnam is most indignant at the suggestion that this amounts to cronyism, insisting that salaries and support for overheads amount to just 45 per cent of his costs after tax.

> I work with about 20 people in the House of Lords who are working their arses off. There is not one who does not lose money in terms of resourcing themselves to do jobs for the public sector.
>
> What really upsets me is that I never asked for a peerage. I was never accused of being a Thatcher crony or a Major crony, and I find it unacceptable. I gave up the film industry . . . I only work for the state, and yet I have to put up with all this rubbish about Tony's cronies.[14]

He remains interested in a leading post at the BBC, professing himself 'thoroughly pissed off' at being passed over for the part-time job of vice-chairman.[15]

Alec Reed founded what is now Britain's largest recruitment company in 1960. The chairman of Reed Executive gave a £100,000 personal donation to Labour in 1996. With Labour in power the following year, a subsidiary of his company Reed Personnel Services won the contract to oversee the Government's Welfare to Work programme pilot project in Hackney. Meanwhile, the Reed Health Group subsidiary charges commissions of up to 20 per cent on the supply of healthcare professionals to understaffed NHS trusts. Alec Reed has proved a dependable source of high-value cheques in most years since his first gift, and has advised Blair on ways of boosting teacher recruitment, especially in the south-east.

Lord Simpson, former chief executive of Marconi, was one of the first batch of Blair business Lords in 1997, with a peerage designed both to underline New Labour's business-friendly attitudes and to reward his participation in the pre-election IPPR Commission on Public Policy and British Business. This man has one of the most impressive CVs in Britain, having been chairman of Rover, chief executive of Lucas, deputy chief executive of British Aerospace, and a director of Pilkington, ICI, Nestlé and the Bank of Scotland.

But since his elevation to the Lords, his personal stock has fallen even more rapidly than that of the company he once headed. Simpson transformed staid old GEC from an old economy defence and electronics business into a communications company, rebranded Marconi. The strategy was badly mistimed. Thanks to the downturn in telecoms, what was once the bluest of blue chips has been reduced to a struggling debt-burdened also-ran.

As late as the start of 2001, everything in Marconi's garden seemed lovely. Then came 3,000 redundancies in April, followed by an abortive attempt to reprice share options. A mishandled profits warning in July – which followed a series of positive announcements from Marconi about its limited US exposure – severely dented City confidence and the share price headed south. A second profits warning and further job losses just two months later saw Simpson ignominiously booted off the board. To make matters worse, the outcry over his £1m pay-off reignited public concern over fat-cat handouts for failure. Such was the furore, that Simpson ultimately walked away with a much reduced £300,000.

Previously a high-profile Tory supporter close to both Thatcher and Major, and widely regarded as the Essex Man's Essex Man, **Sir Alan Sugar** switched sides when he gave Labour £100,000 through a private holding company in 1997. His change of allegiance was loudly heralded in a full-page article in *The Sun* during the election campaign, when he made it quite plain that he was backing Labour as a party of business, not as a nod to his working-class upbringing.

> I never thought I would hear myself say this, but after much consideration I am voting Labour on 1 May. New Labour, that is. I believe Tony Blair is totally sincere when he says there's no going back to the old ways . . . I did very well out of the Tory years. I was proud to be considered one of Margaret Thatcher's favourite businessmen, but today's Tory Party has lost its way.
>
> Tony Blair understands how business works and he's committed to the spirit of enterprise . . . I'll be honest. If he hadn't pledged not to raise income tax there's no way I would vote for him. Nor would I support him if he wanted to go back on the trade union reforms of the 1980s. But he doesn't. Those days are gone.[16]

As chairman of Amstrad and subsequently computer manufacturer Viglen, Sugar was asked by Blair to tour the country to promote youthful entrepreneurship. He became chief executive of Tottenham Hotspur plc in 1998, and was given a knighthood two years later.

Sugar's conversion to Labour parallels the reorientation of his businesses towards the public sector. Viglen – feeling the squeeze from low-cost competition in the PC market – reinvented itself as Learning Technology, and 72 per cent shareholder Sugar has restructured the company to concentrate on the education market. Spending on IT in the education sector is forecast to quadruple by 2010. Learning Technology already has more than two-thirds of UK universities as clients, and is the main IT supplier to more than half of them. It also provides hardware, software or management services to 2,000 schools.

Eton and Oxford educated **Martin Taylor** is a man at the opposite end of the class spectrum to East Ender Sugar. Following jobs at Reuters and the *Financial Times,* he quit journalism to become chief executive first of textiles major Courtaulds and then of Barclays Bank, who ousted him with a £4m pay-off in 1998. He is currently chairman of WH Smith.

Taylor has undertaken a review of the tax and benefits system for the Treasury. As the banking unions bitterly point out, while Taylor has no first-hand experience of life on benefits, the same cannot be said for the 20,000 people he made redundant at Barclays. He has also headed an inquiry into tobacco smuggling, again at the Treasury's behest, as well as the IPPR's recent Commission on Public–Private Partnerships.

Lord Thomas of Macclesfield was elevated to the peerage shortly after Blair's first election win. As managing director of Labour's bankers the Co-op Bank from 1988 to 1997, plain old Terry Thomas arguably kept the party alive in the dark days outlined in chapter one, and has been a regular personal donor.

British by birth, **Lord Trotman** spent much of his career in the US, where as Alex Trotman he was chairman of Ford from 1993 to 1998 and a director of the New York stock exchange. He became a Lord in 1999, and remains a powerful businessman with his recent appointment as chairman of ICI. Trotman advised Labour on its University for Industry policy on education in the workplace, and was recruited by Gordon Brown to head a review of small business policies.

The law is another profession where the closed-circle nature of New Labour becomes all too apparent. Both the Blairs are from legal backgrounds, and time after time, their personal friends have secured important positions in public life in preference to other candidates.

The best-known example is Lord Chancellor **Lord Irvine**, the highest-paid member of the Government. Irvine was Blair's mentor during the Prime Minister's legal career, introducing the promising youngster to Cherie Booth when they were both pupils at his chambers in the 1970s. A longstanding Labour supporter, Alexander 'Derry' Irvine was an unsuccessful parliamentary candidate in 1970. He was close to Kinnock, who arranged his peerage in 1987 after Irvine devised legally watertight ways to expel supporters of the Militant Tendency. John Smith, an old pal from Glasgow University debating circle, appointed him shadow Lord Chancellor.

Irvine has openly sought Labour Party donations from lawyers, who are well aware that he makes the ultimate decisions over appointments to the judiciary, a lucrative career option for many of them. Early in 2001, he wrote to selected barristers and solicitors to invite them to a fundraising dinner with Cherie Blair, where they were asked to pledge a minimum of £200 to Labour's campaign funds. Irvine's former chambers are known to have picked up at least £1m in government work between 1997 and 2000. They are now headed by James Goudie, husband of donor peer Baroness Goudie, and a past head of the Society of Labour Lawyers.[17]

Another lawyer to see preferment is Blair's old flatmate, **Lord Falconer**. As a commercial silk, Charlie Falconer was earning £500,000 a year. Much of his advocacy was on behalf of causes that would once have been anathema to Labour. He advised such clients as British Nuclear Fuels in cases against leukaemia victims and Greenpeace activists, and British Coal when faced with a union legal challenge to pit closures. But Blair was determined to have his friend alongside him once in government.

Just before certain victory in the 1997 election, the party leader offered veteran MP John Gilbert both a place in the Lords and a job as Defence Procurement minister if only he would step down from his constituency. Gilbert, in his early 70s, accepted with alacrity. The intention was to shoe-horn Falconer into Gilbert's seat. But Falconer's insistence that his children would remain in private schools if he was chosen as Gilbert's replacement proved a sticking point with the traditionally minded local party in Dudley North, and he decided to drop out of the selection process.

Blair's plan B was simply to declare that his mate was now a peer of the realm, and appoint him Solicitor General, despite the convention that the job should go to a member of the Commons. The post gave Falconer a place on 14 cabinet committees, more than either Brown or Prescott. Falconer inherited much of the responsibility for the Dome on Mandelson's second ousting, and during Blair's second term he has served as Housing minister.

Barrister **Lord Goldsmith**, a friend of Falconer's, was made a life peer in 1999, after making at least one high-value donation to Labour. Two years later, he was appointed Attorney General, effectively the Cabinet's in-house lawyer, and head of the prosecution system in England, Wales and Northern Ireland.

Another Labour insider from the legal fraternity is **Lord Grabiner**, the £1m-a-year silk who is probably the highest paid lawyer in Britain, and who was made a Labour peer in 1999. Grabiner acted for Levy in his bid to stop the *Sunday Times* revelations concerning his taxation affairs. He has also compiled a report on the black economy for the Treasury.

Meanwhile, **Garry Hart**, godfather to Blair's daughter, Kathryn, was hired as Irvine's special adviser in December 1997, the same year in which Hart made a high-value donation to the Labour Party. As a partner at top

City law firm Herbert Smith, Hart had given Irvine many briefs. The firm also acted for Bernie Ecclestone in the cash for ash affair. The £73,000-a-year appointment was made from a shortlist of one, without the post even being advertised. An employment tribunal later ruled that Irvine had acted illegally, although the decision was overturned on appeal.[18]

There are also large numbers of employees of private companies on secondment to Whitehall. Labour has enthusiastically embraced the so-called Interchange Initiative launched by the Conservatives. Some 450 people are known to have taken part in the scheme between 1997 and 2000.[19] Many of the companies that pay their wages regularly win major public contracts. Marconi had staff working for the Ministry of Defence when it secured a £12bn warship deal. Other defence contractors that have provided Interchange Initiative staff for the MoD include BAE Systems, Rolls-Royce, Vickers and Vosper Thorneycroft, all heavily reliant on the military contracts it awards.

Around half of first-term secondees to the Department of the Environment, Transport and the Regions came from companies with interests in housing or commercial development, including Bovis, Bellway, Kvaerner Construction and the National Grid. Secondees from housebuilders thus worked at the ministry responsible for planning at a time when a major review of green belt policy was in the works. Construction company Christiani and Nielsen sent one of its staff to the DETR after winning a £30m contract to build the Avon ring road.

Yet the Government has been noticeably coy about revealing the identities of business secondees, claiming that to make such information available would be to breach the Data Protection Act. Gordon Brown admits that the Treasury has enjoyed the services of fifteen secondees, but was only willing to identify seven. Ironically, one of those he refused to list – Julian McCrae of the Institute for Fiscal Studies – was openly named on his employer's website as being on secondment.

Such secrecy has been challenged by the Campaign for Freedom of Information pressure group, which argues that people dealing with the Government should have the right to know whether they are talking to a real civil servant or to a paid employee of a private company. Following extensive lobbying, the Government is set to make the information available in an annual register, subject to the consent of the secondees themselves.

Other companies to provide staff to the Treasury include oil majors Esso and BP, both beneficiaries of Treasury tax breaks. Consultants Pannell Kerr Forster, PricewaterhouseCoopers and Ernst & Young have all seconded employees, and have all won government consultancy contracts.[20] The latter two firms, which regularly advise clients on tax minimisation, have also lent staff to the Inland Revenue, which admitted to 13 secondees as of February 2002. The Department of Trade and Industry has owned up to 112 secondees.

Many placements are arranged by the Whitehall & Industry Group, a private organisation funded by 105 leading companies, including banks, arms manufacturers and pharmaceutical and construction businesses. Founded in the Thatcher period, it now lists Lord Haskins as patron. Backers include Accenture, Abbey National, Astra-Zeneca, Balfour Beatty, BP, BAT, KPMG, Merck, Bupa, Camelot, Carillion, Conoco, Exxon, Glaxo, Pfizer, Shell, Texaco, Thames Water and HSBC.

Under its auspices, executives from Marks & Spencer have been placed with the Food Standards Agency, while bankers from Barclays work in the Cabinet Office. Staff from Ready Mixed Concrete are at the Highways Agency, employees of Conoco and Esso are at the DTI, and PPP private healthcare provides secondees to the Benefits Agency.[21]

If Labour wants to make the case that such arrangements are in the public interest, giving the public full information about what is going on would seem an appropriate starting point.

NOTES

[1] *Guardian*, 26 January 1998
[2] *Sunday Times*, 5 December 1999
[3] *Observer*, 30 August 1998; e-mail from House of Lords information office 5 April 2001
[4] *Financial Times*, 28 June 1997
[5] *Guardian*, 7 August 1997
[6] *Financial Times*, 6 June 1997
[7] www.itn.co.uk/specials/politics/politics/010102labour.shmtl
[8] *Guardian*, 6 August 2001
[9] *Financial Times*, 29 November 2001
[10] *Guardian*, 5 January 2001
[11] *Daily Telegraph*, 5 January 2001
[12] *Private Eye*, 13 March 2001
[13] *Observer*, 8 October 1996
[14] *Financial Times*, 27 January 2001
[15] *Guardian*, 13 July 1998
[16] *The Sun*, 24 April 1997
[17] *Financial Times*, 19 February 2001; *Observer*, 5 November 2000
[18] *Daily Mail*, 27 March 1999; *Daily Telegraph*, 21 November 2001
[19] *Sunday Express*, 27 February 2000
[20] *Observer*, 17 June 2001
[21] *Private Eye*, 25 January 2002

7. 'INTIMATE WITH EVERY ONE OF THEM': THE WAGES OF SPIN

SEEN but not heard. In the past, the process of securing favourable political outcomes in Britain followed the standard advice to well brought-up Victorian children. For those with the contacts, most paths could be smoothed over at an agreeable lunch.

These days, cash beats out old school tie connections. Anyone with the money can play the game, or at least hire somebody else to play it for them. The post-privatisation era has seen the rise of a whole new profession in the form of the lobbying industry. Public relations is now politicised as never before.

Lobbying and political PR provides an appreciable living for middle men and women who offer a bridge between business and the cash-starved public sector, to an extent that would have been considered suspect throughout the relatively gentlemanly years of the post-war consensus. Such a state of affairs is now seen as natural by the Conservatives and Labour alike. Both parties share the belief that allowing business to run ever-greater proportions of essential services on a for-profit basis is the only efficient means of delivering them at all, whatever the evidence to the contrary.

These already murky waters are further muddied by Labour and Conservative readiness to accept sizeable corporate donations, frequently from the same companies that tender for government and local authority projects. For New Labour, the symbolism is even more important than the bottom line. Donations from private companies are a tangible measure of its success in securing the support of the business community.

The so-called 'cash for access' affair of 1998 saw some lobbyists claiming the ability to secure advance delivery of market-sensitive information, or facilitate meetings with just about anybody at all in the corridors of power. Industry reaction has been defensive, with lobbyists insisting that they do not engage in influence peddling. That argument rather misses the point. The issue is not the degree of finesse with which lobbyists operate, but the very existence of a means to plough up an ostensibly level playing field in favour of business.

Companies that stand to make hefty profits from the Private Finance

Initiative can easily afford the tax-deductible cost of bringing in professionals to advise them on how to go about it. Community groups and grassroots voluntary organisations, such as those campaigning against PFI projects, simply cannot pay for comparable expertise.

The rise of Labour-sympathetic lobbyists is a comparatively recent phenomenon, although examples of the breed could certainly be found by the early 1990s. Chief among them were the late Jenny Jeger, a partner in GJW, and Richard Faulkner of Westminster Communications. Both mixed in Labour Finance and Industry Group circles.

Jeger was retained by big retailers seeking deregulation of Sunday trading, and was successful in splitting the Labour vote on the issue, persuading many MPs to vote against the shopworkers' union's stance. The role played by supermarket owner David Sainsbury would presumably bear further research.

Hobsbawm Macaulay Communications – founded in 1993 by Julia Hobsbawm and Sarah Macaulay, later to marry Gordon Brown – cut itself a niche market as monopoly supplier of political marketing services to Labour-aligned interests. Before founding the business, Hobsbawm had been employed in Labour's fledgling high-value donor unit between 1991 and 1992. Her company effectively took some of that work into the private sector, managing the party's 1000 Club for high-value donors and the £500-a-plate annual gala dinners.

Other clients have included the Industry Forum, *New Statesman* magazine and think tank Demos, as well as such public sector bodies as the Arts Council and the Victoria and Albert Museum. Hobsbawm Macaulay's ethical stance has certainly paid off in terms of the bottom line. Profits between 1995 and 2000 increased twentyfold, albeit from a small base.[1]

But Hobsbawm Macaulay was then the exception rather than the rule. Most mainstream PR and lobbying concerns during the years of Tory hegemony saw little point in shelling out to have a Labour insider on the payroll. That began to change as soon as it became obvious that Labour was about to return to power. The lobbyists wanted to hit the ground running. By 1995, a *New Statesman* article listed 16 Labour activists working for lobbying companies.[2]

A comparable list today would be several times longer. In Westminster alone there are at least 50 to 60 former Labour staff members now earning a living from this kind of activity. Many more are party members, whether by conviction or commercial interest.[3]

One of the first to make the transition from Labour to lobbying was Colin Byrne – Labour's chief press officer between 1988 and 1991 and effectively number two to Mandelson during the latter's stint as director of communications – who has since risen to become joint chief executive of Weber Shandwick, the UK's largest PR firm. He still maintains close contacts with the party. In September 1996, for instance, Shandwick released him to work alongside Mandelson for one day a week. He continued to work for the company's clients up to the beginning of the following year's election campaign, then took unpaid leave to work for Labour full time. During the 2001 election he was seconded to Labour's business relations unit, headed by Lord Hollick. Another Shandwick consultant, Peter Bowyer, also worked for Labour during the campaign.[4]

The going rate for senior lobbyists such as Byrne is upwards of £225 an hour, so the benefits of such election campaign secondments are worth thousands, or even tens of thousands, of pounds. Byrne insists that his clients were 'comfortable' with the arrangement.[5]

That is hardly surprising, given that many are Labour backers, including PricewaterhouseCoopers and French multinational Vivendi, which funds the party through its Connex rail subsidiary, and supports the New Local Government Network of Blairite councillors through its UK waste management operation Onyx. Other Shandwick clients actively seek public sector work, including arms manufacturers the T.I. Group, Northrop Grumman, and Carillion, the trendy new name for construction outfit Tarmac.

Another pioneer Labour lobbyist was Nicki Lewis, who joined the party staff in 1994 from Dewe Rogerson – the PR company that handled many of the Tories' privatisation campaigns – to become head of corporate relations. Among her early successes was to persuade pharmaceuticals giant Glaxo, which had only the year before given the Tories £60,000, to attend a meeting at Labour headquarters in Walworth Road. Three years later, Lewis was appointed a director of lobbyist A.S. Biss & Co, just before Labour was to take office.

Chairwoman Adele Biss described Lewis's signing as a major coup, and left little doubt about why she was hired: 'Her particular experience is in creating constructive dialogue between clients and Labour's public policy makers on all fronts and she will therefore have responsibility for developing ASB's expertise and links with the Labour Party,' commented Biss.[6]

Lewis herself was even more explicit in asserting that, in her case, the personal was indeed the political: 'I remain on excellent terms with my colleagues at John Smith House [Labour headquarters at the time] with whom I plan to stay in close touch.'[7]

But perhaps the lobbyist to take fullest advantage of the coming political sea change was Westminster Strategy, a Grayling Group subsidiary founded in 1987 and currently boasting a client roster including Asda, Aventis, BAA, BT, the government of Gibraltar, Goldman Sachs, Norwich Union, Sainsbury's and Serco.[8] Westminster Strategy has consistently provided a bridge into the private sector for Labour backroom boys and girls, some of whom subsequently return to party work.

Its first important recruit from Labour was Mike Lee, special advisor to David Blunkett when the latter was health spokesperson, who went on to become director of communications for the Football Association, a Westminster Strategy client. In September 2000 he joined UEFA, European football's governing body, as director of communications and public affairs.[9]

Westminster Strategy proceeded to take on a number of Lee's key party colleagues. Recruits included a certain Jo Moore, later the most infamous Labour spin doctor after Peter Mandelson himself. Moore, an old adversary of mine from when we were both active in the National Organisation of Labour Students in the early 1980s, went on to work as press officer for Labour councils in Haringey and Islington. Talent-spotted by Mandelson, she rapidly rose through the ranks to become head of press and broadcasting at Millbank, specialising in spinning decisions made by Labour's national executive in ways that suited the leadership.

Westminster Strategy snapped her up as an account director in November 1997, at what was coyly described as 'a suitably handsome salary' for a three-day week.[10] But, by February 1999, she was back with Labour as media adviser to Trade secretary Stephen Byers.

After Byers took over the Department of Transport, the hitherto obscure Moore achieved overnight national notoriety with a simple 18-word e-mail to a colleague sent just one hour after the first Al Qaeda jet slammed into the World Trade Centre: 'Alun, it's now a very good day to get out anything we want to bury. Councillors' expenses? Jo.' When the text was leaked a month later, the spin became the story.

Somehow she hung on to her job, despite demands from many quarters for her resignation. But Moore had already damaged her credibility to the point where she could no longer realistically push the Government's plans to reorganise Railtrack into a non-profit trust. Instead, a £55,000-a-month contract went to Finsbury, a PR company and regular Labour gala dinner ticket buyer, run by Roland Rudd, a former *Financial Times* journalist and a friend of Mandelson.

The Tories made political capital from the move, claiming that the taxpayer was being forced to pay for spin twice over. The department has spent £4m on external PR agencies over the last four years.[11]

Moore and her big mouth were back in the news the following year, after privately telling journalists that when her boss Byers described opponents of the Government's reform agenda as 'wreckers', those targeted 'included some in the movement'. This obvious reference to trade unionists sent many general secretaries ballistic.[12]

The plot was rapidly moving towards its denouement. Whatever Moore's abilities in influencing people, she certainly hadn't mastered the art of making friends. Relations between her and Department of Transport head of communications Martin Sixsmith – a civil servant rather than a special adviser – had by this point broken down completely. According to one departmental press officer: 'Jo and Martin couldn't stand the sight of each other. Martin felt there were issues where Jo wasn't keeping him informed. Jo felt Martin impeded and hindered Stephen Byers' profile.'[13]

Ironic, then, that the *Daily Mirror* chose Valentine's Day 2002 to publish a purported e-mail from former BBC journalist Sixsmith to Moore, accusing her of seeking to announce poor rail safety and punctuality statistics on the day of Princess Margaret's funeral. The claimed wording was a direct dig at her earlier gaffe: 'Princess Margaret is being buried that day. I will absolutely not allow anything else to be.' Ouch.

The timing was terrible for the Government, already up to its neck in the Lakshmi Mittal affair, and the spin machine moved into overdrive. The e-mail was 'a pack of lies' and 'completely made up', Moore insisted. It was, according to Robin Cook 'a fabrication' and according to Blair himself, 'a fiction'. The *Mirror* stood by its story. It was later confirmed that an e-mail making substantially the same point had indeed been sent, although the wording was slightly different. But who was behind the leak? The *Mirror* revealed that Sixsmith himself had used the press to undermine his rival, no small matter for a civil servant.[14]

By the end of the week, Byers announced that both Sixsmith and Moore had resigned. Sixsmith immediately insisted that this was not the case, claiming that the first he heard of his 'resignation' was on the radio following a hospital appointment that afternoon. Effectively, he was accusing his boss of lying. There were days of claim and counterclaim, and growing clamour for Byers' resignation. A lifeline was eventually provided by permanent secretary Sir Richard Mottram, who broke the tradition of civil service anonymity and issued a statement that Sixsmith had 'agreed that he was willing to resign', providing Moore went with him and that a generous financial package was worked out. Sixsmith's defenders pointed to the difference between being willing to resign on certain conditions, and actual resignation.

Three months later, Byers was forced into an embarrassing climbdown in a Commons statement, which accepted that Sixsmith did not resign in February, even though the announcement to that effect had been in good faith. Sixsmith secured a £200,000 compensation package. Shortly afterwards, Byers too was out of a job.

Another Westminster Strategy alumnus is Tom Engel, who worked alongside Mike Lee in Blunkett's office as a relatively lowly researcher before spending two years with the company. He then went back to his old boss, this time as senior adviser to a politician who was now Secretary of State for Education.[15]

The move raised eyebrows. Civil service rules precluded Engel from working on issues where former clients had an interest. Yet Westminster Strategy worked for several education sector concerns, while the Football Association was involved in a number of social exclusion projects falling within the remit of Blunkett's department.

Where Westminster Strategy led, other lobbying companies soon followed. Dave Hill, who had spent 26 years working his way up the Labour ladder, starting as Roy Hattersley's researcher and ending up with the title chief spokesperson – stood down in April 1998 to take a directorship with Bell Pottinger Good Relations, on a reported £100,000-plus salary.

Since making the switch, he has become most insistent on being referred to as David rather than Dave.[16] Whatever he chooses to call himself, his high standing in the party makes him one of the few people whose calls automatically get put straight through. And as if that wasn't connectivity enough, his partner Hilary Coffman works in Blair's Downing Street office.

On starting his new position, Hill spent much of his time advising GM food manufacturer Monsanto on media strategy. He has also offered political advice to private prisons operator Securicor on issues such as union recognition. Bell Pottinger claims to have facilitated meetings between Securicor and a number of Labour notables. These include Prisons minister Lord Williams; Welsh Secretary Alun Michael; Lord Warner, an adviser to the Home Secretary; the Downing Street Policy Unit; Adrian Montague, head of the PFI taskforce; and a number of backbench MPs. Hill denies that he personally played matchmaker.[17]

Like Byrne, Hill has made a point keeping up contacts, and was seconded back to the party for the 2001 election campaign in a senior campaigning role.

The company also recruited Cathy McGlynn, who had spent six years as an aide to Jack Cunningham, then Agriculture, Fisheries and Food minister, in 1998. Her specialist knowledge would have been invaluable to GM concerns. McGlynn had also built a strong business contacts book after serving on the secretariat of Cunningham's pet project, the Industry Forum.

Other clients of Bell Pottinger, founded by Thatcher advertising mastermind Lord Bell, include many companies that have fallen foul of environmental and Third World campaigners. Among them are Nestlé, accused by its critics of promoting formula baby milk in the Third World to the detriment of breast feeding; Nike, a frequent target of the anti-globalisation movement; and oil majors Texaco and BP.

Elsewhere in the lobbying world, Nick Pecorelli, formerly an aide to Margaret Beckett, worked for Politics International before returning to the party payroll, now serving as assistant general secretary. Luke Akehurst, who stood for Labour in Aldershot at the last election, works for GJW.[18]

Larger companies typically maintain extensive in-house communications teams. When Labour entered office in 1997, many comparative youngsters were instantly catapulted into well-paid jobs. Pete Metcalfe, then a 24-year-old researcher for energy spokesperson John Battle, doubled his salary overnight, with a £30,000-a-year job as head of public affairs for British Nuclear Fuels Ltd. BNFL commented: 'We wanted someone with a knowledge of the industry, used to communicating with Whitehall and political audiences.' It added, seemingly without irony: 'Obviously his Labour contacts help.'[19]

Even better off was Tim Allan, a former television researcher who went to work for Blair in 1992 while the politician was still home affairs spokesperson. After the election, Allan became deputy press officer to Alastair Campbell. In April 1998, still not yet 30, he secured an overnight £60,000 salary increase by taking a £100,000-a-year post as director of corporate communications at BSkyB. One media analyst neatly summed up the task at hand: 'Tim Allan was part of the team which sold Labour to the middle class. Now he's got to sell the same people BSkyB.'[20]

Allan announced in 2001 that he is setting up his own PR business on the back of a deal with BSkyB, which will be the company's first client. The *Financial Times* commented: 'He will give guidance on government affairs, where his political expertise and inside knowledge of Whitehall will prove invaluable to BSkyB and future clients.'[21]

Gez Sagar, a former writer in Blair's election campaign office, who had worked for the party since 1988, was appointed head of press and parliamentary affairs for Millennium Central, the body set up to organise the Millennium Dome. Sagar himself told trade magazine *PR Week*: 'As the project is currently under review and key decisions about the project have still to be taken, it is useful to understand how the Labour Party works.'[22]

This trend continued throughout Labour's first term in office. Faz Hakim left the political office at 10 Downing Street in 2000 for a new post as vice-president in charge of press strategy across Europe for financial giant J.P. Morgan. Hakim had worked for Labour in both opposition and government for seven years. J.P. Morgan insisted: 'We hired her because of her skills in dealing with the press, not because of her political contacts.'[23]

Sometimes lobbyists are able to use their quasi-political jobs as a springboard to elected office. Before becoming an MP, Charles Clarke – the cabinet-ranked Labour Party chairman – ran his own lobbying concern, Quality Public Affairs.

Rochdale MP Lorna Fitzsimons, a past Labour-aligned president of the National Union of Students, started her career with Rowland Sallingbury Casey, a firm run by former Tory MP John Maples. Clients included the Water Companies Association and Amersham International, one of the first Thatcher privatisations. Such was her skill in the job that *PR Week* even awarded her the title of Young Communicator of the Year.

The 1997 election underlined the rewards of Rowland Sallingbury

Casey's ecumenical approach to politics. Maples became a so-called parliamentary 'retread' after being returned as Conservative MP for Stratford-on-Avon, while Fitzsimons was elected for Rochdale on a Labour ticket. That must represent a considerable come-down for a woman who once swooned: 'I'd rather be a venture capitalist with a jet-set lifestyle than a Labour MP.'[24]

But after settling for second-best and embarking on a parliamentary career, her perception of who she was at Westminster to represent appeared to extend beyond the citizens of Rochdale. *PR Week* quoted her shortly before the election as claiming: 'The value to Rowland's clients is that they've got one more person in the House who really understands them.' The magazine itself added: 'Should she get in . . . she thinks that she will be an asset to her clients.'[25]

Hoping to follow Fitzsimons into parliament is Howard Dawber, a Bell Pottinger employee who fought Cheadle for Labour in 2001. Dawber handles the PR account for the PPP Forum, a group that lobbies the Government for more Public–Private Partnerships. Backers include the Royal Bank of Scotland, the Halifax, Laing, W.S. Atkins, Amec and City lawyers Clifford Chance. It is headed by the ubiquitous Cathy McGlynn.

Lobbying also offers employment to politicians who have fallen foul of the electorate. Former Labour MEP Carole Tongue has signed up with Labour donor Citigate, which until recently included Enron on its client roster. Citigate director Rex Osborn is former deputy director of campaigns at the Labour Party.[26]

This rapid interchange between influential backroom jobs in a governing party and highly paid posts in the private sector can leave both lobbyists and their mentors open to criticism. One case in point is the relationship between John Prescott and Mike Craven, his researcher for much of the 1980s. Craven went on to become managing director of Market Access International. Following an internal dispute, he went on gardening leave, continuing to receive a salary from the company.[27]

In September 1998, Craven was named as temporary replacement for Dave Hill as Labour's acting chief press officer, declining to take the job on a permanent basis as he was already formulating plans to start his own consultancy. Given the extreme sensitivity over the party's links with lobbyists after the cash for access affair, there was some surprise that he got the job even on a caretaker basis.[28]

Craven ultimately did start up his own show, in the shape of Lexington Communications. Its clients have included many companies with interests in transport. Among them are numbered British Airways, tube privatisation consortium Metronet, and Serco.[29] At the last election Craven followed the example of Byrne and Hill, and spent the campaign working with his old boss. So it was that a man with clearly transport-oriented business connections ended up volunteering his services to the politician in overall charge of Britain's transport sector.

Stephen Hardwick, chief lobbyist for BAA, also worked on Labour's election team, where he established a good relationship with Prescott's team.[30] BAA was at that time anxious to secure a government go-ahead for a fifth terminal at Heathrow, a move fiercely opposed by local residents. A vast amount of money was at stake. So important was this project that BAA had already spent £320m on preparatory work for the £2bn scheme.[31]

Permission for Terminal Five finally came in November 2001, and it is expected to open in 2007. Two months later the Government confirmed it was considering the case for additional runways at BAA's Heathrow, Gatwick and Stansted airports. The Prescott link can hardly have damaged BAA's chances of seeing its wish list so completely fulfilled.

As it became apparent that New Labour would walk home for a second term, the gravitational pull of Blairism became irresistible even to one-time Conservatives. Ceri Evans, former adviser to both Tory leader William Hague and London mayoral candidate Steve Norris, jumped ship. Evans is managing director of public affairs at PR firm Golin Harris Ludgate, regarded as having poor ties to Labour on account of the overt Conservative allegiance of its senior staff. The number of Ludgate lobbying clients had fallen from 40 to just 17 between May and November 2000. Evans' defection bolstered the company's Labour links, neatly combining political conversion and shrewd career move.[32]

As businesses in their own right, some lobbyists are themselves financial backers of the Labour Party. Labour is well aware of this, and courts them accordingly. Lobbying company personnel, including former Labour staffers, are invited to drinks parties at Westminster, where they happily mix with Labour fundraisers on the look out for financial support. Sponsorship possibilities are openly discussed. A Labour spokesperson explained after one such bash: 'We just invited lobbyists in. You know we are looking for sponsorship for various things.'[33] While lobbying companies could send who they liked, some of the guests would inevitably turn out to be former Labour Party employees, she conceded.

Perhaps the most surprising lobbyist to have given Labour money is the now defunct Ian Greer Associates, a £5,000-plus donor in 1996. The firm's founder, Ian Greer, was forced to step down as chairman after press accusations over his role in getting Conservative MPs to table Commons questions on behalf of Harrods proprietor Mohammed al Fayed in return for cash.

Other lobbyist donors tend to have more on-side track records. Paul Adamson, the multimillionaire founder of Brussels-based Adamson BSMG, whose clients included McDonnell Douglas, SmithKline Beecham, Shell and Glaxo Wellcome, gave £10,000 in 1999. This was, Adamson insisted, inspired purely by the Government's positive approach towards Europe.[34]

Adamson BSMG is now a subsidiary of Byrne's Shandwick group, trading as Weber Shandwick Adamson. It is particularly noteworthy for its pro-globalisation stance. Adamson and two colleagues are members of the Global Services Network, a body that seeks to 'build global support for the liberalisation of international services trade, and to create a global services community of business people, government officials and academics who are committed to increase trade in services'.[35] In plain English, then, its main aim is to see ever greater tranches of the public sector opened up to service sector multinationals.

In line with this internationalist perspective, Adamson has also supported the Foreign Policy Centre think tank, established by Robin Cook during his time as Foreign Secretary. Blair is listed among the patrons, while Levy sits on its advisory council. Other backers include Accenture, BP, Diageo, Hiscox, Interbrand, KPMG and Rio Tinto, and two companies that supply mercenary forces, Control Risks and Armor Group.[36]

Concern over Labour's links with the lobbying industry reached its apex in July 1998 as a result of the cash for access affair. Parallels with the cash for questions scandal that so damaged the Conservatives under John Major were only too obvious. Journalist Greg Palast secured this considerable scoop by approaching lobbyists, purporting to represent unnamed 'Texan energy interests'. If the name Enron sprung to the lobbyists' minds, that was probably the intention. His clients, he explained, were seeking exemption from the rule that all new power plants had to use coal rather than gas.

Palast spoke to former aides to Blair, Brown and Mandelson, by then working for private lobbying companies. Between them, they claimed to have passed confidential government information on to their clients, arranged meetings with ministers and senior advisors, and secured places on government taskforces for selected business people.

The first Labour insider implicated was Karl Milner, one-time communications advisor to Gordon Brown, but now on the payroll of lobbyist GJW Government Relations. GJW is a financial supporter of Labour, spending £5,000 or more on sponsorship or dinner tickets in 1997, 1998 and 1999. Its clients include BUPA, Premier Oil and Goldman Sachs.

Milner, who incidentally worked for Hillary Clinton during the 1994 US presidential campaign, produced a confidential select committee report on energy policy the day before it was officially published. 'This report is embargoed,' Milner explained. 'As I've told you, we have many friends in government. They like to run things past us some days in advance to get our view, to let them know if they have anything to be worried about, maybe suggest some changes.'[37]

Milner may have been talking himself up here. Many government documents are routinely circulated in advance to interested parties, including friendly journalists. Keen to impress, Milner may simply have been hyping up his readiness to break an embargo. Either way, such braggadocio must have caused considerable embarrassment to his employers. GJW's managing director Andrew Gifford was chairman of the lobbyists' self-regulatory body, the Association of Professional Political Consultants, whose code of conduct provides that members must 'act in good faith and in an honest manner . . . with proper regard to the public interest'. There is nothing to suggest that Gifford knew of, or approved, the leak. But he did not consider Milner's actions a hanging offence, allowing him to keep his job.

The second former aide caught out was Ben Lucas, erstwhile head of research for building union UCATT, who led Blair's political briefing unit in the 1997 election. Afterwards he worked for Lowe Bell, where he met another former New Labour backroom boy, Neal Lawson. Lawson had some degree of clout in Blairite circles through his role as managing editor of little-read moderniser journal *Renewal*. The two men, together with their friend Jon 'Jonny' Mendelsohn, founded a lobbying firm under the unimaginative name Lawson Lucas Mendelsohn. Financial backing for the venture came from businessman Steve Rubin, one-time owner of the Reebok sportswear brand.[38]

Mendelsohn had headed the Union of Jewish Students in the late 1980s, and became a protégé of Labour MP Greville Janner. He was instrumental in building support for the War Crimes Act 1991, allowing Nazi criminals to be tried in British courts. He also served as director of the British-Israeli Parliamentary Group and the Inter-Parliamentary Council Against Anti-Semitism, and trustee of the Holocaust Educational Trust. After catching Blair's eye, he worked on Labour–business liaison between November 1995 and May 1997, a role ideal for a future lobbyist.

Despite being a new kid on the lobbyist block at the time, LLM's ties to Blair and Brown provided it with off-the-peg credibility. It had also been careful to contribute to New Labour coffers, spending over £5,000 on dinner tickets in the year of the scandal. Lucas certainly considered himself in with the in-crowd, telling Palast he knew 'intelligence which in market terms would be worth a lot of money'. LLM could 'reach anyone', he added. 'We can go to Gordon Brown if we have to.'[39]

Lucas boasted of knowing the contents of the Chancellor's Mansion House speech – a key annual City fixture – some days in advance, and also of providing a client with advance warning of Brown's decision to create a new housing directorate. LLM took full advantage of New Labour's professed non-ideological nature, Lucas argued. 'The Labour Government is in two minds. It operates in a kind of schizophrenia. On big issues especially, they don't know what they are thinking. Blair himself doesn't always know what he is thinking . . . This Government likes to do deals.'[40]

The sales pitch continued in this vein. Not only could places on government taskforces be guaranteed, but the Government was desperate for an ever-expanding supply of business people willing to serve on them, Lucas insisted.

LLM sought fees of £5,000–£20,000 a month to assist Palast's non-existent clients. As evidence of past success, it cited work done for Tesco. The supermarket chain is a regular high-value Labour sponsor, and gave substantial financial support for the Millennium Dome. Other clients included News International and Railtrack, which was another Labour Party sponsor before it was forced into administration.

Even after the story broke, LLM was resolutely unrepentant. 'We can hold our heads high,' Mendelsohn maintained.[41] The business is still up and running.

But undoubtedly the highest-profile casualty in the story was Derek Draper, director of lobbyist GPC Market Access. Son of a British Leyland shop steward from Chorley, Draper got involved in Labour student politics at Manchester University before working for MP Nick Brown in Newcastle. In 1992, he was hired by Mandelson, and the two became very close.

Draper is one of life's natural true believers, and New Labour got to him before the Moonies. I vividly remember our first meeting at a midsummer champagne party thrown by a lobbyist in Westminster, *circa* 1993 or 1994. Both he and I were members of Vauxhall Labour Party at the time, and our mutual reputations preceded each other. It was a hot evening, and we had both been drinking plenty of the free booze on offer that night.

Within minutes of being introduced, Draper and I were engaged in a full-on public shouting match on the respective merits of Blairism and socialism. Draper very early on aggressively initiated four-letter obscenities. This was one of his standard debating tactics, designed to intimidate. While at one stage matters looked like coming to blows, things fizzled out rather tamely. We simply agreed to differ.

Draper indicated to Palast that he had secured political advantages – ranging from confidential information to actual changes in government policy – for a range of important business clients. For starters, he boasted he had provided US investment bank Salomon Smith Barney with a week's advance notice of a spending cap from the Treasury. Here, bragged Draper, was genuine 'inside information'. He added: 'If they acted on it, they'd have made a fortune.'[42] Salomon Smith Barney declined to comment on the affair. There is no suggestion that it either asked for this material or subsequently traded on it.

Draper maintained he had special access to the Treasury and Downing Street. GPC had secured the appointment of the chief executive of British Gas to the Government's Welfare to Work taskforce, he insisted. This was denied by the company, who said that David Varney's invitation had come directly from the Government. This was a company that Labour in opposition routinely pilloried as a bastion of corporate greed. It is now a regular high-value sponsor.

Draper spoke of his friendship with key Labour figures. He claimed to have facilitated a meeting between the chief executive of the House Builders' Federation and Blair advisor Geoff Norris over the development potential of several tracts of green-belt land.[43]

As a further example of his lobbying prowess, Draper insisted that GPC had cleared the way for privatised electricity generator Powergen to realise its long-harboured ambition to buy a regional electricity company. Conservative Secretary of State for Trade and Industry Ian Lang had been against such a step, as was his Labour successor Margaret Beckett, on competition grounds. But Draper had arranged meetings between Powergen chairman Ed Wallis and Treasury officials, and the company now had the green light, Palast was told. Powergen admitted using GPC for political intelligence gathering, but denied reaching a deal with the Government. Whatever the truth here, it was later given the go-ahead to buy East Midlands Electricity for £2bn, in one of the first decisions taken by Draper's former employer Peter Mandelson on becoming Secretary of State for Trade and Industry.

Palast asked how his clients could go about getting exemptions from pollution restrictions. The most obvious solution would have been to lobby Environment and Industry ministers. Draper advised against this course. Environment minister Michael Meacher was written off as 'very weak . . . basically irrelevant' and 'a nobody going nowhere' who wouldn't be in the job much longer. Four years later, Meacher is still in post, rather more than can be said for Draper. Similarly, Beckett was dismissed as 'useless', while her minister John Battle was highly regarded by comparison, being only 'pretty useless'.

But what was really damning for Draper – and New Labour as a whole – was that all of this was more than sales talk. He really did have direct links to Number 10. Draper first entered the lobbying sector with Prima Europe, a management buy-out from leading PR firm Burson-Marsteller by a clutch of former SDP figures. Given such parentage, it is ironic that Prima, whose clients included Unilever, Glaxo Wellcome, Abbey National, British Nuclear Fuels, Rio Tinto, Powergen and British Gas, made great play of its Labour links following Blair's first election victory.

In a mailshot that May, the company argued:

> The Labour election victory last Thursday was a major watershed in British politics. Many companies like yours will now be considering the effect of the new government on their business.

As you can see from the attached brochure, Prima Europe has unrivalled knowledge of the Labour Party's policies and personalities. I am therefore writing to you to tell you a little more about the unique service we offer our clients.[44]

Great play was even then being made of Draper's government contacts. Soon Prima Europe was able to offer an even more influential connection to the top through one of its founders, Roger Liddle, co-author with Mandelson of a book called *The Blair Revolution*. Liddle had spent 14 years in the SDP and Liberal Democrats, three times standing against Labour candidates in parliamentary elections. Just two years after rejoining Labour, he was put in charge of European affairs in the Prime Minister's policy unit. As a result, his 25 per cent stake in Prima Europe, worth around £260,000, went into a blind trust. The company insisted that therefore no conflict of interest could arise.

Its managing director did admit that the company traded on the basis of its 'understanding of the different policy currents in the Labour Party', but promised that it would not play up its link to Liddle. He added: 'There could be people to whom we could say, Roger used to work for us and we know Roger.'[45] But that would be improper, he insisted.

In February 1998, Prima Europe was purchased by Canada's GPC for a reported £2m, and adopted the new parent's name. Draper made a reported £150,000 out of the deal, and secured a six-figure salary from his new employers. Liddle was to be paid off on an 'earn-out' basis, with the proceeds conditional on profit targets over the following three years being met. In other words, Liddle stood to gain financially if GPC's new purchase did well.

When Palast asked Draper to provide a senior figure who could vouch for his influence with the Government, Draper introduced him to Liddle at a GPC party in Westminster. Liddle was more than happy to sing Draper's praises. He told the journalist: 'There is a circle and Derek is part of the circle. And anyone who says he isn't is an enemy . . . Derek knows all the right people.' Liddle then handed Palast his business card, complete with Downing Street and home telephone numbers, and added: 'Just tell me what you want, who you want to meet, and Derek and I will make the call for you.' Draper then made his now notorious comment about the extent of his influence. Britain's Government comprised a surprisingly narrow circle, he maintained. 'There are 17 people who count and to say I am intimate with every one of them is the understatement of the century.'[46]

Crowing aside, Draper – today an outcast as a result of the affair – wielded real influence in New Labour circles. He owned *Progress*, the Blairite house journal, and wrote a regular column for the *Daily Express*, faxing the copy through to Mandelson for approval before sending it to the paper that paid him to write it.

There were more examples of Draper's big-headedness in the days to come. 'What I really am is a commentator-fixer,' he self-importantly opined. 'Your Mayor Daley has nothing on me.' Nor was he acting from any residual socialist desire to make the world a better place. 'I just want to stuff my bank account at £250 an hour,' Draper candidly admitted.

Cash for access was to be Draper's downfall. He was immediately suspended from GPC and stripped of his *Express* column. Draper maintained he had done nothing wrong, although he did confess in a radio interview: 'I am a bit of a tosser.'[47] Those who knew him heartily concurred.

Subsequent career moves flopped dismally. Draper convinced one gullible national newspaper to run the story that he was writing a television thriller satirising Labour cronyism, which would see BBC and ITV competing for the rights to the six-part thriller. Television viewers have mercifully been spared that particular blockbuster.[48]

Hired by former *Sun* editor Kelvin MacKenzie as a presenter on Talk Radio, he was sacked in April 1999 after a prank on-air telephone call, in which the self-confessed tosser claimed to be sitting in the jacuzzi in an Amsterdam brothel with a prostitute called Claudia. Later that year he launched an advertising agency called Farm, on the premise that 'the people who listened to the New Labour message are the same ones who will buy beer or soap'.[49] Word of its launch was one of the main stories in the *Sunday Times* business section. Draper was last heard of in Los Angeles seeking spiritual enlightenment. From New Labour to the New Age.

When cash for access made it into print, Palast's scoop dominated the headlines for days. But Blair stood by Liddle. Without mentioning him by name, he stressed that, although he expected the highest standards of probity from his officials, he would not take action against them without proof. Liddle remains in post to this day. But Palast paid a heavy personal price for the story, finding himself the subject of not one but two vitriolic front page splashes in the mass circulation *Daily Mirror*, traditionally Labour's strongest supporter in the national press.

The first onslaught came just three days after the story broke. Palast woke up that Wednesday morning to find his photograph plastered all over *The Daily Mirror* front page under a huge headline proclaiming him 'The Liar'.[50] The story centred on comments made by a New York judge in a court case two years earlier, who had rejected Palast's evidence on the grounds that it was evasive and biased.

The judgment 'left a huge question mark against Palast's claims that he had uncovered government sleaze', the *Mirror* claimed. It did nothing of the sort, of course. Whatever the wrongs and rights of the earlier judgment, the two issues were entirely separate. For his part, Palast maintains that if anyone involved in the court case was biased, it was the judge, an overt Republican and thus more than happy to discount anything said by Palast, then a government investigator for the Democrat administration.

Worse was to come in September, when the *Mirror* breathlessly informed readers: 'A sex pest scandal rocked Labour's Blackpool conference last night after a top investigative reporter was found in a woman delegate's hotel room.'[51]

Margaret Payne, Blairite candidate for the national executive, alleged that Palast had pestered her for a date in two phone calls from New York, having met her at a function two years previously. Although she had spurned his advances, she went on, Palast had nevertheless bluffed the hotel's reception desk into giving him access to her room. As a result of these claims, Palast had his media pass withdrawn, a rather convenient outcome for Millbank. From journalist of stature, he found himself downgraded to male bunny boiler.

Palast insists that he had set up an interview with Payne, and that he has a sworn affidavit from the hotel clerk, saying that Payne instructed the front desk to let Palast into her room for a prearranged appointment. He also has a statement from a witness who overheard Alastair Campbell thank *Mirror* editor Piers Morgan for running the story.

Reflecting on cash for access several years later, Palast is scathingly dismissive of the New Labour defence line that the whole affair was over-cooked, and based on the deluded boastful raving of a few youngsters. The very word 'boastful', he points out, is an ambiguous term. There is all the difference in the world between idle boasting, and boasting that you can do something and then going on to do it. In most cases, the lobbyists were able to deliver on their promises.

As Palast puts out: 'If you think that British Gas, Powergen and Rupert Murdoch are so dumb they paid people to lie to them, you have got to be kidding. The whole idea of "boastful lobbyists" is bullshit.'[52]

If anything, *The Observer* undersold the story, Palast maintains. Liddle was on good personal terms with *Observer* editor Will Hutton, and thus able to launch a confidential appeal for mercy. 'Liddle called up Hutton at home and admitted, "I said those stupid things but I was drunk." Later he would say I fabricated the whole thing,' Palast argues. Hutton confirms the call took place.[53]

In the wake of the Draper scandal, the Association of Professional Political Consultants hired a former senior civil servant and a leading barrister to investigate the claims. Spot checks were made on several companies, and the code of conduct toughened up.

The Observer returned its attention to lobbyists the following year. In 1999, Scotland got its own parliament for the first time in nearly 300 years, immediately transforming the Edinburgh political scene. The cash for access scandal saw a repeat performance north of the border, with the added dimension of nepotism. This time the accusations centred around a lobbying firm called Beattie Communications, which kept the sons and daughters of several leading Scottish Labour figures on its payroll. This was another sting operation, in which a reporter posed as a US businessman anxious to use Beattie's services to help it secure PFI contracts for schools and hospitals. The meeting was filmed and taped.

Beattie sent along media director Alex Barr and Kevin Reid, erstwhile head of Labour's monitoring unit and son of Secretary of State for Scotland John Reid. Reid reeled off a list of Labour contacts to the pretend client, culminating in a probably well-rehearsed line: 'I know the Secretary of State very, very well because he's my father.'[54]

Kevin Reid's career has also included a spell working for Dad as a parliamentary researcher, with his salary met from allowances paid to Reid senior as an MP. A complaint was lodged with Elizabeth Filkin, then parliamentary commissioner for standards, that Reid junior engaged in Labour Party campaigning in working time, contravening applicable rules. Filkin upheld the complaint, and reported that John Reid had attempted to intimidate witnesses to mislead her inquiry. But MPs on the Committee on Standards and Privileges overturned Filkin's report.

Kevin Reid was not the only offspring of senior Scottish Labour politicians on the Beattie payroll. Another employee was Malcolm Robertson, son of the Secretary of State for Defence George Robertson. Robertson junior went on to become parliamentary officer for the Scottish Airports Authority. Robertson senior was made a peer and is now head of NATO.

Jack McConnell, former general secretary of the Scottish Labour Party, was also hired by the company. Barr told the undercover journalists that McConnell got the job 'in the certain knowledge that Jack would get a safe seat and in the hope and expectation that he would also get a cabinet position'.[55]

He did rather better than that. In November 2001, McConnell was confirmed as Scotland's First Minister, despite the fiasco of a press conference halfway through his campaign confirming that, yes, he had had an affair with a Labour Party press officer. McConnell was paid £15,000 during his six months at Beattie subsidiary Public Affairs Europe. Public Affairs Europe had no clients on its books at the time, indicating that the workload may not have been unduly onerous.

While with the firm, McConnell took Sports minister Sam Galbraith along to a Rangers game, in order to meet Scottish Premier League chief executive Roger Mitchell. There they discussed the need for financial support for youth soccer academies. Labour subsequently pledged £10m in backing.[56] Another former Beattie worker, Christina Marshall, is daughter of Glasgow MP David Marshall. She was later employed as McConnell's personal assistant.

Beattie later got into more trouble when it was alleged to have orchestrated a dirty tricks campaign on behalf of a US multinational. Trade unionist Jim McCourt began to investigate a spate of miscarriages, cancers and fertility problems among workers at a National Semiconductor's computer factory in Greenock.

Two of Beattie's female staff targeted McCourt for surveillance, and posed as National Semiconductor workers to get information out of a BBC Scotland team looking into the claims. Bill Spiers, leader of the Scottish TUC, described the incident as 'the biggest anti-union scandal to hit Scotland in many years'.[57]

Of course, Beattie doesn't have a monopoly on the Edinburgh lobbying scene. Its rival PS Communications has seen its former employee Lord Watson appointed Tourism minister in McConnell's cabinet.[58]

But in both Holyrood and Westminster, UK lobbying remains in its infancy. Top 'inside the beltway' equivalents in Washington are paid ten or twenty times the salaries pulled down by their British counterparts. But then, the stakes are ten or twenty times higher. In 2000, General Electric's lobbying bill came to $16m. Defence giant Lockheed Martin spent $14.4m, cigarette manufacturer Philip Morris $11.2m and telecoms group Verizon $10.5m. With the increasing Americanisation of British politics, under a Government whose admiration for the US knows few bounds, this may be a window to our own future.[59]

Prospects for the public affairs industry look strong enough, with big law firms and accountants now trying to get in on the act by offering clients lobbying services. However, with the growing control of Brussels over areas such as financial services, mergers and taxation, the action may now shift to the continent.

Concrete pay-backs from their services may not be as extensive as lobbyists like to make out. Given the overtly business-friendly nature of New Labour, many companies could have achieved their goals entirely through their own efforts. But that does not mean that the impact of lobbying on politics is irrelevant.

The interface between government and business seems to be dominated by a magic circle mentality. Lobbyists market themselves to companies on the implicit premise that they are somehow part of the loop, incorporating words like 'access' and 'good relations' in their company names. Thus they hint of their ability to secure input into decision-making – for a fee. Cross our palms with silver and the democratic process can be circumvented. The net effect is substantially to devalue the integrity of politics in the public eye, feeding the apathy that so reduced the turnout at the last general election. What's the point of voting when business gets to take all the decisions anyway? Welcome to the world of politics as a service industry.

NOTES

[1] *Sunday Times*, 15 April 2001
[2] *New Statesman & Society*, 23 June 1995
[3] *Independent*, 24 March 1998
[4] *PR Week*, 27 September 1996; *Observer*, 18 March 2001; *Guardian*, 6 June 2001
[5] *Private Eye*, 18 May 2001
[6] *PR Week*, 14 November 1996
[7] Ibid.
[8] Association of Professional Political Consultants register for the second half of 2001
[9] *Financial Times*, 6 July 2000
[10] *Daily Telegraph*, 11 November 1997
[11] *Guardian*, 20 October 2001; *Daily Telegraph*, 5 March 2002
[12] *Daily Telegraph*, 4 February 2002
[13] Department of Transport, Local Government and Regions press officer, comments to author
[14] *Daily Mirror*, 14 February 2002; *Daily Mirror*, 15 February 2002
[15] *Observer*, 23 May 1999
[16] *Daily Mail*, 13 February 1999
[17] *Guardian*, 2 November 1998
[18] Association of Professional Political Consultants register
[19] *Observer*, 4 May 1997
[20] *Guardian*, 20 April 1998
[21] *Financial Times*, 26 April 2001
[22] *PR Week*, 16 May 1997
[23] *Financial Times*, 11 August 2000
[24] *Times*, cited in *Private Eye*, 30 May 1997
[25] *PR Week*, cited in *Tribune*, 7 June 1996
[26] *Private Eye*, 23 March 2001; *Private Eye*, 8 March 2002
[27] *Observer*, 18 March 2001
[28] *Times*, 13 September 1998
[29] *Observer*, 18 October 1998
[30] *Observer*, 18 March 2001
[31] *Guardian*, 19 April 2001
[32] *Private Eye*, 18 May 2001
[33] *Independent*, 24 March 1998
[34] *Daily Telegraph*, 17 September 1999
[35] *Socialist Review*, July/August 2001
[36] *Red Pepper*, April 2002
[37] *Observer*, 5 July 1998
[38] *Guardian*, 7 July 1998
[39] *Observer*, 5 July 1998
[40] Ibid.
[41] *Jewish Chronicle*, 10 July 1998

[42] *Observer*, 5 July 1998

[43] *Daily Telegraph*, 6 December 1997

[44] Quoted Tom Easton's article, 'Liddle and Lobbygate: Reflections on a Downing Street Drama' in *Lobster* 36, Winter 1998/99. Read this for chapter and verse on the SDP connection.

[45] *Daily Telegraph*, 6 December 1997

[46] *Observer*, 5 July 1998

[47] *Sun*, 8 July 1998

[48] *Sunday Times*, 16 August 1998

[49] *Sunday Times*, 8 October 1999

[50] *Mirror*, 8 July 1998

[51] *Mirror*, 29 September 1998

[52] Greg Palast, interview with author

[53] Ibid.; Will Hutton, interview with author

[54] *Observer*, 26 September 1999

[55] Ibid.

[56] Ibid.

[57] *Scottish Socialist Voice*, 17 August 2001

[58] *Private Eye*, 14 December 2001

[59] *Financial Times*, 14 March 2002

8. PFI OR BUST

FOLLOWING the collapse of Railtrack, the premise that private enterprise is an inherently superior method of delivering public services surely stands shredded more comprehensively than the last set of Enron accounts. Yet under New Labour, even incarceration and the armed forces – regarded even in right-wing political theory as core governmental functions – are increasingly being outsourced to the private sector. Through the continual extension of privatisation, the Government has taken the Thatcherite programme of 'rolling back the frontiers of the state' into a second phase, with deleterious consequences for public service users and employees.

New Labour's favoured method of achieving this aim is through Public–Private Partnerships, the catch-all term for any arrangement bringing together the private and public sectors in a common project. PPPs can take on a number of forms, including concessions, franchises and joint ventures. The Private Finance Initiative is just one version, albeit by far the most common. But however such deals are structured, they share one basic flaw.

Private companies prioritise the interests of shareholders over and above every other factor. Indeed, as company law stands at the moment, they are legally bound to do so. And the interests of shareholders are narrowly defined as maximising profits. If maximising profits entails minimising service standards, health and safety, cleanliness, employment conditions or anything else, so be it.

Quaint notions that hospitals should be administered in the interests of patients, that schools should be run for the good of their pupils, or that the primary function of public transport is getting passengers as cheaply as possible from A to B are increasingly rejected by New Labour.

In most areas of public services, no alternatives to PPP and PFI are even being considered. Let's take hospitals as an example. As Health minister Alan Milburn proclaimed in July 1997, while still new to the job: 'When there is a limited amount of public sector capital available, as there is, it's PFI or bust.'

As of December 2001, some 68 NHS hospitals had been built privately since New Labour took office. Out go the crumbling relics of Victorian philanthropy, in come shiny happy superhospitals . . . or so the

119

Government would have us believe. Here comes the supposedly clever bit. Capital spending hasn't come from the state, but from the private sector. Once built, the hospitals are leased back for NHS use, typically for 30 years. But at the end of that period, they remain the property of the owner, to do with as they please. It's like paying off your mortgage and then giving your house back to the building society.

It is blindingly obvious why private construction companies are up for such deals. Research compiled by the London Health Emergency pressure group estimated returns for PFI hospital contractors of up to 25 per cent. The study found that the first six completed schemes had a capital cost of £423m, yet involved payments of £2.4bn over the life of the contracts. Fourteen further projects under construction involved total payments of a further £7.5bn. This is money that could and should be ploughed back into provision of health services.

The only logic in doing things this way is that the payments do not count against public sector borrowing requirement. PFI is an Enron-style off balance sheet financing vehicle *par excellence*. That was particularly an important consideration during New Labour's first two years in office, as it pledged to stick to inherited Tory spending plans. Yet the public sector borrowing requirement is simply a question of definition. Other countries solve the problem by changing the definition to exclude capital expenditure.

Another justification sometimes advanced for PFI is that it results in extra investment. The figures used to substantiate such claims are again based on manipulation of the particular accounting methods used in the public sector. The notional cost of providing investment through the public sector is what is known as the 'public sector comparator'.

A high notional value is assigned to the 'transfer of risk' supposedly borne by the private sector in undertaking the project. But many contracts are practically risk-free. It would be politically impossible for an NHS trust to be allowed to go under. PFI hospitals are guaranteed three-decade cash cows. On top of that, calculations frequently do not take into account the millions spent on legal fees and consultancy bills to bring the projects to fruition.

The roots of PFI lie in the early 1990s, when the Tories forced local authorities to subject council services to compulsory competitive tendering. Chancellor Norman Lamont developed PFI as a design/build/finance/ operate model. The private sector was being given the opportunity to deliver public services for private profit.

Early PFI projects included the Manchester Metro and a number of road and prison schemes. But in its early incarnation, PFI hardly set the world on fire. In the event, the Tories signed fifty PFI contracts in five years. Labour routinely denounced PFI in strong terms until a few months before the

1997 election. But, once in power, the party found itself keen to expand infrastructure without shelling out from the public purse. The Blair administrations have seen the good times roll for PFI.

Within months of taking office, Labour decided to set up a new body to oversee the operations of the Private Finance Initiative. The PFI taskforce, under the auspices of Geoffrey Robinson at the Treasury, was charged with deciding which schemes should go ahead. Most of its members came from the private sector. Many had business links with PFI players. Chief executive Adrian Montague, for instance, was recruited for the expertise he garnered on the Channel Tunnel and British Rail privatisations while working at Dresdner Kleinwort Benson merchant bank.

Taking the logic inherent in the scheme to its conclusion, the PFI taskforce was itself privatised in June 2000, as a merchant bank with a 49 per cent government shareholding under the name of Partnerships UK. P:UK now advises public authorities purchasing PFI deals, in some cases even investing in them itself.

The 51 per cent private sector stake in the company includes Jarvis, Serco, Barclays and Bank of Scotland. The potential conflicts of interest inherent in joint ventures between governments and private companies engaged in commercial projects should be obvious.

By December 2001, more than 450 PFI deals had been signed, with a lifetime value of £100bn, equivalent to a quarter of current total public spending. Over 300 more were in procurement. Moreover, PFI is now becoming an export product. Countries such as Finland, Canada and South Africa are turning towards the model pioneered in the UK. Often this gives British companies with PFI experience a head start in overseas markets, with foreign competition virtually absent.

Within the UK, PFI is for many companies the business opportunity of a lifetime. Many staid established concerns are restructuring themselves from top to bottom to become thoroughbred creatures of PFI. Businessman Paris Moayedi, for instance, was moved to comment: 'When I saw the Labour Party manifesto, I said "if you wanted to fashion a company to benefit from its programme of investment in infrastructure, that company would be Jarvis".'[1] Moayedi's job? Chief executive of Jarvis, the company responsible for rail maintenance at Potters Bar.

For its part, the Treasury is determined to sell the idea to a sceptical public, and a major drive to mould public opinion is planned, reportedly on the orders of Blair himself.[2] The need for this propaganda blitz stems from real fears that public confidence in the omniscience of private enterprise has taken a severe battering.

The private sector is well aware of the danger. John Gains, chief executive of Mowlem and president of the Construction Confederation, has argued that attacking the initiative has become 'a dangerous national sport' that could see PFI 'killed off'. Amey director Robert Osborne even went as far as to predict: 'I can imagine the forces against us prevailing.'[3]

With any luck, they just might. Trade unions – fearful that many workers could see their public sector terms and conditions, particularly occupational pension schemes, undermined by a transfer to private sector employers – are leading opposition to PFI. More than a century of loyalty to Labour is being called into question. The GMB is reducing its financial support for the party by £2m over the next few years, largely as a result of PFI, and may even begin to back non-Labour candidates in local elections standing on a pro-public services platform. Others unions are likely to follow suit.

There have already been repercussions at the ballot box. One of the few moments of real interest for those sitting up half the night to watch the results roll in at the last election was the victory of independent Richard Taylor in Wyre Forest, who ousted a sitting Labour MP after standing on a 'health concern' ticket. This small earthquake in the West Midlands constituency was almost entirely down to a PFI hospital.

The costs of building a PFI replacement for the Worcester Royal Infirmary rose by 118 per cent between 1996 and 2000. As a result, the local health authority was forced to inflict cuts at Kidderminster General, most notably in accident and emergency services. The population – a small but representative sample of Middle England – was horrified and willing to express its displeasure in the voting booth.

The critique of PFI hospitals focuses on inflated costs, poor quality, inflexibility, lack of accountability and the knock-on costs to other parts of the NHS, as well as the huge profits that are being made.

The Government's so-called 'design tsar' Sir Stuart Lipton has described many of the new hospitals as 'urban disasters'. He may well have had the likes of Cumberland Infirmary in Carlisle in mind. Blair gave his personal blessing to the privately built and managed hospital by performing the opening ceremony. Within weeks, ceilings had collapsed and operating theatres were flooded with sewage. The following year, surgery had to be cancelled after the electrical wiring caught fire.

Still more PFI hospitals have been heavily delayed. The new hospital for the Barts and London Trust, announced in 1998, will not be open until 2007 at the earliest. A new hospital for Swindon was announced in 1997, but the final contract had not been signed by early 2002. Yet over the next 30 years, the taxpayer will have to fork out £500m, when facilities could have been provided for the public sector at an estimated price of just £76m.[4] By contrast, some recently constructed NHS-funded hospitals have been completed on time and to budget. Indeed, a hospital in Bury recently came in below the expected cost.

Nowhere is the case against market delivery of public services clearer than in healthcare. Only through universal provision can the costs of more expensive treatments be pooled across society as a whole, for the benefit of the vast majority of us who could never afford them as individuals. Recent statements from Labour and Conservative politicians alike should worry those who want to see the NHS remain a comprehensive provider and free at the point of use.

But PFI hospitals are only one aspect of a generalised increase in private sector involvement in a health service that is rapidly becoming a gigantic adventure playground for business. NHS use of private beds trebled between October 2000 and February 2001, following a 'concordat' between private providers and Secretary of State for Health Alan Milburn. Some 60,000 NHS patients are likely to be treated by private companies in 2002, and a projected 100,000 in 2003.[5]

Private hospital operators have been quick to respond. A BUPA hospital in Redhill, Surrey, has contracted to provide surgery for 12,000 NHS patients a year. General Healthcare, another leading player, is looking for similar deals, and planning a £40m fast-track diagnostic and treatment centre at its own risk, hoping that the NHS will contract for diagnostic services and waiting list surgery such as hip and cataract operations. It is unlikely to find this expectation disappointed.

Discussions have taken place with Swedish hospital group Capio over the use of Swedish doctors at such facilities. Meanwhile, former minister Frank Field is pushing the charms of a company called German Medicine Net, which is offering to set up prefab units across Britain offering surgery to 500,000 waiting list patients. They would be served by hundreds of German freelance doctors, moonlighting for one week a month. The plan would cost the NHS £725m or so.[6]

Such developments bring with them a ratchet effect. For instance, NHS accounting practices are being forced into line with the private sector's, a move that will considerably facilitate further private sector involvement. Meanwhile, there are plans to bring both NHS and private healthcare providers under a common inspectorate. A spokesperson for the private healthcare trade association was quick to point out what that could one day mean: 'The NHS could eventually become only the funder and regulator of healthcare, not the provider.'[7]

The thrust of government thinking couldn't be clearer. The Department of Health has created a special unit to push through more partnerships between the NHS and the private sector. Private management will run NHS hospitals deemed to be failing, while successful ones will be allowed to become 'foundation hospitals', with rights to buy and sell assets, keep the proceeds of land sales, and adjust pay scales. Four 'failing' NHS trusts – Ashford and St Peter's Hospitals, Dartsford and Gravesham, Portsmouth

Hospitals and Barnet and Chase Farm – have already seen their management contracts put out to franchise.

Meanwhile, private health industry representatives have been appointed to the NHS Modernisation Board, including General Healthcare chief executive Charles Auld. Milburn even presents such increased business input in quasi-sexual terms: 'This is not a one-night stand, it's a long-term relationship, and the private sector has got to be involved in the planning.'[8]

For a glimpse of what Milburn's long-term relationship might involve, it is worth looking at the many hospital services, such as cleaning and catering, that are already handled by contractors. Hard information on contractor standards is difficult to come by. A parliamentary question in 2000 revealed that in the three preceding years, private companies providing support services to the NHS had been fined more than £2m for failing to meet performance standards. Ten companies had contracts terminated. But the Government refused to give full details, citing commercial confidentiality.[9]

Such details as are made public hardly inspire confidence. For instance, the Commission for Health Improvement produced a particularly damning report on hygiene standards at the Epsom and St Helier NHS Trust in Surrey, which covers one of the most affluent areas of Britain. Cleaning services are provided by French multinational Sodexho. The wards were filthy and 'a strong smell of urine' was in evidence.

Some New Labour figures are even doing nicely, thank you, out of private sector input into the NHS. Lord Sawyer was once plain Tom Sawyer, a union official central to the organisation of the 1979 'winter of discontent' public sector dispute. He must be one of the few members of the Lords with a working knowledge of anarchist theory. During his time as general secretary of the Labour Party, he once took me to lunch, where small talk turned to the ideas of Peter Kropotkin. Sawyer still patronises second-hand bookshops in search of collector's item literature on labour movement history.

These days, however, his various interests include a £35,000 a year part-time job as non-executive director of Reed Health Group, a private agency providing hard-pressed NHS trusts with nursing and other healthcare professionals, at commission rates of up to 20 per cent. The company – run by Alec Reed, a major Labour Party donor – makes profits of over £5m a year. Sawyer defends himself with arguments that fall a long way short of Kropotkin's ideals of mutual aid: 'Here we have a situation where there is a growing labour market shortage, where it is very difficult to get nurses and some health authorities ask private companies to do it . . . This is what business does, it provides help in difficult market situations.'[10]

Presumably the Sawyer of old would have recognised that the appalling levels of pay endured by nurses – some of whom still earn less than £10,000 a year – might have something to do with the recruitment picture.

Schools have not been exempt from the drive to harness market forces. In opposition, Blair defined Labour's priorities as 'education, education, education'. In office, education policies have boiled down to privatisation, privatisation, privatisation.

Resource-starved schools have increasingly come to depend on free exercise books emblazoned with advertising logos extolling tooth-rotting soft drinks and sundry teenybopper bands, while computers come courtesy of vouchers from Tesco, and books thanks to Murdoch's News International, a publisher of barely literate tabloids. Marks & Spencer, Littlewoods, Burtons Biscuits and Black & Decker are among 30 brands that have banded together to launch the Schools Plus initiative, under which schools will sell booklets of discount vouchers to the parents of their pupils for £10. The schools get to keep £7, less VAT. If a successful pilot scheme in the south-east is anything to go by, Schools Plus expects to get through two million booklets a year.

These are marketing exercises, not giveaways. Consumer magazine *Which?* calculates that parents have to buy around £250,000 worth of shopping at Tesco to secure a £1,000 PC. Nike has established a soccer coaching scheme that will take in 500,000 kids. No prizes for guessing the official football boot manufacturer here. Meanwhile, high street banks are paying for CD-roms and games machines with information on personal finance, a subject now on the national curriculum.

Education is nowadays increasingly regarded as a market and even something of a growth sector. Capital Strategies – a corporate finance house specialising in education – believes education will be worth £5bn to the private sector by 2006. That figure could reach £25bn in the long term.

Private companies now work alongside head teachers and education authorities in setting attainment targets. Outsourcing extends to everything from teacher recruitment to payrolls, stationery, IT supplies and classroom maintenance. Pressure is placed on education authorities, particularly in inner cities, to outsource, even where this proves more expensive than keeping services in-house. The money lost, which can run to millions of pounds annually, is effectively denied to education.

Construction company Amey's schools PFI activities in Glasgow – singled out by Blair for praise in a speech shortly after the last election – have been especially controversial. Some 29 secondary schools under the company's control have lost the use of games halls, while eight swimming pools have shut. Some schools have even lost classrooms. Five were not ready to open at the start of the 2001 autumn term, and one had to close almost immediately. In September alone, the ceiling fell in on a class at Shawlands

Academy, with one child taken to hospital, while St Roch's primary was evacuated after builders set the roof on fire, and a power surge at Holyrood school led to the evacuation of 2,200 people, as computers burst into flames and light bulbs exploded.[11]

The Education Action Zone scheme was touted as an attempt to attract public sector cash and managerial dynamism towards disadvantaged schools. By any yardstick, it has proved a crashing flop, underlining the stupidity of relying on business altruism as a catalyst for regeneration.

The 73 EAZs are each based around a cluster of two or three secondary schools and their supporting primary schools. For up to five years from the launch of each local scheme, management is shared between local education authorities, businesses, parents and community representatives. The zones have the power to take over school governance, vary teachers' terms and conditions, and even disapply parts of the national curriculum.

On paper, some major business names are part of the scheme. Shell is involved in Lambeth, while Manchester Airport plc has signed up in Manchester Wythenshawe. BAE Systems participates in Hull, Plymouth and Teesside. Other companies nominally engaged include Tesco, ICI, Cadbury Schweppes, Kelloggs and McDonald's.

Each EAZ gets up to £750,000 from the Department for Education, in return for which it is theoretically required to raise £250,000 a year from the private or voluntary sectors. In this way, claimed Schools Standards minister Estelle Morris in 2000, additional funding to the tune of £43m could be secured. Sounds good. But the money hasn't materialised. And much of what is theoretically contributed by the private sector isn't actually cash, but rather 'donations in kind', sometimes of little real value.

Thus the mere agreement of local business worthies to join the Blackburn EAZ management committee was booked as an £80,000-a-year donation in kind. In Newham, construction firms Laing and Mowlem invited action zone kids to workplaces to tell them how great it is to work in construction, an industry facing recruitment problems. That was deemed to be worth £40,000. Pride of place probably goes to the Blue Planet aquarium in Ellesmere Port, which offered half-price admission for zone pupils. That counted as a £12,500 contribution to the EAZ.[12]

The Liberal Democrats analysed all 37 available EAZ accounts for 1999–2000, and found only five of them met sponsorship targets. The average amount of cash raised was just £47,000 a zone. Five zones failed to attract any support from business whatsoever, in either cash or kind. Ten others received some support in kind but no money.[13] Such has been the resounding lack of success that Morris's successor Stephen Timms confirmed that none of the zones will have their life extended beyond the initial five years. The lesson is so simple that even a dunce could grasp it. Business simply has no motivation to participate in education unless a profit is to be had.

126

In order to ensure that there *is* a profit to be had, Labour is in the process of legislating wholesale deregulation of state education. State schools will be split into three groups. Around 350 secondaries – 10 per cent of the total – will qualify for 'earned autonomy'. That will enable them to seek private sector partners for just about anything. Earned autonomy schools will even be able to set themselves up as companies and undertake a range of business activities, including outsourced education authority contracts.

In the case of somewhere between 30 and 70 schools judged consistent failures, the Department of Education will get reserve powers to compel local authorities to open them up to business takeover. The majority of schools that fall into neither camp will be able to apply for permission to opt out of restrictions for up to three years if they have a business proposal they want to try.

So much for existing schools. The Government plans open competition for new ones, which could see private education companies building, running and delivering state education. Chris Woodhead – the right-wing former chief inspector of schools – is seeking £70m backing to set up a chain of private schools. The Church Schools Co., which runs fee-paying private schools with a Christian ethos, will probably get the contract to run a school in Manchester's deprived Moss Side.

Local government is also now an important market for the private sector, with contracts on offer worth something like £5bn a year. Council-oriented contractors enjoy a ready-made circle of influential New Labour friends, in the shape of the New Local Government Network. Endorsed by the Prime Minister himself, this group is an ideologically Blairite caucus of around 1,750 Labour councillors and others, seeking to develop a 'modernisation agenda' for local government. In plain English, this largely entails advocating increased private sector input into public services. NLGN often works closely with the Confederation of British Industry in organising road shows, away days and other events.

NLGN has heavily pushed the mayor/cabinet/manager model of local governance as a replacement for traditional local democracy. Such arrangements facilitate direct dealings with business, without the tiresome need to win the vote of the majority of councillors.

In its own words, NLGN is 'a relatively small independent research and campaign organisation' with six full-time staff and a turnover of £650,000 a year, but one that 'continues to have an influence and an impact that is arguably well above and beyond this limited resource'.[14]

The network is chaired by Professor Gerry Stoker of the University of Manchester, also a member of the Institute for Public Policy Research Commission on Public–Private Partnerships. Founder Lord Filkin is a former head of the Association of District Councils, and the husband of sacked parliamentary watchdog Elizabeth Filkin. Other key figures include Professor Paul Corrigan, partner of former Local Government minister Hilary Armstrong. Corrigan lobbies on behalf of firms pitching for NHS contracts, while at the same time advising Secretary of State for Health Alan Milburn on PPPs.[15]

He is joined on the executive by figures such as Ben Lucas of cash for access lobby firm Lawson Lucas Mendelsohn, CBI official Amanda McIntyre and KPMG corporate affairs director Neil Sherlock. Just to illustrate that the traffic travels both ways, former NLGN executive director John Williams has recently been appointed market development director of PFI player Serco.[16]

The NLGN's 37 sponsors – openly thanked for providing 'intellectual and financial support' – include Andersen Consulting, Amec, Amey, BT, Capita, Carillion, the CBI, the Corporation of London, Deutsche Bank, Jarvis, KPMG, ICL, Nord Anglia, Onyx, Serco, Serviceteam, Sodexho, W.S. Atkins and Xerox. Many of these companies stand to benefit from the policies they pay the NLGN to push forward.

Let's look at one of the NLGN's supporters in particular. Founded in 1984, Capita has moved on from its local authority roots to become a FTSE 100 company. It holds 150 large contracts across the country, most of them IT related, in central government, health, education and the private sector. Several of them have proved less than successful.

Capita was sacked by Lambeth after bringing the south London borough's housing benefit service to near collapse, with tens of thousands of unprocessed claims leaving many families in danger of eviction. The decision cost the cash-strapped authority £1.5m. Yet the council felt unable to invoke its right to force the company to pick up the tab, as this might affect Capita's work on council tax, call centre and cashier services. In other words, Lambeth was essentially locked in to a single supplier, and may also have been deterred by the prospect of a lengthy legal battle on the issue.

Other authorities have also had problems with the company. One year into a 15-year contract with Blackburn Council, hailed at its launch by local MP Jack Straw, housing benefit claims were taking an average of 74 days to process, again leaving claimants at risk of eviction. Benefit Fraud Inspectorate checks on Capita operations in Westminster and Bromley found significant shortcomings, while a Metropolitan Police audit found that the company's handling of its payroll may have resulted in staff getting expenses and overtime to which they were not entitled. This from a company that provides intellectual support to Blairite councillors.

Shortcomings in Capita's IT security were a factor in the collapse of Individual Learning Accounts, the Government's nationwide £260m flagship training support programme. Individual Learning Accounts relied on personal identification numbers, giving holders access to money to pay for training needs. Yet somehow, Capita's online system was breached. Computer disks containing account holder names and PINs began to circulate on the black market, allowing unscrupulous education providers to get their hands on the cash. Estelle Morris, by now Secretary of State for Education, had no choice but to scrap the entire scheme. How much the sting – dubbed by wags 'the great training robbery' – cost the taxpayer remains unknown.[17]

The Government is still keen on Individual Learning Accounts, and wants them restored as soon as possible. Incredibly, Capita may even get the contract again, in order to avoid a long tendering process.

Elsewhere in education, Capita acts as management consultant to Education Leeds, the council-owned company that employs all the city's education staff. Capita stands to pick up both consultancy fees and a performance-related bonus, and may soon get the opportunity to offer further services.[18]

It also runs Connexions, the new name for what many of us will remember as the careers advisory service. School-leavers get swipe cards, on which they accumulate points when they turn up for careers advice. These can be exchanged for discounts on consumer goods via the Connexions website. Information on their choices is made available to such 'commercial partners' as McDonald's and *PlayStation* magazine for marketing purposes.[19]

Despite its decidedly mixed track record, Capita is the preferred bidder for both a £500m ten-year contract to collect television licence fees for the BBC, and a £230m five-year contract to run London's proposed congestion charging scheme.

Just to underline that there are no no-go areas for PPP, the concept has even been extended to the armed forces, which are increasingly finding their capability impaired as a result of obsolete weaponry. The highly sophisticated military equipment of today inevitably comes with a hefty price tag. As part of efforts to cut costs, the Ministry of Defence has proposed PFIs for leasing planes, sharing military satellites with commercial operations, hiring hospital ships, and greater use of civilian support staff.

As of December 2001, some 39 military PFI deals were said to have brought in £2bn in investment. A further 50 or so – valued at £12bn, about half the annual budget of the MoD – were under consideration. Companies involved include Serco, Amey and Electronics Data Systems.[20]

Privatisation of the Royal Navy's warship maintenance and support divisions in Faslane, Portsmouth and Devonport will save £200m a year as work shifts to the private sector. Some 1,000 job losses are expected to result. Beneficiaries include DML, the Brown & Root subsidiary that owns Devonport; Babcock International, owner of Rosyth dockyard, which will take over Faslane's work; and Fleet Support, a joint venture between BAE and Vosper Thornycroft, which operates parts of the Portsmouth naval base.[21]

Military contracts up for grabs in 2002 include the supply of tanker planes for air-to-air refuelling, apparently something of a Royal Air Force speciality. Aircraft would remain the property of the contractor, and be crewed by a mixture of RAF servicemen and company employees. Some of the latter would be deemed 'sponsored reserves' and subject to call-up.

When the RAF does not need the aircraft – basically modified civil airliners – they will be available for charter elsewhere. Two rival consortia have been formed, using Boeing and Airbus aircraft respectively as platforms. AirTanker, based around the offer of Airbus A330-200s, includes Brown & Root again, Rolls-Royce, Thales, Cobham and European Aeronautic Defence and Space Company, the 80 per cent owner of Airbus. Tanker & Transport Service Company – offering a Boeing 767 platform – includes BAE Systems, Serco and specialist financier Spectrum Capital.

Elsewhere in the armed forces, six roll-on roll-off ferries are being built to provide heavy equipment transport for tanks. A consortium of Andrew Weir, Bibby Line, Houlder Offshore Engineering and quoted company James Fisher is the preferred bidder.[22]

The biggest military PFI scheme of all is a £2bn contract for satellite services, which has gone to the Paradigm consortium, effectively led by EADS and BAE Systems. BAE was also involved in the rival consortium, in what must have been a no-lose bet. Bandwidth will be sold to other governments, with profits from third-party sales split between the contractors and the MoD. Paradigm now has its sights set on a similar contract with NATO.[23]

Prison privatisation began under the Tories in 1992, and Britain now glories in one of the largest 'commercial penal industries' in the world. Justice is now a market worth £2.5bn a year. But this rapid growth is not the result of private prisons proving an unquestioned success.

True, statistics indicate that private prisons are 8–15 per cent cheaper to run than their public counterparts. That is only to be expected, given they employ fewer staff, pay lower wages for longer hours, and offer less generous pensions and other benefits. But even so, several have had to be returned to Prison Service management after private companies have failed to hold contracts. Yet privatisation continues to be used as a stick with which to beat prison unions, with threats to bring in outsiders to run London's Brixton jail in the name of 'market testing'.

In opposition, Labour opposed prison privatisation resolutely. As Home Affairs spokesperson, Jack Straw declared it 'morally unacceptable for the private sector to undertake the incarceration of those whom the state has decided need to be imprisoned'. Straw had, he wrote in the Prison Officers'

Association journal, 'a fundamental objection to prisons run by the private sector . . . We cannot break contracts that already exist. But we should certainly make no new ones, and within the existing budget, shall take back into the public sector the privatised prisons as soon as contractually possible.'[24]

Within one month of becoming Home Secretary, Straw agreed to sign prison PFI contracts already in the pipeline. The following year, he began to sign new contracts. So much for his fundamental objections. Politicians break promises all the time, but rarely so brazenly and with such alacrity.

All new prisons are now to be built by the private sector, Prison Service director general Martin Narey announced in late 2001. Private jails have demonstrated 'enormous' strengths in design, finance and construction, and led the way in the more flexible use of staff.[25] Superb property development opportunities will be provided through the sale of 30 older prisons, frequently in prime city-centre locations. They will be replaced with eight superjails, each capable of holding 1,500 inmates. Private companies will provide maintenance, healthcare, workshops and shops.[26]

One PPP project patently falling apart at the seams is Britain's air traffic control system, the first attempt at privatising this crucial service seen anywhere in Europe. Within weeks of the sell-off, the company running it was in serious difficulties, underlining just how monumentally stupid it was to embark on this particular flight path in the first place.

Originally mooted by the Major government, even the Conservatives soon dropped the plan as unworkable. That didn't stop Andrew Smith, Labour's transport spokesperson, lambasting the Conservatives for this 'crazy idea'. Smith famously told the 1996 Labour conference: 'Our air is not for sale.' But within the space of a year, the crazy idea became somehow sensible, with the new Government pledging to give it consideration. A proposal to dispose of a majority holding in the air traffic system duly made it onto the statute books, despite considerable parliamentary opposition. Up to 43 Labour MPs rebelled against the bill, with key sections twice voted down by the Lords. It was all to no avail. Our air was for sale after all.

In March 2001, Prescott announced that a 46 per cent stake in air traffic control was being sold to the Airline Group consortium of seven airlines, namely British Airways, Virgin Atlantic, British Midland, EasyJet, Airtours, Britannia and Monarch. Unsuccessful bidders included BAE Systems and Serco. Employees were to get a 5 per cent holding, with the Government maintaining 49 per cent, a golden share, and the right to appoint three directors.

An information memorandum published during the privatisation process described the 'primary objective' of the sell-off as 'to provide the UK with the world's best air traffic services in terms of safety, efficiency and capacity to meet increasing demand'.[27] Some aviation commentators saw the real big idea as the creation of a private sector British company capable of taking over in other countries after expected future Europe-wide liberalisation of air traffic control.

The Airline Group – rebranded National Air Traffic Services – was due to take over air traffic control at the start of June 2001, but the deal was delayed while the two sides haggled over the price. Eventually they settled on £750m, and the handover took place in late July.

The buyers were confident that the service's debt-laden balance sheet could be serviced from the future revenue stream. In the year to March, it had made a steady if unspectacular pre-tax profit of £32.6m on a turnover of £595.5m. But just to make certain, one of the new owners' first actions was to axe 20 per cent of the 5,700 strong workforce, as part of a drive to cut overheads by £200m.

The results were quite predictable. Staff shortages recently saw a belt of airspace 200 miles either side of a line from Hull to Copenhagen closed for nine hours after one single controller rang in sick. A colleague commented: 'Management knew many hours in advance that there was going to be a problem, but they could not find anyone willing to volunteer for overtime to fill the gap. The morale here is absolutely dreadful.'[28]

A long-awaited new control centre at Swanwick in Hampshire finally went live in January 2002. In another example of just how amazingly efficient PPP can be, it was six years late and, at £623m, one-third over budget. Getting the facility up and running inevitably meant more disruption for Britain's overcrowded skies. UK airspace capacity was cut by 30 per cent from summer peak levels, with around 1,000 flights a day subjected to delays of an hour or more.

Even then, safety standards have been compromised. Controllers complain that characters appearing on computer screens are too small, causing users regularly to confuse the digits 0, 6, 8 and 9. These software glitches were identified as long ago as 1995. The Civil Aviation Authority later confirmed that the problems breached safety rules, yet did not issue an enforcement order on the matter, presumably for fear of generalised aviation breakdown.

Pilots also complain of being unable to hear radio instructions. One commented:

> London air traffic control now has the worst quality transmission of anywhere in Europe. We have all been putting up with it, but in busy sectors with loads of other aircraft on the same frequency it is verging on the unsafe. We have a brand new state-of-the-art centre that cost millions and the radio doesn't work properly. It's pathetic.'

Another pilot likened Swanwick to Dakar in Senegal, as 'the Third-World ATC system of Europe.[29]

In just one seven-week period at the start of 2002, there were four major interruptions to air traffic services, causing delays and disruption for hundreds of thousands of people. One day tragedy in the skies will inevitably result. And when it does, privatisation will be every bit as much to blame as it was for the Paddington rail crash.

A similar centre at Prestwick in Scotland, due to become operational in 2007, is already two years behind schedule, with no date even set for commencement of the work. Despite an anticipated one million more flights a year by 2011, NATS is seeking to cut costs by delaying the project further.

Yet the company is responsible for air traffic not only above Britain, but for all eastern Atlantic airspace, and handles over two million flights a year. If it is to maintain the capability to do so, a projected £1bn capital spend across ten years is required. The big question is, will NATS be able to come up with the cash?

The airline industry may take years to recover from the impact of Ms Moore's good day to bury bad news. The downturn in air travel after 11 September could even see one or more of the seven NATS consortium members go bust. The bankers that funded the acquisition – Barclays Capital, Abbey National, HBOS and Bank of America – have had difficulty syndicating their loan to other banks, and are concerned about the company's ability to support its debt, let alone fund investment. Such were NATS' cashflow problems that some staff were even paid late just before Christmas 2001.

The airlines have now whipped out the begging bowl, claiming that, despite haggling down the price, they overpaid and should be given some of the money back. One of their major bargaining chips is the Government's obligation under international law to keep air traffic control up and running. Secretary of State for Transport Stephen Byers was forced to authorise a £30m bail-out, backed by further commercial loans of another £30m, in February 2002, simply to ensure that NATS stayed operational for at least a further year.[30]

NATS is seeking a new partner prepared to invest at least £50m. Privatised airports operators BAA is the leading contender, although Serco – an unsuccessful bidder to buy NATS in the first place – is also in the race. Unions are threatening industrial action if Serco is allowed any involvement.

If air traffic privatisation represents 'Railtrack in the skies', the forthcoming sell-off of London's overcrowded, filthy and unbelievably expensive underground railway network is surely Railtrack in subterranea. The tube is a service on the brink of collapse, with one in twelve services simply cancelled. It is worse than unreliable. It is dangerous, and in need of an estimated £1.2bn backlog in repairs.

New Labour plans to rectify matters through a PPP involving private sector consortia – infrastructure companies, or in the jargon, 'infracos' – to renovate and run the ailing infrastructure for the next 30 years. Trains will still be operated and stations staffed by London Underground. London Underground will in turn be under the direction of Transport for London (TfL), a public sector operating company headed by the Greater London Authority's transport commissioner. Contracts for new rolling stock will go out for tender.

In this way, around £16bn of investment will be unlocked, we are told. Some 60 miles of track will be replaced or refurbished. More than 50 stations will be modernised. There will be new signalling on the Victoria and Northern lines, and CCTV in trains and stations. All this can be achieved at a cost £4.5bn less than leaving the tube in public hands for the next 15 years. Sounds like great news for harassed strap-hangers from Mill Hill East to Morden.

Yet somehow this is the Millwall FC of PPP. No one likes it, the Government doesn't care. Few even pretend to be convinced that the underlying assumptions stack up. Nine out of ten Londoners are against the idea. So, too, are *Financial Times* leader writers and rail union militants. A report from the Commons Transport Committee on the subject is one of the most damning critiques a parliamentary body with a Labour majority has ever penned against Labour policy. It is also a symbolic issue for London mayor Ken Livingstone, serving as his main political justification for running against Labour as an independent candidate.

While happy enough to see the private sector actually undertake infrastructure work, Livingstone and his transport chief Bob Kiley want to keep full control of both day-to-day maintenance and the schedule of works required. They also want to pay for the renovation through issuing bonds, a process that would be substantially cheaper than a PPP.

The big problem with New Labour's tube privatisation is that it mimics the privatisation of the rail industry, enshrining a divorce between infrastructure providers and operating companies that proved the root cause of subsequent problems with Britain's railways. Entrenched separation of track and rolling stock made unified decision-making in the best interests of the railways as a whole completely impossible and will soon achieve the same on the tube.

Under the tube PPP plan, performance 'outputs' for the infracos will be specified by the Government, in return for public subsidy to the tune of £1bn a year, with the contractors themselves deciding how to go about delivering them. If they fail to do so, penalty payments for lost customer hours will operate, although there is no public interest termination clause. TfL argues that contractors may sometimes find it cheaper to make such payments than undertake work. More resources will be needed to monitor maintenance, and arguments over performance are inevitable, TfL adds.

There are also real grounds for safety concerns. A 1997 report for the Government written by PriceWaterhouse Coopers – only publicised when leaked to the press four years later – admits that a unified system would be safer, and is the option preferred by the Health and Safety Executive. The HSE, incidentally, was subsequently given just one month to monitor the tube's PPP safety case.

The scheme certainly hasn't proved a quick fix, either. At the time of writing, the PPP was already 18 months behind schedule, with no firm date for commencement. New rolling stock for District, Circle, Metropolitan and Central Lines is not expected until 2015 at the earliest, while the Bakerloo Line may have to wait until 2019, and the Victoria line until 2030. Only four of the eleven lines will see increased service frequency before 2010, and overcrowding could worsen on most lines until 2010.[31]

Even the claimed financial advantages evaporate on closer examination. Initial calculations were rigged against the public sector alternative. Public sector costs were automatically assumed to over-run by 11 per cent, with a notional 15 per cent then added to compensate for 'passenger inconvenience'. And because the initial bids are for just seven and a half years of a 30-year contract, private infrastructure companies were given a strong incentive to tender an unrealistically low price.

The Department for Transport has admitted that whatever happens, at least £6bn of the £13bn needed to stop the tube falling to bits over the next 15 years will come from the public purse. During the first seven and a half years, the Government will invest 45 per cent of the money needed and the private sector 25 per cent, with the rest generated by passenger revenue. Fares – already astronomical by the standards of most European cities – may have to rise sharply to make the sums add up. The department declines to comment further, citing commercial confidentiality.

Despite all the talk of transferring risk to the private sector, the Government is even ready assume the risk of the infracos going bankrupt, and has agreed to underwrite 95 per cent of the money private companies borrow, further distorting financing costs in the private sector's favour. TfL's analysis of figures from PricewaterhouseCoopers argues that 'when the full weight of financing costs to the PPP are taken into account, total public funding would have to rise to £12.3bn, or 98 per cent of the funding for the 15-year period'.[32]

Lastly there is the political dimension. The City is mindful both of Livingstone's opposition and the mishandled winding up of Railtrack. 'The Tube PPP is a weird animal,' commented one source close to the negotiations. 'The amount of political interference that has gone on is an order of magnitude greater than any other PPP deal.'[33]

The Government has responded by promising that the infracos will be able to terminate their contracts if London Underground is deemed to act unreasonably, but will still be guaranteed their projected profits under the full 30-year contract, which could amount to as much as £500m.

Many of the major companies that will profit extensively from the developments outlined in this chapter are listed below.

WHO'S WHO IN PPP
CONSTRUCTION AND ENGINEERING:

Amec is involved in seven PFI schemes, including three roads, two hospitals and offices for the Department of Social Security in Newcastle. PFI still represents a relatively small part of its profits, as its projects are in their early stages and still carry debt. The company approached the Export Credit Guarantee Department to underwrite its £68m involvement in the Yusufeli dam project in Turkey, which would have displaced 15,000 ethnic minority Georgians. The application proved controversial, both because of the nature of the project and because Amec director Liz Airey also serves as head of the ECGD advisory committee. Amec has since pulled out of the dam scheme. But it is now likely to be built instead by French company Spie Batignolles, in which Amec holds a 46 per cent stake.

Amey participates in three PFI schemes and a further four PPPs. As well as Glasgow's schools, its other projects include Croydon's trams and maintenance of the A19 and M6 motorways. Amey is also a major contractor on mainline railways, and is part of one of the consortia due to run London Underground. Shares in the company rose 12 per cent in a single day in May 2002, when it announced that it expected to make a profit of up to 20 per cent from its involvement in the tube.

Balfour Beatty is involved in eleven PFI projects, and is preferred bidder for three more. In all cases it participates as part of consortia, and takes an equity stake in the project. These investments account for up to 33 per cent of operating profit. Margins, at up to 18 per cent, are massively more favourable than the 3–4 per cent clocked up by its traditional civil engineering businesses.

Like Amec, Balfour Beatty made headlines for its involvement in a similar but even more environmentally detrimental Turkish dam scheme. The Ilisu dam would have displaced 78,000 people and destroyed the ancient Kurdish town of Hasankeyf, a cultural centre for a minority the government ruthlessly represses. It would also have given Turkey the power to prevent water from the Tigris reaching Syria and Iraq. But the company has pulled out of the project, after a campaign led by satirist Mark Thomas and Friends of the Earth.

Carillion is the new name for what was the construction firm Tarmac. The company runs ten rail maintenance projects, is involved in five hospital schemes and six prisons, and has contracts with local authorities and GCHQ.

Interserve, formerly Tilbury Douglas, has equity stakes of 20–50 per cent in 14 PFI schemes in construction, facilities management or both. The work ranges from healthcare to prisons and government offices. PFI accounts for 50 per cent of operating profits at Interserve's facilities management division.

Jarvis acquired Northern Infrastructure Maintenance Company Ltd from British Rail in June 1996. It is now responsible for 60 per cent of mainline track renewals and the maintenance of 6,500km of track. Jarvis is involved in 28 PFI schemes, and another 10 partnerships to provide university accommodation. It also holds a third of all PFI projects related to the provision and operation of schools. These include a contract to build Colfox School in Bridport, Dorset. The capital cost is £15.2m, but the contract will be worth £22m to Jarvis. Indeed, the final contract price was only 2 per cent below the public sector comparator. Jarvis is also rebuilding 15 schools in Liverpool and refurbishing three others, and building the Army Foundation College in Harrogate for the MoD.

John Laing participates in 14 PFI projects – from roads and rail to hospitals, schools and military establishments – through various consortia, and puts together and sponsors new projects. Its Laing Investments division makes around 65 per cent of its profits from PPPs in Britain and abroad, even though they represent only 40 per cent of turnover.

Mowlem's main PFI deal so far is a contract to build and manage the South Tees Acute Hospital. But the one-time construction firm is sufficiently enthused by the NHS services market to have bought Britain's fourth-largest contract cleaner, Pall Mall. Mowlem's services arm – which trades as Acumen – has a £60m management contract for MoD property in the Thames Valley region, and a £140m contract to maintain and clean some 250 Inland Revenue properties.

Serco has clocked up 14 consecutive years of double-digit profit growth, winning over 120 outsourcing contracts in 2001. It is now responsible for everything from the Docklands Light Railway to the Commonwealth Games swimming pool in Manchester and Abu Dhabi airport, and evaluating contract opportunities worth as much as £15bn.

The company traces its roots back to 1929, when American movie giant RCA set up a UK subsidiary to provide services to British cinemas. Three decades later, RCA Services installed and commissioned the radar system at RAF Fylingdales, which despite the RAF nomenclature is essentially a US military base. The company became Serco following a management buy-out in 1987, with a stock exchange flotation the following year. Since then it has grown worldwide, particularly in the Asia Pacific and North American markets.

Serco is a 'strategic partner' of the National Crime Squad, offering consultancy on IT, communications and the ominously named 'crime-related technologies'.

W.S. Atkins has equity stakes in ten PFI projects, ranging from the armed forces to healthcare, education and transport. It was founded as a civil engineering group by Sir William Atkins in 1938, and first came to prominence with post-war projects such as Drax power station and the development of Selby coalfield. Now it is seeking to reinvent itself as a 'global integrated solutions provider' with a heavy PFI orientation.

The company now provides virtually all education services to the London borough of Southwark, and has a £148m PFI contract to build and manage schools in Cornwall through its New Schools joint venture. It has been named preferred bidder to build a new £900m PFI garrison town for the 5,500 army staff in Colchester.

LOCAL GOVERNMENT:

Capita's sorry track record in local government and other sectors is detailed above. Competitors include both Deloitte and Touche subsidiary **CSL** and **ITNet**. The latter – the latest incarnation of what was once the computer department of Cadbury Schweppes – was sacked by Hackney council for its failings in handling that authority's housing benefit.

Parkwood has 60 predominantly local government contracts across Britain, in areas such as grounds maintenance and sports and leisure facilities. **Serviceteam** broke new ground when it signed a deal to handle all direct services work for Lambeth, in what was then the first-ever local government PFI deal. Serviceteam specialises in refuse collection, street cleaning and grounds maintenance, with some 77 contracts, mainly in the south of England and the Midlands. Its main rival is **SITA**, a subsidiary of French multinational Suez Lyonnaise des Eaux, with a similar number of UK local government contracts.

CONTRACT CLEANING:

Sodexho's rivals include **Compass**, demerged from the Granada Group of New Labour convert Gerry Robinson. Compass has around 190 catering and cleaning contracts in the NHS and education, and offers both services as a package for PFI schemes. Danish owned **ISS** concentrates on NHS cleaning, catering and portering. Also active in local government, it is involved in eight PFI projects.

OCS has 82 NHS cleaning and property services contracts in England and Wales. Another player is **Rentokil Initial**, led by unreconstructed Thatcherite Sir Clive Thompson, with around 100 catering and cleaning contracts, mainly in the NHS but also in education and local government.

EDUCATION:

Serco acquired Quality Assurance Associates – a major provider of school inspection services and head teacher training – in December 2000, in a cash and shares deal valuing the company at £2.55m. Now known as **Serco QAA**, it undertakes around 250 school inspections a year, and manages the local education authorities in Bradford and Walsall. The local education authority in Tower Hamlets, one of Britain's poorest boroughs, is now, in the words of corporate financiers Capital Strategies, 'explor[ing] the benefits of being treated as an operational unit of Serco, subject to its business disciplines and management systems'.

Cambridge Education Associates holds a seven-year contract to run education services in Islington, where it has sometimes failed to meet specified targets. In 2001, it was fined half its annual management fee of £400,000 on account of under-performance, measured by results of GCSEs and tests for 11 year olds.

Tribal Group is a 50 per cent partner in **Ensign**, a joint venture with security firm Group 4 that seeks to win local education authority outsourcing contracts. Tribal is also active in the local authority, NHS and government agency outsourcing markets.

Founded in 1972 by former teacher Kevin McMeany, Cheshire-based **Nord Anglia** is a rapidly expanding group of over 50 companies, employing around 2,500 people. It operates over 20 private schools, both in Britain and abroad. In 1999, the Government forced Hackney to hand over some of its education services to Nord Anglia, the first time the Government has made use of such powers of intervention.

Nord Anglia's outsourcing division has contracts with well over a dozen local education authorities. It also works for the Department for Education and Science and the Office for Standards in Education.

PRISONS:

Four companies are in the private prisons sector, all making substantial profits. Market leader is **Group 4**, Europe's biggest security company, with operations stretching from Thailand to Canada. While British-based, it is registered in the Netherlands Antilles, a Caribbean tax haven. It was one of the first off the blocks in the justice market, taking over prisoner escort duties in the East Midlands in 1993, and hitting the headlines after an embarrassing string of prisoner escapes. More recently it was severely criticised by the social services inspectorate for the use of excessive force at the Medway young offenders' prison.

Group 4 runs Wolds prison in Humberside and the controversial detention centre for asylum seekers at Campsfield in Oxfordshire, although it was stripped of the contract for Buckley Hall prison in Lancashire in 1999. No reasons were officially given. Among its other contracts, it has provided the computer system that gives access to the Pentagon, and guards the Treasury in Whitehall.

Securicor Custodial Services, which runs Parc Prison in Bridgend and electronic tagging in Greater Manchester, is part of the Securicor Group.

United Kingdom Detention Services is a joint venture between Sodexho and the Corrections Corporation of America. CCA is the world's leading private prisons multinational, with facilities in the US, Puerto Rico and Australia as well as the UK.

Premier Custodial Group is a consortium of Serco and Florida-based Wackenhut Corporation, and runs five prisons and an asylum detention centre, as well as undertaking prisoner escort services and electronic tagging in London, the Midlands and Wales.

Wackenhut – long regarded by American union federation AFL-CIO as one of the country's most anti-union employers – has a long history of ties to the far right in the US. Its founder kept files on the political opinions of 2.5 million Americans, selling the information to employers. To this day, it continues to offer 'pre-employment screening services'. The company has lost prison contracts in Texas and Florida, amid allegations of sexual abuse of inmates and misuse of public money.

Among Premier's prisons is Doncaster – nicknamed 'Doncatraz' – which suffers from some of the highest assault and suicide rates in the country.

Group 4 bought Wackenhut for $573m in March 2002, and Serco was at the time of writing intending to exercise a contractual option to buy out the Wackenhut interest in Premier in the event of a change of control. Wackenhut was disputing Serco's interpretation of the contract.

LONDON UNDERGROUND:

Several of the main PFI players have formed consortia in order to win London Underground infraco contracts. With only two bidders for three contracts, it was a case of don't all rush at once. The **Tube Lines** consortium is preferred bidder for the Jubilee, Northern and Piccadilly Lines, and is made up of **Amey**, **Bechtel**, **Hyder** and **Jarvis**.

As a major contractor on mainline railways, Amey was responsible for signals and track in the Paddington area, including signal SN109, passed at danger by a Thames Train turbo in October 1999. Some 31 people died and hundreds were injured in a collision with another train. The signal had been passed at danger several times previously, with drivers complaining that it was difficult to sight.

US-based Bechtel became project manager for the Jubilee Line extension in late 1998. A strike of electricians and mechanical fitters over safety conditions followed immediately afterwards, with the project coming in both late and two-thirds over budget.

Hyder was formed in 1996 from the merger of Welsh Water and

electricity company SWALEC. It has since faced numerous prosecutions on pollution charges. In November 1999, Hyder was fined £50,000 after one of its electricians lost both arms following a 33,000 volt shock at a Swansea substation. The company had forgotten to put up warning signs on its cables.

Jarvis is another mainline railway contractor. In August 2000, its Jarvis Fastline subsidiary was fined a total of £500,000 for breaches of health and safety regulations following two freight train derailments.

Worse was to come in May 2002, when seven lives were lost in a rail accident in Potters Bar, on track that Jarvis was contracted to maintain. The company has claimed that sabotage might have been to blame, although investigators are focusing on a maintenance error or technical problem as the most likely cause.

The other consortium is known as **Metronet**, and is led by **Balfour Beatty**, with **W.S. Atkins** and Canada's **Bombardier** also participating. Metronet is set to take over the eight lines not going to Tube Lines.

Balfour Beatty deserves another mention here as the company responsible for inspecting the railway track at Hatfield at the time of a fatal accident that killed four in October 2000. Broken track was the cause of the disaster. The company has since lost the East Coast mainline maintenance contract. Nevertheless, it has hung on to three Railtrack contracts covering Kent, Wessex and the Anglia and Great Eastern regions.

NOTES

[1] *Daily Telegraph,* 13 June 2001

[2] *Financial Times,* 12 October 2001

[3] *Guardian,* 1 August 2001; *Financial Times,* 12 October 2001

[4] *Observer,* 10 June 2001

[5] *Observer,* 25 February 2001; *Guardian,* 7 January 2002

[6] *Financial Times,* 19 September 2001; *Financial Times,* 5 December 2001; *Guardian,* 4 March 2002

[7] *Financial Times,* 17 January 2002

[8] *Daily Telegraph,* 29 December 2001

[9] *Red Pepper,* August 2001

[10] *Daily Telegraph,* 26 November 2001

[11] *Private Eye,* 18 October 2001

[12] *New Statesman,* 26 November 2001

[13] *Guardian,* 27 November 2001

[14] New Local Government Network annual report 2000–01

[15] *Guardian,* 17 August 2001; *Daily Telegraph,* 26 November 2001

[16] *Private Eye,* 5 April 2002

[17] *Financial Times,* 16 January 2002

[18] www.capitalstrategies.co.uk/press/5theducreport.pdf, as of 10 December 2001

[19] *Guardian,* 8 January 2002

[20] BBC News Online, 3 December 2001

[21] *Financial Times,* 23 March 2002

[22] *Financial Times,* 3 December 2001

[23] *Financial Times,* 27 February 2002

[24] Michael Barratt Brown, *The Captive Party* (Socialist Renewal pamphlet, 2001); *Guardian,* 26 August 1998

[25] *Financial Times,* 2 October 2001

[26] *Guardian,* 27 February 2002

[27] *Financial Times,* 24 October 2001

[28] *Guardian,* 25 February 2002

[29] *Financial Times,* 26 January 2002; *Observer,* 1 January 2002; *Guardian,* 1 March 2002; *Daily Mirror,* 13 March 2002

[30] *Daily Mirror,* 20 February 2002; *Guardian,* 20 February 2002

[31] *Financial Times,* 20 August 2001; *Daily Telegraph,* 8 February 2002; *Guardian,* 15 March 2002

[32] *Guardian,* 28 December 2001

[33] *Financial Times,* 26 October 2001

9. MITTAL ENGLAND

EVERY year since coming to power the Government has given away a billion pounds in state support to industry.[1] Sometimes that statistic seems hard to credit. Britain's manufacturing base has never been in worse shape, and Labour's macroeconomic policies must bear much of the blame.

Thanks to the persistent overvaluation of sterling, businesses that actually produce things have been hung out to dry. But instead of developing a thought-out strategy to maintain manufacturing employment, subsidies have been selectively applied like elastoplasts to amputations.

Regional assistance money has backed investments by Nissan in Sunderland and Marconi in Coventry, while Airbus got £530m in repayable aid for its A380 superjumbo. The 1998 energy review saw the mining industry – mainly in the shape of a single company, RJB – pocket £100m. Then there was £28m of public money for a semi-conductor plant on Tyneside: constituency MP Stephen Byers, Secretary of State for Trade and Industry.

Perhaps the kindest adjective that can be applied to this approach is 'incoherent'. The consistent message seems to be, if you want to make steel, you are better off doing so in Romania than in South Wales.

This chapter looks at the fortunes of the motor industry, steel, pharmaceuticals and aerospace under New Labour, and examines how some of the businessmen that have given money to the party have fared. Given the Government's hit-and-miss approach, little sign of rhyme or reason emerges.

Labour has presided over the decimation of volume car manufacture, which now has little future in Britain. Nissan and Honda are surviving, if not exactly thriving. While British-born former Ford chairman Alex Trotman has picked up a peerage and written a couple of policy reviews, the company is no longer making cars in the UK. General Motors has considerably scaled down its Vauxhall operation, despite the willingness of chairman Nick Reilly to serve on quangos.

But it is the fortunes of Rover – once the nationalised British Leyland – that undoubtedly has had the most political impact. Byers' first brush with speculation that his job was on the line, something of a recurring theme for several years until his eventual departure from the Government, was marked by the Rover closure crisis.

Under the Conservatives, British Leyland returned to the private sector with a trade sale to British Aerospace. BAe in turn sold the company to BMW in 1994. But losses mounted steadily, to the point where the Germans first threatened it with closure in 1998.

Peter Mandelson, then Secretary of State for Trade and Industry, took a hard line and insisted there was no question of a government bail-out. As Mandelson's successor, Byers had something of a more measured view. After all, Rover was a crucial underpinning of Britain's traditional manufacturing heartland in the West Midlands. Its plant at Longbridge, Birmingham, employed 14,000 workers directly, and indirectly supported a further 50,000 jobs across the region.

Nevertheless, by 1999 it was losing £2m a day, half of that attributable to sterling's high exchange rate, inevitably a serious problem for a plant that produced half its output for export. With BMW now threatening to switch production to Hungary, Byers declared his readiness to come up with state aid after all. He put together a package worth £152m for Longbridge, provided that BMW in return would commit to investing billions of pounds in the development of new models. Sceptics in Brussels countered that BMW was bluffing, and that Hungary was not a real option. In December, the EU announced that it would investigate the rescue plan under competition law.

Faced with this delay, BMW decided to sell up to venture capitalists Alchemy Partners. When the story broke early the following year in German newspaper *Suddeutsche Zeitung*, Byers was forced to confess to a cabinet meeting that despite the DTI's ongoing negotiations with BMW, he had not been given advance notification of the disposal. Blair was furious that BMW had strung the Government a line, encouraging it to fight Brussels over the aid question, while secretly arranging a sale behind its back. He made a personal phone call to BMW chairman Joachim Milberg to ensure that displeasure was felt.

But Milberg had a different story to tell *The Sunday Times,* insisting that he had previously rung Byers and made it clear to him that Longbridge faced the axe. This sparked further animosity with the DTI. A spokesperson as good as called Milberg a liar: 'The notes of the various contacts between the Secretary of State and Professor Milberg show that . . . BMW gave no indication that the sale of Longbridge and the break-up of Rover was being considered.'[2]

Alchemy's plans for Rover did little to reassure anybody that it was taking a long-term view. It stated openly that heavy redundancies were inevitable, and that even if it succeeded in turning the company round, it would be looking for another buyer within four years. Trade union protests grew, culminating in a march through Birmingham that was probably Britain's largest labour movement demonstration in a decade. Byers – heckled by workers during a visit to Longbridge – was determined to save face, and publicly announced that he did not want to see Rover go to Alchemy.

In the event, the deal broke down of its own accord. BMW had been prepared to write off an estimated £2bn of debts, and effectively give Rover away. But the two sides were unable to reach agreement on residual liabilities of a relatively minor £300m. The day was saved by a consortium of West Midlands businessmen, headed by former Rover chief executive John Towers, which bought Rover for a tenner.

At times 2000 seemed like one long multiple pile-up of bad news for the car industry. Ford weighed in with the announcement that it was to close its plant in Dagenham and transfer Fiesta production to Cologne and Valencia, and the year ended with a particularly unwelcome Christmas present. General Motors subsidiary Vauxhall announced the closure of its Luton plant, with the loss of 2,000 jobs. The first the workforce heard of the news was on local radio. It came as a cruel blow. Installation of plant and equipment for the new Vectra model was already underway.

Now Byers looked foolish not because he did not know about the redundancies in advance, but because he did. Perhaps on account of the company's closeness to the Government, the DTI had been fully briefed.

Vauxhall is a high-value sponsor to the Labour Party, and chairman Nick Reilly had earlier in the year been awarded a CBE. Only months before the closure announcement, David Blunkett had given Reilly the job of chairman of the Adult Learning Inspectorate, a kind of Ofsted for further education, paying over £10,000 a year for just two days' work a month. Reilly also had a seat on the Commission for Integrated Transport and the Training Standards Council.

This time there was no rescue package. Luton was closed in 2002. The future of production at Vauxhall's other major UK plant, Ellesmere Port, was in the balance at the time of writing. General Motors has warned that it must hit demanding targets or go the same way as its southern counterpart. Dagenham has also shut down, marking the end of Ford's volume car production in Britain.

Rover somehow survives, producing 200,000 vehicles a year, making it something of a minnow by world standards. Luckily, a Communist nation has thrown what was once one of Britain's industrial flagships a lifeline. Rover recently signed a strategic alliance with China Brilliance Group, which will pool development and production, component sourcing and even sales revenue. The Chinese manufacturer will invest £211m in the project.

After cars it was the turn of steel to come under the hammer. Corus – the

Anglo-Dutch steelmaker that includes what was once state-owned British Steel – announced 6,000 redundancies in February 2001, blaming the move on both the strength of sterling and the overcapacity afflicting the European steel industry. In its heyday, the steel industry in Britain employed 300,000 workers. By the time the lay-offs were revealed, that figure had fallen to just 22,000. Yet even at that depleted tally, the company remained an important blue-collar employer in several industrial areas.

Hardest hit was Llanwern, the plant near Newport in South Wales, with 1,340 redundancies. The nearby facilities at Ebbw Vale were to close altogether, with the loss of 780 jobs, while there would also be redundancies at Shotton in North Wales and Redcar in Teesside.

Welsh First Minister Rhodri Morgan had visited Llanwern only months before and bent over backwards to help the company. The agenda included relief on business rates, a concession worth £8m. Meanwhile, the DTI was looking at ways of assisting Corus with research and development, while the Welsh Assembly offered to buy any surplus property. Yet the Government had no idea of the redundancies until the day the company was ready to go public with the news. Downing Street was once again furious, even hinting that jobs could have been saved if only the matter had been discussed first.

But Corus chairman Sir Brian Moffat was unmoved. In a clear reference to what had happened at Vauxhall just two months before, he argued: 'We were not prepared to go into details with the Government before first talking to our employees. Leaks from the Government have been all too prevalent in the past.'[3]

The Corus crisis provides the backdrop for the subsequent furore over Lakshmi Mittal, a man hailed by the *Wall Street Journal* as the 'Andrew Carnegie of a brave new world in the global steel industry', and praised by Credit Suisse First Boston for running 'arguably the best steel company on the planet', in the shape of his master company LNM Holdings. Its steel production arm Ispat International.[4]

Mittal is an Indian national born in a small village in western Rajasthan. His parents moved to Calcutta, and, after graduating from the prestigious St Xavier's College, Mittal began working in his father's small family-owned steel mill. Frustrated by India's bureaucracy, he left the country in 1976 to set up his first overseas venture in Indonesia.

Since then, his modus operandi has been to pick up loss-making state-owned steel plants on the cheap and turn them round. In 1989, he snapped up a mill in Trinidad and Tobago, then losing $1m a day. Within a year, Mittal had doubled output and restored profitability. He repeated the trick with Sicartsa in Mexico in 1992, bought for just $220m despite government investment of $2bn over the previous few years. Output soon increased fivefold. Kazakhstan's steel industry got the same treatment in 1995.

But remember that this businessman's name is Mittal, not Midas. Not everything he touched turned to gold. In 1996, Mittal bought Irish Steel for a token £1, and renamed it Irish Ispat. The deal involved a debt write-back and grant from the Irish government, worth the equivalent of £38.2m, in return for the promise to invest £30m and guarantee jobs. John Major lobbied against such state aid, arguing that it would undermine the British steel industry. In the event, the UK steel sector managed to do a perfectly good job of undermining itself.

By this stage, Mittal had been resident in Britain for about a year, buying a £6m house in Hampstead's Bishop's Avenue dubbed the Summer Palace. Britain's richest Asian soon developed friendly links with New Labour. Like the Hindujas – who feature extensively in the next chapter – Mittal is a noted party giver and has met Blair on social occasions. He is also on good terms with Keith Vaz, and Mittal's wife Usha has donated to Vaz's campaign funds. Mittal himself gave Labour sizeable donations before both of the last two elections. He handed over £125,000 in late May 2001, with press reports that Lord Levy was instrumental in securing the money.

Within four weeks of Mittal signing the cheque, Blair lent his support to LNM's £300m bid to take over a state-owned Romanian steel concern. The Romanian government had understandably been cautious about the deal. Irish Ispat – one of Europe's more expensive steel producers – was by now losing £750,000 a month. Even as the negotiations with the Romanians were taking place, Mittal's Irish operation closed, with £36m in debts and 400 job losses.[5]

In such circumstances, Blair's letter to his Romanian counterpart Adrian Nastase, dangling the considerable carrot of helping to ease Romania's path to EU membership, must have done a lot to put Nastase's mind at rest. 'I am delighted by the news that you are to sign the contract for the privatisation of your biggest steel plant, Sidex, with the LNM Group,' Blair reassured him. 'I am particularly pleased that it is a British company which is your partner. And it will, I hope, set Romania even more firmly on the road to membership of the European Union, an objective of which the British government remains a staunch supporter.'[6]

Much of the subsequent controversy turned around the adjective 'British'. Fewer than 100 of LNM's 125,000 employees worldwide – less than 0.1 per cent of its staff – are based in the UK. The holding company is registered in the Netherlands Antilles. Only LNM's corporate headquarters are in London, thanks to the capital's standing as a financial centre. Ispat International is based in Rotterdam and quoted on the New York and Amsterdam stock exchanges.

Otherwise, LNM's claims to Britishness hinge on a small steel wire manufacturing operation in Kent. If having a few dozen staff in this country makes a business British, then virtually any multinational from Coca-Cola to Sony is, by that definition, British.

Mittal himself does not have British nationality, and, as a beneficiary of the non-domicile tax loophole, does not pay tax in Britain, presumably saving millions of pounds as a result. However, as a Commonwealth citizen registered to vote, he is still permitted to make political donations.

Yet Blair's assertion of LNM's credentials may have swung the deal. Nastase had clearly been worried about the company's provenance, and is quoted as commenting: 'Some have considered our partner somewhat ineffable, dwelling somewhere in the isles and with a postal box office as its headquarters.'[7] But after the letter, LNM had Blair's personal endorsement. Two days later, Nastase confirmed the deal, which was eventually finalised in November. Mittal had beaten off a rival bid from Usinor, which had the backing of French prime minister Lionel Jospin and had been confident about its chances.

Sidex went cheaply for just $500m, the purchase subsidised by a $100m loan from the European Bank for Reconstruction and Development. The new owner promised to invest £350m over the next decade, and not to reduce the 27,500 workforce – other than through natural wastage – for the next five years. The employees will be paid around £100 a month.[8]

Meanwhile, Mittal has gone on to secure exclusive negotiating rights for a plant being privatised at Nova Hut, in the Czech Republic. The country's finance minister considers him 'a very promising strategic partner'.[9]

The *Sunday Telegraph* got hold of Blair's letter to Nastase in February 2002, with publication generating a storm of criticism. In particular, Plaid Cymru were unhappy that, where Major had opposed Mittal's overseas expansion, Blair was backing a competitor to Corus despite the massive job losses of just one year before.

Downing Street maintained that the Prime Minister had been unaware of Mittal's £125,000 donation when he wrote the letter, and had only intervened on the advice of Richard Ralph, Britain's ambassador to Bucharest. It later emerged that Ralph's partner, Jemma Marlor, worked for the Bucharest office of British lawyers Linklaters and Alliance, the firm that advised Sidex on the sell-off. Marlor had joined after the signing of the draft contract, but before the deal was finally closed.

Returning from one of his global statesman trips to Senegal, Blair himself insisted that he couldn't see what all the fuss was about: 'If people have got a complaint to make, let them make it. It's just Enron chapter number 55, I suspect.' What unwitting testimony to how routine these affairs have become.[10]

The Prime Minister clashed with Tory leader Iain Duncan Smith in the Commons, branding the affair 'garbagegate not Watergate'. But the Mittal letter continued to hog the headlines. The spotlight turned on Jonathan Powell, who during his diplomatic career had served alongside Ralph in

Washington, but was now heavily involved in party fundraising. Powell's other roles include advising Blair on which Foreign Office papers should be signed, which amended, and which rejected.

Early drafts of the letter, drawn up by Ralph, referred to Mittal as a 'friend' of Blair. The offending word had been deleted before the letter was signed. Could Powell, who would likely have known that Mittal was a Labour benefactor, have been the one who struck it out? At Prime Minister's Questions, Blair three times refused to answer Duncan Smith's direct questions on the extent of his chief of staff's involvement.

Soon there were further revelations that the Home Office had passed on to the Belgian authorities – with a supporting letter of its own – a request from Mittal's lawyers asking for information about a corruption inquiry over a £39m oil and gas pipeline deal in Kazakhstan. While Mittal was not personally involved in the matter, any insight could obviously have been of commercial benefit. The Belgians rejected the request, which did not conform to their legal procedures.[11]

It was also discovered that Clare Short's Department for International Development had since 1997 backed three loans to Mittal businesses, provided by the European Bank for Reconstruction and Development and the International Finance Corporation, an offshoot of the World Bank. Collectively they totalled £153.6m.[12]

To round off this spectacular New Labour own goal, the press also learned that Ispat's American operation Ispat Inland, which follows the Enron policy of donating to Republicans and Democrats alike, had spent $600,000 lobbying president Bush for tariffs on steel imports. These are likely to be imposed at a rate of up to 30 per cent, a move severely to the detriment of the tattered remnants of the British steel industry. Up to 5,000 jobs may go as a result. But one City banker observed that the tariffs could boost Mittal's bottom line by as much as $800m a year. Ispat Inland's profits would rocket from $20m to $300m, while Mittal operations in Trinidad, Romania and Indonesia would enjoy exemptions given to Third World nations.[13]

That could prove the difference between life and death. Mittal's empire is currently laden down with massive debts. Analysis of its accounts indicates that Ispat may have negative net assets, and experts foresee a 20–30 per cent chance of collapse in the coming period.[14]

It is left to aeroengine manufacturer Rolls-Royce to prove that blast-from-the-past-style state aid is still alive and well. But then here is a company that has been a beneficiary of bail-outs from governments of all stripes. When Rolls-Royce's aeroengines division faced collapse in 1971, the 'Selsdon Man' Tory administration of Ted Heath nationalised it inside 24 hours. New Labour wouldn't dream of being anywhere near as radical as that. But in February 2001, Byers announced a £250m soft loan to the very same business, long since back in private hands, to assist development of its Trent superjumbo engine series.

Byers justified the move as safeguarding around 7,000 jobs. It has achieved nothing of the sort. Before the year was out, Rolls-Royce announced 5,000 job losses, within weeks of the 11 September terrorist outrages that sparked an aviation downturn. Ironically, the loan received formal European Commission approval the following month, despite claims from US rival Pratt & Whitney that it constituted illegal state aid.

Byers argued instead that Rolls-Royce is to pay the government a percentage on each engine sale and each repair and maintenance contract, making full repayment by 2035. Taxpayers can expect a 'direct return from the sales of engines', he maintained.[15] This begs the question of why, if a commercial return was to be had on the outlay, the money was not available from a commercial source.

But what now looks most questionable about the deal is the initial justification that it would maintain employment. In fact, the money has effectively subsidised mass sackings. Rolls-Royce will save millions on what it would have cost to raise £250m on the money markets. The directors will continue to pay themselves the kind of inflated salaries to which they have become accustomed. Dividends will be enhanced. And thousands of ordinary employees will be signing on.

Pharmaceuticals is generally regarded as one of the few industrial sectors where Britain has maintained some sort of international standing. Companies like Glaxo SmithKline are among the world leaders.

One example of Labour's consistent support for industry came when the major drug companies seized the moral low ground by banding together to sue South Africa, in a bid to prevent the import of cheap anti-AIDS, malaria and tuberculosis drugs. The ensuing international uproar forced the drugs barons to back down. Yet Science minister Lord Sainsbury and Health minister Lord Hunt were among those who worked on a joint Government/pharmaceuticals industry report that saw Britain stand up to be counted in support of intellectual property rights, rather than affordable treatment for people dying in the Third World.[16]

Let's stay on a South African theme for a while. Isaac Kaye, chairman of pharmaceuticals manufacturer Norton Healthcare, has switched his political allegiance away from the parties that ruled that country under apartheid and towards New Labour. Presumably that must be considered progress of sorts.

An Irish citizen entitled to vote in the UK, Kaye first came to Britain from South Africa in 1985, becoming the major shareholder in a company called Harris Pharmaceuticals. Five years later Harris was sold to Ivax Corporation

– a Florida-based holding company with subsidiaries involved in the research, development, manufacture and marketing of both branded and generic pharmaceuticals worldwide – and renamed Norton.

Kaye did rather well out of all this. The £23m he got from the sale now resides in a Channel Islands trust fund. Moreover, Kaye got to stay on as Norton's chairman, and was also appointed deputy chief executive of Ivax. His stake in the parent company is thought to be worth a further £12m.

Norton is now the number one supplier of generic medicines in Britain. It is also one of six companies raided by police investigating an alleged £400m fraud on the NHS in April 2002. Claims of overcharging, and possibly even price-fixing collusion, are at the centre of the probe, although the investigations may of course give Norton and the other companies a clean bill of health.

Kaye was a high-value donor to New Labour in 1997, 1998 and 1999. In the latter year, his support reportedly totalled £100,000. He also backed Frank Dobson's ill-fated bid to be elected mayor of London in 2000 with a cheque for £10,000. Dobson is, of course, a former Secretary of State for Health who ordered NHS doctors to use generics wherever possible.

Generic medicines are essentially cheaper substitutes for expensive products developed by the big pharmaceutical multinationals. But Norton has in recent years consistently squeezed the highest possible profits out of the NHS, frequently hiking the price of its products to just below those of the copyright equivalents. In 1998, a pack of Norton thyroxine tablets – a treatment for goitre and thyroid cancer – cost the health service £6.84. The following year, the price rose to £44.89, negating much of the savings that would otherwise have been made. Such tactics saw Ivax's profits rise over 70 per cent in 2000, despite a 12 per cent decline in turnover.

Other of Norton's business activities in Britain have given cause for concern. In 1996, for instance, it was censured by the Association of the British Pharmaceutical Industry for offering rather enticing incentives, ranging from Marks & Spencer vouchers to mountain bikes, to high street chemists that ordered its products.

Meanwhile, Kaye has refused to recognise trade unions, arguing that they are 'not in line with company philosophy'.[17] In May 2000, a Kentucky judge ruled that Norton unlawfully violated the rights of its nurses at one of its US hospitals, by barring them from union activity in their own time. This was held to be in violation of the National Labor Relations Act.

Before he became a chequebook-wielding New Labourite, Kaye enjoyed friendly ties with politicians back in South Africa, where he spent much of his life. Between 1977 and 1982, he served on the board of South African Druggists, a major supplier to the country's healthcare market. Company documents from the period show that SA Druggists subsidiaries offered lavish gifts to hospital administrators and other medical figures. These included cars, payment of credit card and garage bills, swimming pools and trips to Europe and the Far East. The comparison with the tactics later adopted in the UK is obvious.[18]

SA Druggists executives were also seconded to assist the election efforts of the Afrikaaner-led National Party. Kaye is not likely personally to have supported the racist party. But South Africa's erstwhile National Party minister for health Dr Lapa Munnik – an apartheid stalwart who threatened to close Catholic schools if they dared to admit non-white pupils – claims that Kaye offered him the use of cars to transport supporters to the polls at a crucial 1979 by-election. Another National Party candidate remembers Kaye as a 'substantial' backer.[19]

These claims are contested by Kaye's lawyer, who insists that the only South African party his client supported financially was the liberal opposition Progressive Party. Even so, it was admitted that Kaye did back one National Party candidate on grounds of childhood friendship.

Evidence gathered by the police during the April raids is being considered by the Serious Fraud Office. There is no suggestion that Kaye was personally complicit in or even aware of any malpractices. But if it does emerge that Norton has a case to answer, this could certainly prove a political news story worth watching.

Another Labour financial backer from the pharmaceuticals industry is Dr Paul Drayson, chief executive of PowderJect. Drayson wrote out a personal cheque for £50,000 towards Labour's campaign costs in 2001 after his company had been awarded a £17m contract to supply tuberculosis inoculations to the NHS, at a cost four times higher than the previous supplier.

After the election, PowderJect began negotiations with the Government for a £32m contract to supply emergency stocks of smallpox vaccine. During these talks, Drayson handed over a second £50,000 gift. The subsequently concluded deal was initially kept quiet on national security grounds, but leaked out from industry sources unconnected with PowderJect, and unbeknown to them, boosting the company's share price as a result. Rivals were furious that the contract did not go out to open tender.[20]

PowderJect will not manufacture the vaccine itself, but instead purchase 20 million doses from Germany at a cost of around £10m. As a result, it stands to pick up a profit in excess of £20m.

In his role as chairman of the Bioindustry Association, a trade body, Drayson has also led a successful lobbying campaign for tax breaks for the sector, including his own business. Drayson asked the Government to allow tax relief on research and development spending, which totals hundreds of millions of pounds every year.

Treasury officials wanted to give relief only on spending above present levels. But following meetings between the Bioindustry Association and Treasury minister Andrew Smith, Chancellor Gordon Brown caved in to the industry's demands. As a result, PowderJect will see its corporation tax bill fall from £3m to £750,000. Overall the measure will cost taxpayers some £400m a year.

Incidentally, another member of the association is the venture capitalist Apax, which is chaired by Sir Ronald Cohen. Cohen has given the Labour Party at least £200,000.[21]

It seems that when offered cash injections from drugs companies, New Labour cannot follow its own advice and 'just say no'.

NOTES

[1] *Financial Times,* 13 June 2001; Department of Trade and Industry press release 13 June 2001

[2] *Sunday Times* interview with Milberg, quoted by BBC News website at hhtp://news.bbc.co.uk/hi/english/business/newsid_698000/698406.stm

[3] *Daily Telegraph,* 2 February 2001

[4] *Observer,* 29 March 1998

[5] *Guardian,* 14 February 2002

[6] *Observer,* 10 February 2002

[7] *Guardian,* 13 February 2002

[8] *Guardian,* 14 February 2002; *Daily Telegraph,* 20 February 2002

[9] *Daily Telegraph,* 19 February 2002

[10] *Daily Telegraph,* 11 February 2002

[11] *Daily Mail,* 7 March 2002

[12] *Daily Mail,* 8 March 2002

[13] *Observer,* 10 March 2002

[14] *Private Eye,* 8 March 2002; *Guardian,* 6 March 2002

[15] *Financial Times,* 14 February 2001

[16] *Guardian,* 31 March 2001

[17] *Private Eye,* 1 October 1999

[18] *Daily Express,* 28 September 2000

[19] Ibid.

[20] *Daily Telegraph,* 18 February 2002; *Guardian,* 13 April 2002; *Guardian,* 8 May 2002

[21] *Observer,* 28 April 2002

10. DOME WASN'T BUILT IN A DAY: MANDELSON AND FRIENDS

DISGRACED lobbyist Derek Draper – once one of Peter Mandelson's closest associates – believes that his former boss 'should stay away from rich glamorous people, because he seems to go gaga every time he meets one'. Rupert Murdoch made the same point somewhat more crudely, reportedly referring to Mandelson by the Rolling Stones song title 'Starfucker'.[1]

Both observations are supported by considerable empirical evidence. Rich businessmen have not once but twice caused Mandy to lose cabinet office. His position as Secretary of State for Trade and Industry became untenable thanks to a clandestine loan from Geoffrey Robinson, the MP who built a fortune through his large stake in ill-fated engineering concern TransTec. He was also forced to quit the Northern Ireland Office after suggestions that he had helped one of the billionaire Hinduja brothers obtain a passport in exchange for a £1m gift to the Millennium Dome.

Such has been the backlash from these two affairs that it is difficult to see how Blair could ever again raise Mandelson to cabinet status. But never say never. As Mandelson himself reminded the electors of Hartlepool on election night 2001, he is a fighter, not a quitter.

Mandelson – one-time Young Communist, trade union researcher and TV producer – first started accruing enemies through his 'black briefing' tactics while Labour's director of campaigns and communications between 1985 and 1990, all too often knifing colleagues in preference to knifing Tories. By the time he became an MP in 1992, he was actively disliked by many of his colleagues. Not least among his detractors was leader John Smith, who effectively put Mandelson's career on hold.

But Smith's death and his replacement by Blair transformed Mandelson's prospects overnight. Much of his recent spin-doctoring efforts had been devoted to talking up the Blairite cause, and he also played a key backroom role in the leadership campaign. Yet such was his unpopularity among his peers, the assistance could not even be acknowledged until Blair's victory speech. Mandelson was the supporter who dare not speak his name. Ever since that day, the Brown camp has never forgotten what they regarded as his act of treachery in backing the wrong moderniser.

Despite now having established himself as a leading figure in one of

Britain's major parties, Mandelson professed himself depressed that his abode – a flat in the fashionable inner London district of Clerkenwell – ill behoved a man of his status. As early as 1996, he sowed the seeds of his first downfall two years later, when Robinson responded to his plight with a £373,000 personal loan, enabling Mandelson to step up to a £475,000 house in Notting Hill. The two men considered the arrangement a private affair. It was not declared either on the register of members' interests or to the Britannia Building Society, who put up the rest of the money.

After Labour took power, Mandelson's preferment was a foregone conclusion. Initially this came in the form of a job as Minister Without Portfolio in the Cabinet Office, which gave him overall responsibility for the Millennium Dome, a celebration of Britain in the year 2000 initially dreamed up by the Tories. The appointment had some historical resonance, given that Mandelson's grandfather Herbert Morrison had been in charge of the Festival of Britain celebrations in 1951. Mandelson visited the Dome site to give staff a pep talk, asking them to ensure that it became a 'thrilling' and 'must-see' event 'which every child would beg their parents to take them to see'.[2] Part of the brief was to ensure sufficient sponsorship from business. In fulfilling this task, he set in train the events that led to his second departure from the Cabinet. Much in the manner of a Greek tragedy, hubris not once but twice led to disaster.

Promotion came the following year when Mandelson was appointed Secretary of State for Trade and Industry, arguably the key job in the New Labour/big business interface. This was a job in which he should have proved a natural born killer. Yet somehow he found it difficult to build a rapport with the business milieu. 'He lost interest in me when he discovered that I only have a couple of million in shares,' an unnamed senior businessman close to Blair told the *Financial Times*.[3]

Politically, Mandelson made little impact at the DTI. No major policy initiatives taken during his stint at the helm are indelibly associated with his name, although, to be fair, he didn't exactly have long to make his mark. The general tenor of his term in office was deregulatory. He also made plain his opposition to public ownership. Looking back on the Thatcher and Major years, he argued: 'Practically in every single instance, the Labour Party was wrong to oppose privatisation.'[4]

Mandelson continued to hold responsibility for the Dome, leading to him being dubbed the 'Dome secretary'. In this capacity, he began to court the Hindujas. Gopichand, Srichand, Prakash and Ashok Hinduja are among India's most colourful business people. Together they run the Hinduja Group, founded by their late father, which was originally based in Iran. Since the Iranian revolution of 1979, many of its businesses have been headquartered in London.

The Hindujas have certainly prospered since coming to Britain. Today

156

their worldwide empire spans media, petrochemicals, energy, transport and many other sectors, taking in everything from a Swiss bank to Bollywood movies. The group is probably worth somewhere between £1bn and 2bn.

Nevertheless, there is a dark side to their success. There have been persistent claims that much of the Hinduja fortune is based on the supply of arms to the Shah of Iran's tottering regime in the 1970s. These suggestions have always been strongly denied by the Hindujas themselves, who argue that such activities would be against their strict Hindu moral code.

Whatever that moral code might entail, much attention has also been paid to their role in a 1986 arms deal, in which Swedish company Bofors sold 400 Howitzer field guns to India. Massive kickbacks from the contract somehow ended up in the coffers of Rajiv Ghandhi's government. India's Central Bureau of Investigation has since 1990 alleged that the Hindujas' Swiss bank accounts served as the conduits. But investigations were for the best part of a decade hampered by a long-running legal battle waged by the brothers in the Swiss courts to prevent access to their bank records. The documents were only handed over in 1999, and the Central Bureau of Investigation filed a so-called 'charge-sheet' alleging criminal conspiracy and corruption against the Hindujas.

The Hindujas staunchly maintain they are victims of a politically motivated prosecution. In June 2002, a Delhi court rejected the charge sheet because of a procedural error by the bureau. But the Hindujas are not yet off the hook. The charge sheet is likely to be re-presented once the error is rectified.

As the scandal first surfaced, Gopichand Hinduja sought British citizenship. His application – lodged in 1990 – was refused by the Conservatives, who considered that he could not meet the requirement to demonstrate 'good character' while the accusations were still in place.

There is no doubt that Mandelson knew about all this. As has frequently been pointed out, Britain's intelligence services were briefing the Government about this matter. But it's not as if this stuff was privileged information. Any regular reader of the world news pages of a quality newspaper would have been aware of the accusations. Yet Labour chose to ignore the warnings. One reason may well have been the Hinduja's social standing, particularly among wealthy Asians in the UK.

Both the Indian elite and the British establishment can often be caught mingling at regular bashes at Hinduja Group headquarters on the 13th and 14th floors of an office block above the New Zealand embassy in London's Haymarket.

A columnist for *India Today* – one of that country's leading magazines – notes: 'There is a huge amount of clout behind a Hinduja's invitation. If you get one you go, because you know that you are going to see people who matter at one of their parties. And I think it's a great source of pride to them that they have that much influence.'[5]

These are truly A-list bashes. US President Bill Clinton and the Queen have both been seen in public with the Hindujas, while Tony and Cherie Blair attended their 1999 Diwali party, Ms Booth looking resplendent in her £1,000 salwar kameez. Many ministers – including at least one-third of the first-term Cabinet – have met at least one of the brothers. The Hindujas are not peripheral players. So it is worth listing some of their top-level New Labour contacts.

Mandelson's successor Stephen Byers first met the brothers at the DTI in April 1999, and then again at a New Zealand House reception in September the same year. There were telephone conversations and a third meeting in November. In 2000, there were further meetings at the department and in Cambridge, with discussions centred on a joint venture in India between the Hindujas and privatised Powergen.

Trade minister Richard Caborn also met the Hindujas while at the DTI. E-commerce minister Patricia Hewitt dropped in at their home in Bombay during an official visit to India. She later met Srichand at his London home for lunch.

Secretary of State for International Development Clare Short got together with Srichand in 2000 to discuss investment in a number of government activities, including an AIDS-related project and a pamphlet aimed at Hindus. As Secretary of State for Culture, Chris Smith met the Hindujas once at a party and once for lunch. Foreign Secretary Robin Cook also met the brothers, although the Foreign Office declined to give details.[6]

Not that the Hindujas are in any way partisan Labour supporters, you understand. They maintain close links with many senior Tories too, including Thatcher herself, and threw an especially lavish party to celebrate William Hague becoming Tory leader.

There was a £2,000 gift to Edward Heath's constituency association in 1994. Indeed, it was the former prime minister who had signed Gopichand's application for a British passport. Another Tory insider recalls the brothers at a Conservative fundraising event: 'A bottle of House of Commons whisky autographed by Thatcher was auctioned off. They paid £25,000. They are teetotal and they returned it.'[7]

Even the Liberal Democrats were courted, with at least one brother in attendance at their conference each year. It appears to be a case of covering all available bases.

Such was the Hinduja reputation for general helpfulness towards politicians that there was little surprise when, by the middle of 1998, it emerged that the Dome Secretary had successfully tapped them for financial support for the Dome's Faith Zone, a celebration of vaguely defined religiosity considered essential in marking the 2000th anniversary of the birth of Christ. As observant Hindus, the Hindujas had made a major donation towards the construction of the huge Hindu temple in Neasden, North London. Nevertheless, they were also ready to bail out Mandelson with a major contribution towards a Christian knees-up at a time when the entire Dome project was struggling. The subsequent controversy turns on whether strings were attached to the generosity.

At the same time as Mandelson was talking to the Hindujas about the extent of their backing, Srichand was seeking a British passport. That was not in the Secretary of State for Trade and Industry's power to grant, of course. Opinions differ on whether or not Mandelson telephoned Home Office minister Mike O'Brien in June 1998 regarding Srichand's chances. O'Brien insists that Mandelson did. Mandelson equally insists that he does not recollect doing so.

Four months after the call – at that stage entirely confidential – either did or did not take place, it was announced that the Hindujas were ready to underwrite the Faith Zone to the tune of £6m. They would not necessarily stump up that huge amount themselves, but would seek to raise the cash from others and make up any shortfall. In the event, this offer to raise £6m was dropped in favour of a straightforward handout of £1m. At that stage, the reasons for this change of plan were not revealed.

By December 1998 – just five months after Mandelson took office at the DTI – whispers were growing in the Brown camp that their enemy would soon be in deep trouble. A biography of Mandelson, written by Brown-friendly *Mirror* journalist Paul Routledge and due out in January, was set to tell all about the secret loan from Robinson, by now Paymaster General. If that wasn't bad enough, Routledge was intending to point out that the DTI was currently investigating Robinson's links to fraudster Robert Maxwell's company Hollis Industries. Given that Mandelson was the head of the DTI, the question arose of whether he might be compromised.

Just to compound the situation, *The Guardian* soon got hold of the information as well. Both newspapers splashed the story and Mandelson was forced to resign, admitting only to an error of judgement and not to actually doing anything wrong. He had, he insisted, only kept quiet at Robinson's request, and had also ensured that he was 'insulated' from his department's investigation into Hollis. Robinson was forced out of office as well. Collateral damage included Brown spin doctor Charlie Whelan, widely assumed to be Routledge's source.

The affair was subsequently investigated by parliamentary standards commissioner Elizabeth Filkin, who ruled that loans between friends did not necessarily have to be recorded in the register of members' interests. However, she added that Mandelson had breached the MPs' code of conduct by withholding the full facts from the Britannia Building Society. After all, not revealing everything to a financial institution from which one is seeking a loan is no small matter for the Secretary of State for Trade and Industry, a brief that includes financial services.

None of this should have been the end of the world, or even the end of Mandelson's career. He was able to sell the house, and, thanks to London's crazy house price inflation, made a profit of around £300,000.[8] He must also have known that such was Blair's political dependence on him, he could expect rapid rehabilitation.

In March 1999, Srichand Hinduja received a British passport with highly unusual alacrity. Normally, fast-tracking is only possible in exceptional circumstances, such as a parent without a passport urgently needing to visit a dying child overseas or a South African athlete required for the British Olympic squad. For the time being, there the passport issue seemed to rest.

By October, Mandelson was back in the Cabinet, just ten months after his forced resignation. Blair appointed him Secretary of State for Northern Ireland, where he played an important part in getting the power-sharing executive off the ground.

It was only in November 2000 – when *The Observer* ran a story explicitly linking the Hinduja's Dome donation with the success of Srichand's citizenship application – that Mandelson's difficulties began anew. The broadsheet suggested that the primary reason Srichand wanted British nationality was to give him an additional layer of protection against any fall-out from the Bofors accusations back in India.

The article aroused the interest of Liberal Democrat MP Norman Baker, who tabled a written question to the Home Office, asking if it had received representations on the Hindujas' behalf from either Mandelson or Europe minister Keith Vaz. Civil servants dug out the relevant files, and claimed that Mandelson had made such an approach.

In January 2001, the newspaper used the reply Baker received as the basis for a follow-up article. Baker was allowed to get in a soundbite that put the matter rather succinctly: 'We have a rich businessman in the middle of a corruption scandal who gets a British passport in record time after donating £1m to the Dome. It now appears that the minister responsible for the Dome helped to get him a passport.'[9]

But even that story might not have proved fatal, were it not for Mandelson's response when approached for comment the day before publication. Mandelson briefed his special advisor Patrick Diamond to say that he had not himself made a personal approach to O'Brien. The statement, issued in Mandelson's name, said: 'To the limited extent I was involved in this matter I was always very sensitive to the proprieties. The matter was dealt with by my private secretary. At no time did I support or endorse this application for citizenship.'[10] In parliamentary parlance, this may have been something of a terminological inexactitude.

New Labour took Mandelson at his word, loyally backing the cabinet minister. The day after the *Observer* claims, Blair's press secretary Alastair Campbell briefed the lobby that there had indeed been no direct contact between Mandelson and O'Brien. It was only when Downing Street asked O'Brien for his version of events, which O'Brien forthrightly gave, that the game was up. Mandelson admitted to Campbell that he might have spoken to O'Brien, but then have failed to recollect the call.

Campbell was furious at being made to look foolish. At Tuesday's lobby briefing, he told the assembled hacks that the call had in fact taken place. He also confirmed that Gopichand, whose second application for UK citizenship had been successful in 1997, had written to Mandelson about a possible passport application from Prakash.

A clearly flustered Mandelson did his best to explain his forgetfulness to an increasingly sceptical media. Labour's explanations seemed to be shifting all over the place. As one minister commented: 'The trouble is that Peter speaks for Tony. If he makes a call he's saying "Tony wants this passport".'[11]

By Wednesday's lobby briefing, Campbell as good as confessed that he had been misled, citing 'difficulties and contradictions' in Mandelson's version of events. By midday, Mandelson was forced to resign. To lose one Cabinet post may be regarded as a misfortune. To lose two looks like carelessness.

A statement from Srichand Hinduja tried to lower the temperature, to little avail: 'We are sad to see Mr Mandelson go. I wish to reiterate that I have never at any time linked our support for the Faith Zone with our request to Mr Mandelson for information in 1998.'[12]

Blair ordered an inquiry into the matter, headed by Sir Anthony Hammond QC, Knight Commander of the Order of the Bath, standing counsel to the General Synod of the Church of England, former Treasury solicitor and general purpose pillar of the establishment. In his findings, published in March, Hammond concluded that the disputed conversation had 'probably' taken place, but that Mandelson's original explanation of forgetting the call was 'honestly held'.

Mandelson hailed the outcome as vindication. Such a claim entirely misses the point. The real axis of this affair is not a bout of temporary amnesia on the part of a senior politician painted into a corner, but whether or not Mandelson facilitated a passport to a businessman facing arms kickback charges back home, in return for a £1m bung to a New Labour vanity project.

Hammond was most insistent that this was all one long string of coincidences: 'As a matter of timing, discussions with the Hindujas over sponsorship were being carried out over the same time as their efforts to obtain citizenship. But I have found no evidence that they have sought to link these discussions to their desire to obtain citizenship.'[13]

The Hindujas were furious at Hammond's verdict, feeling that the inquiry exonerated Mandelson while damaging their reputations. They pointed out that they had not even been asked to give evidence and even claimed to have posted a package of relevant documents to Hammond, which, according to Hammond, never arrived.

Former Hinduja aide Darin Jewell was in possession of draft agendas for two meetings between Mandelson and the Hindujas in August and October 1988, which indicate that both the passport application and the Dome donation were to be discussed in parallel. Yet Hammond felt happy to say: 'I have not considered it necessary to contact Mr Jewell. I accept Mr Mandelson's explanation.'[14]

Jewell has provided a statement to *The Observer* that a secret meeting between the brothers and Lord Levy took place on 29 October 1998, shortly after Srichand applied for a passport. Jewell, who was present, claims that Levy made it 'perfectly clear' that he was acting on the personal instructions of the Prime Minister.

Levy said he had been playing tennis with Blair, and that while 'Tony' appreciated the offer to find £6m for the Faith Zone, there was media concern that other religions were not equally involved. Instead, Blair would 'appreciate' a straight £1m donation, while Levy cast around for the same sum from the Christian, Muslim and Jewish communities. Srichand agreed to pay, resulting in a hug from Levy.[15]

Controversy was rekindled in February 2002, when Mandelson produced a previously lost civil service memo which he insisted cleared his name. The document appeared to confirm that Mandelson consulted officials when asked to make inquiries on Srichand Hinduja's behalf. Blair reopened Hammond's inquiry, but didn't get the result he may have been hoping for. Hammond ruled the new evidence insufficient to prove that the disputed phone call did not take place, although he once again cleared Mandelson of impropriety or lying. Lib Dem inquisitor Baker memorably dubbed the second set of conclusions 'a whitewash whitewashing a whitewash'.

Keith Vaz, Labour's chief conduit to the wealthy Asian business community, was inevitably also sucked into the Hinduja affair. There is is no doubt of the proximity of Britain's highest-ranking politician of Indian extraction to the brothers. It is no secret, for instance, that Vaz frequently signed letters they had drafted. Ties went back even to Labour's time in opposition. In 1995, for instance, the Hinduja Foundation – a charity controlled by the brothers – paid nearly £1,200 to Mapesbury Communications, a company run by Vaz's wife Maria Fernandez and Vaz's mother, in return for help in organising a reception at the Commons.

On joining the Foreign Office as Europe minister in October 1999, Vaz raised a few eyebrows by actively asking to be put in charge of visa applications, a task that had not hitherto been part of the job. A parliamentary question later revealed that Vaz intervened on 18 occasions to overrule decisions by the British High Commission in India not to allow Indian nationals to enter the UK. The Tories immediately claimed a potential conflict of interest, given that Fernandez is an immigration lawyer whose practice specialises in visa issues, although no impropriety has ever been established.[16]

The Hindujas were not the only prominent Asians linked to Vaz. Lakshmi Mittal's wife Usha has contributed to his campaign funds. Sairosh Zaiwalla, a leading City lawyer, also made two £450 donations, and was subsequently recommended by Vaz for an honour.

Other contacts included Iraqi-born billionaire Nadhmi Auchi. Auchi, whose interests range from banking and construction to shipping, is another of Britain's richest men, worth an estimated £1.7bn. Vaz was director of the British wing of Auchi's corporation General Mediterranean Holdings, only stepping down when he became a minister in 1999.[17]

Auchi enjoys impeccable political connections. A glitzy party in April 1999 to mark General Mediterranean's 20th anniversary saw Lord Sainsbury present the billionaire with a painting of the House of Commons, signed by Blair himself and over 100 other parliamentarians, including opposition figures.

Following a series of Tory complaints, Standards Commissioner Elizabeth Filkin spent 18 months investigating Vaz's affairs, publishing her findings in March 2001. The delay she blamed on Vaz's failure to provide 'full and accurate answers' to her questions. Plainly, Filkin had been hamstrung by her lack of powers to force MPs to respond to her inquiries. Of the original 18 complaints about Vaz's conduct, only one – pertaining to Zaiwalla – was upheld. Then again, only nine were actually dismissed. Eight complaints were not proceeded with, simply for lack of evidence. Vaz's refusal to cooperate severely undermined his ability to claim vindication.

Only a fortnight later, Filkin reopened the investigation, after *The Sunday Times* published details of the 1995 payments to Mapesbury Communications. This was all too much for Vaz, who collapsed during the filming of a television interview and went on extended sick leave. After securing re-election in June, he was replaced as Europe minister in the ensuing reshuffle.

Filkin's second inquiry ruled that the Mapesbury payment did not, as the rules stand, have to be disclosed. But, she added: 'It is clear to me there has been deliberate collusion over many months between Mr Vaz and his wife to conceal [the facts] and to prevent me from obtaining accurate information about his possible financial relationship with the Hinduja family.'[18]

The Committee on Standards and Privileges found Vaz to have

committed 'serious breaches' of the Commons code of conduct, and accused him of contempt of the Commons by wrongful interference with the investigation. His penalty was a one-month suspension from the House of Commons.

While neither Mandelson nor Vaz are ministers any longer, both remain MPs. Mandelson's bank balance may even be somewhat healthier than it was while he was in the Cabinet. The 2001 Register of Members' Interests reveals him as one of Parliament's top earners. He is now a director and shareholder of Clemmow Hornby Inge, the advertising agency that won the £4m account to handle Labour's last general election campaign. Details of his salary were not available. He also pockets tens of thousands of pounds on top of his parliamentary salary from giving speeches to international banks and City PR firms, and a further £15,000 a year from his column in glossy monthly GQ.[19]

Mandelson insists he does not want to return to government, but speculation continues that he is in line for such plum jobs as European commissioner or an ambassador to Washington or Paris.

Meanwhile, what of the Dome? After Mandelson's first downfall, responsibility passed to Lord Falconer. By this time, the project was well beyond salvation. That this shambolic scheme was destined to become a magisterial flop could easily have been predicted from day one. True to form, it proved a disaster from start to finish. It was, to paraphrase its own advertising slogan, one amazing mess.

Financial projections were based on the assumption that 12 million visitors would pass through its turnstiles in the single year for which it was to open, four times the attendance at Alton Towers. In the event, only 5.5 million did so. Yet no fallback plan had been developed to make up the revenue, other than to beg for lottery money. While estimates vary, the best guess is that the project cost just over £1bn, including tube access and decontamination of former industrial land on which it was built. Each punter effectively benefited from a £128 subsidy, four times the state handout for patrons of the Royal Opera House.

Even the disposal was spectacularly mishandled. There was a three-year struggle before a 200-acre site on a prestigious riverside location, close to central London and with excellent public transport links, could effectively be given away.

One of the ideological purposes behind the Dome was to exemplify the collaboration of business and the state. Labour was seeking to prove that the private sector could and would work together with government on a patriotic prestige project of a type that would in the past have been funded entirely from the public purse. The Dome was, in its own way, New Labourism in a nutshell.

This is clearly illustrated by the composition of the board of the Government-owned New Millennium Experience Company, legal owner of the building. Its chairman was Robert Ayling, chief executive of privatised airline British Airways. Other directors included Sam Chisholm of Murdoch's BSkyB, former Channel 4 boss Michael Grade and Sir Brian Jenkins, chairman of the Woolwich Building Society. Joining them was the Honourable Sara Morrison, former vice-chairman of the Conservatives. Planet Hollywood burger chain chief Robert Earl offered his 'business advice' on the project at around the same time as his £1m donation to New Labour.[20]

It only later emerged that these risk-taking entrepreneurs were acting in the knowledge that civil servants had secretly guaranteed to bail the company out if it could not cover its losses, something never reported to Parliament.

There were further accusations of cronyism when it was revealed that several high-value Labour donors had secured contracts with the New Millennium Experience Company. 1970s progressive rocker Peter Gabriel was given a four-figure sum to act as musical director of a concert on the first day of 2000. Oscar-winning actor Jeremy Irons was paid a five-figure sum for a voiceover for Dome television commercials. A catering deal worth millions went to the catering arm of Granada, chaired by Labour convert Gerry Robinson. The New Millennium Experience Company insisted it was 'pure coincidence' that the jobs had all gone to Labour backers.[21]

Such was its accent on business the Dome finally materialised as little more than an unimaginative trade fair, with hefty commercial sponsorship paying for the icing on the heavily state-subsidised cake. Boots paid £12m to sponsor the Body Zone, featuring stylised 200-foot figures of a man and a woman bereft of anything remotely resembling genitalia. GEC and British Aerospace supported the Mind Zone to the tune of £6m each, while junk food merchants McDonald's shelled out £12m on the McDonald's Our Town Story, in which towns and cities could stage events in a 500-seat performance area. Other sponsors included BT, Manpower, Marks & Spencer, Tesco, Sky, BAA, British Airways, the Corporation of London, Swatch and Camelot, and, as we have seen, the Hinduja brothers.

Such a roster of backers inevitably raises the question of whether there was a potential conflict of interest for Mandelson, as head of the Department of Trade and Industry, in combining responsibility both for Dome fundraising and for regulating the very companies he was looking to for support. Meanwhile, sponsorship proved to be tax deductible as promotional expenditure. Accordingly, of the £150m raised in this way, £50m was effectively refunded by the exchequer. This made rather a nonsense of Blair's claim that 'not a penny of taxpayers' money' would be spent on the Dome.[22]

The somewhat unattractive 'attraction' lost money from the minute it opened its doors. By February, it was forced to turn to the Millennium Commission for a £60m lottery money bail-out. In May, the Dome picked up a further £29m in state support. This time the cash was conditional on the dismissal of Ayling. The other directors came close to resigning en masse, in a gesture of solidarity that would probably have been illegal had it been contemplated by a trade union. Finally, there was yet another £47m of lottery money, which came in September.

Even halfway through millennium year, the government was looking for someone to buy the building and site, with Nomura International named as the preferred bidder in July 2000. The Japanese-owned bank wanted to turn it into an entertainment complex, and was offering £105m. But it pulled out within months, accusing Dome chiefs of withholding financial and other information it needed to mount a viable bid.

A new frontrunner emerged in the shape of the Legacy consortium, which nursed ambitious plans to transform the Dome into a high-technology business park to be known as 'Knowledge City'. Legacy was to get 63 acres of land, on the understanding that it would not demolish the Dome for 15 years. Any profits in the first ten years would be shared with the Government. And profitable the whole thing should indeed have been. Given the right mixture of luxury and low-cost housing around the technology park, the site could have been worth anything up to £500m.

Legacy was nominally headed by Robert Bourne, a multimillionaire property developer with a taste for navy-blue Armani suits, who had previously donated £100,000 to the Labour Party. That wasn't his first political donation. Under Thatcher, he had given at least £40,000 to the Tories. Nevertheless, Bourne's involvement immediately ran into accusations of cronyism.

Bourne was the son of a Jewish refugee who made his pile in the rag trade. After a private education, he trained as an accountant before working for Mark 'the shark' McCormack's IMG sports management group. He later moved into property development with his brother Graham.[23]

By 2000, his New Labour connections were well established. As well as his own six-figure gifts, there were those of his partner. Theatrical impresario Sally Greene's generosity to the party had been of a similar magnitude to Bourne's. And just to cement those all-important personal contacts, Bourne once held a birthday party for Mandelson at his house in Chelsea's Cheyne Walk, picking up the £5,000 tab.

But had the deal gone through, Bourne would not have been the one calling the shots. His initial stake in Legacy was just 5 per cent. Construction company Sir Robert McAlpine owned a further 10 per cent, and the Bank of Scotland 5 per cent. By far the largest investors were Irish developers John Ronan and Richard Barrett, who held the remaining 80 per cent through their company Treasury Holdings. Ronan and Barrett were the key players in the redevelopment of Dublin's docklands, winning a reputation for being somewhat litigious. At one point, they were involved in nearly 40 legal disputes. They have also given donations to Irish political parties, including a £10,000 to Labour leader Ruairi Quinn in 1997.[24]

Once the Dome had limped through millennium year, the time came to transform Legacy from a shelf company into a development corporation. Sir Robert McAlpine decided it wanted out. As a result, Bourne was forced to increase his initial 5 per cent holding to 15 per cent. But whatever the organisational difficulties, Legacy was touting around an impressive list of potential tenants for Knowledge City. Big names supposedly on board included computer giants Cisco, Sun Microsystems and Hewlett-Packard, as well as Imperial College and the Open University. The trouble is, such claims were, at least in part, marketing hype. While any or all of these clients may well have been interested, none had even gone so far as to sign a pre-letting agreement.

Legacy now needed to raise £150m to fund its ambitions, with the Bank of Scotland ready to commit one-third of the money. Finding such a sum should not have been a problem. Nevertheless, Whitehall became concerned about the viability of Legacy's plans, and talks collapsed in February 2001.

By July, the Government relaunched the Dutch auction. Finally a serious contender emerged in the shape of Meridian Delta, a six-member consortium initially including the BBC, which had plans to transform the Dome into a theme park. Four of the participants were subsequently to pull out, until Meridian consisted of just Lend Lease, the company behind the Bluewater shopping complex in Kent, and Quintain, which was primarily interested in the land.

At the start of December 2001, Meridian announced that the Anschutz Entertainment Group of the US was now involved in its bid, with plans to redevelop the Dome into a 20,000-seater sports and entertainment venue, roughly the European equivalent of Madison Square Garden in New York. The remaining land on the Greenwich peninsula was to be used for homes, shops and offices.

Anschutz is owned by Phil Anschutz, who made his money in oil before moving into railways, real estate and telecoms, so becoming one of the ten richest people in the US. The sports-mad billionaire owns the LA Lakers and LA Kings basketball and ice hockey sides, the London Knights ice hockey team and Swedish football club Hammarby. As an evangelical Christian, he has pronounced rightist political views, giving money to the Republican presidential candidate Bob Dole and also donating to anti-gay rights groups.

Anschutz had a number of business worries on his plate at the time of writing. His telecoms company Qwest – one of the mainstays of his fortune, supplying local telephone services in 14 US states – was reportedly $26bn in debt and with a junk credit rating.[25]

As the sole bidder, Meridian was able to strike an incredibly good deal for itself, in what is essentially a profit-share agreement. The consortium has been awarded a 999-year lease, for which it will pay not a penny upfront. The Exchequer will not receive any return until 2005 at the earliest. The final twist in the dismal saga of the Dome probably has yet to be written.

NOTES

[1] *Guardian*, 24 January 2001; *Observer*, 17 September 2000

[2] *Financial Times*, 21 June 1997

[3] *Financial Times*, 27 January 2001

[4] *Financial Times*, 16 December 1998

[5] Quoted on *Channel 4 News*, 24 January 2001

[6] *Financial Times*, 27 January 2001

[7] *Guardian*, 26 January 2001

[8] *Sun*, 29 January 1999

[9] *Observer*, 21 January 2001

[10] Ibid.

[11] *Guardian*, 24 January 2001

[12] *The Week*, 4 February 2001

[13] Quoted by columnist Nick Cohen in *The Observer*, 17 February 2002. Cohen lays out a devastating case to the contrary

[14] Ibid.

[15] *Observer*, 24 February 2002

[16] *Daily Mail*, 19 March 2001

[17] *Observer*, 27 March 2001

[18] *Guardian*, 24 December 2001

[19] *Guardian*, 19 December 2001

[20] *Observer*, 23 November 1997

[21] *Financial Times*, 13 January 1999

[22] *Financial Times*, 27 November 1998; *Financial Times*, 24 February 1998

[23] For an amusing biography-cum-hatchet job on Bourne, including all the gory details of his failed marriage to an American heiress, see *Mail on Sunday*, 4 February 2001

[24] *Daily Telegraph*, 12 October 2000

[25] *Financial Times*, 30 May 2002

11. MAXWELL'S SILVER

WHEN crooked publishing tycoon Robert Maxwell fell from his yacht in November 1991, explanations for his sudden death ranged from drunken mishap to suicide to Mossad take-out. Many newspapers the next day, not least his own, were filled with tributes to the great man.

Within weeks of his burial on the Mount of Olives came revelations that, towards the end of his life, Maxwell had plundered pension fund assets to the tune of perhaps £450m, in a last-ditch attempt to prop up the share prices of his companies.

By its very nature, this could not have been a solo effort. Yet no one has ever been seriously punished for these crimes. Goldman Sachs in 1993 paid a fine of £160,000 – small change by its standards – for breaches of UK securities rules while acting as Maxwell's broker. Maxwell's sons Kevin and Ian, and a financial adviser, were acquitted of fraud in a criminal trial in 1996. That was that.

It took an extraordinary ten years before the Department of Trade and Industry's report into the affair was finally published in 2001, just months before the general election. The document must have made uncomfortable reading for some of those in the upper echelons of the Labour Party.

After all, Maxwell had been a Labour MP for six years in the 1960s. Thereafter, his wealth, not to mention his role as proprietor of what was then the only Labour-supporting mass-circulation newspaper, had given him influence in Labour circles for decades.

Several erstwhile Maxwell protégés have been important players in New Labour. Three ministers in the first Blair administration – Lord Donoughue, Helen Liddell and Geoffrey Robinson – must have cast their minds back to their earlier careers. All are former Maxwell employees.

All these people insist on their complete ignorance of the criminal activity perpetrated by their erstwhile boss. But even while they were working for him, they can hardly have been unaware of his reputation. Maxwell had been demonstrably exposed as a liar, a cheat and a bully decades before.

Jan Ludwig Hoch was born in Czechoslovakia in 1923. He fled to Britain in 1940, signing up with the army, where he reached the rank of captain and won the Military Cross. Most of his family perished in the Holocaust.

Adopting the new name Robert Maxwell, after the war he worked as a military press officer in the British sector of occupied Berlin. He soon spotted the potential for English translations of German scientific journals, and founded Pergamon Press to this end in 1949. British intelligence saw obvious advantages in access to such material, and may even have arranged the necessary financial backing. Pergamon went on to build extensive ties across the Communist bloc, establishing itself as the leading English-language publisher of scientific work from Eastern Europe and the USSR.

Maxwell was elected as a Labour MP in 1964 and again in 1966, but continued to devote much of his time to his business interests. In 1969, he sold Pergamon to Leasco of the US for £25m. Once the buyer looked properly at the accounts, it soon realised that profits had been heavily overstated through questionable accounting practices. As a result, the Department of Trade and Industry suspended Pergamon's shares and launched an inquiry.

Maxwell, the DTI ruled, had 'made exaggerated claims of sales and orders with a deliberate intention to mislead shareholders'. In consequence, he was 'not a person who can be relied on to exercise proper stewardship of a publicly quoted company'. Ejected by the voters of Buckingham, he settled with Leasco out of court for £6.25m compensation, and in 1974 bought Pergamon Press back for a nominal sum as a private company.

With the help of stockbrokers Grieveson Grant, in 1981 Maxwell launched a successful dawn raid on the British Printing & Communication Corporation, the country's largest printing concern, which was losing £1m a year. Almost at once he took an axe to the workforce, cutting jobs from 13,000 to 7,000 over the following five years. But within four years, the company he acquired for just £10m was making pre-tax profits of £25m a year.

In 1984, Maxwell picked up Mirror Group newspapers from Reed International for a bargain £113m. Two years later, its central London office block alone was worth more than that. Once again, massive job losses were pushed through. Profits rose substantially, even though circulation fell heavily.[1] Maxwell was by now ambitious to build a media empire to rival Murdoch's.

Despite Maxwell's continued protestations that he still supported Labour, the *Mirror* pursued a tough anti-union line, mounting a subsequently discredited smear campaign against miners' leader Arthur Scargill. Meanwhile, Pergamon branched out into Stalinist vanity publishing, releasing such unforgettable classics as *Ceausescu: Builder of Modern Romania and International Statesman*. Maxwell interviewed the dictator personally, inevitably posing such tough questions as: 'What has made you so popular with the Romanians?' Maxwell liked to drop hints that these contacts made him invaluable to the intelligence services of more than one nation.

Warning signs of his ability to play fast and loose were visible early on. In 1986, the Mirror Group was in need of cash. Maxwell took £34m from the pension fund, replacing it with Reuters shares. When these shares were transferred back three years later, the fund took a significant hit on the transaction. This was the trick he was later to repeat, but on a grander scale.

By the late 1980s Maxwell had borrowed heavily to fund a string of acquisitions and his master company Maxwell Communications Corp was £2bn in debt. When recession hit in 1990, he was forced to float 49 per cent of Mirror Group to keep up with the payments. Still the overdrafts continued to mount, however, and his bankers were given Mirror shares as security. But a fall in the share price meant that even they were now effectively devalued.

During 1990 and 1991 Maxwell begged, stole or borrowed £344m and spent it on buying shares in Mirror Group and MCC, essentially to prop up their price. But by August 1991, his position became untenable. Goldman Sachs was threatening to sell the Mirror Group shares it held as security, which would flag up Maxwell's difficulties to the market as a whole. Maxwell's buisness affairs were unravelling fast.

On Maxwell's payroll throughout most of this was Bernard Donoughue, a former academic who served as an adviser to both Wilson and Callaghan. After Thatcher came to power, Donoughue worked first in senior positions in journalism and then in the City, becoming a partner in Maxwell's stockbrokers Grieveson Grant.

A peerage for Donoughue followed in 1985, and from 1988 to 1997, he served variously as opposition spokesperson on Treasury, energy and national heritage issues. In the first Blair administration, Donoughue spent two years as an Agriculture minister, before resigning in 1999. His track record demonstrates his standing in the Labour Party under five of its last six leaders.

In 1988, Maxwell recruited Lord Donoughue as executive vice-chairman of London & Bishopsgate Investments, a company that controlled around 10 per cent of the Mirror's pension funds. By this time, Maxwell was collecting peers much like schoolboys collect stamps, then employing 17 of them, including two former Lord Chancellors.

The presence of Donoughue at London & Bishopsgate instantly conferred credibility on the enterprise, and he was remunerated accordingly. In just three years with the company, he picked up £1.29m, including a £500,000 golden hello payment, an annual salary of £180,000 and £250,000 on leaving. While such rewards would today be nothing out of the ordinary, they were certainly exceptional by the standards of the time, especially considering that the firm made an annual profit of only £180,000.

London & Bishopsgate was central to Maxwell's subsequent malpractice.

Using a device known as stock lending – the temporary transfer of legal title to shares to a lender as a from of collateral – Maxwell was able to siphon off about £70m of its assets, to the benefit of his private companies.

Donoughue subsequently admitted 'misgivings' about the way Maxwell handled pension fund assets. But he has always maintained that his role was strategic, and that he personally knew little or nothing about the stock lending programme, and certainly of 'nothing illegal or improper'. He tendered his resignation in July 1991, at which point the pension fund assets were to the best of his knowledge safe, and finally left the company in mid-October, just four weeks before Maxwell's death. On his departure he pocketed an additional payment of £50,000 to remain silent under a confidentiality agreement.[2]

During his time with the London & Bishopsgate, such an obviously intelligent man, with considerable experience in the ways of the City, can hardly be said to have demonstrated much curiosity about what was going on in the company he was so handsomely paid to scrutinise. The 2001 DTI report found that Donoughue 'ought, as a director, to have ascertained sufficient information about the way Maxwell was moving funds around his business empire'. Had he done so, he might have identified some of the malpractice.[3]

Another of Maxwell's 1980s employees was Helen Liddell, the bus driver's daughter who finally won cabinet ranking when she was made Secretary of State for Scotland in 2001. Liddell first entered parliament in Monklands East in the 1994 by-election caused by the death of John Smith. The following year she was appointed Labour's Scottish spokesperson, and undertook a variety of ministerial posts in the first term, including Economic Secretary to the Treasury.

Liddell's career began with jobs as an economist with the Scottish Trades Union Congress and as a BBC economics correspondent, before she became general secretary of the Labour Party in Scotland for 11 years. During this period she even found time to write a novel, apparently rather on the raunchy side, with a plot centring on a ruthless female Scottish MP who gets to be both Deputy Prime Minister and mistress of a future president of the US. No names, no pack drill.

Displeased at being passed over for the job of general secretary of the Labour Party nationwide, Liddell was in 1986 evidently happy to accept a job with Maxwell that paid £50,000, then a considerable salary. On her own account, the offer came out of the blue. Other reports have it that she wrote Maxwell a letter seeking such a post. Either way, until 1992 she worked as a director of personnel and public affairs of the *Daily Record*, earning a reputation as something of a Maxwell hatchet woman.

One former colleague records: 'She was employed as director of personnel at the Scottish *Daily Record*, but the view of the senior executives was that it was a strictly personal appointment by Maxwell, because she had no relevant skills and was often off doing other things unrelated to the job.'[4]

When questioned about the period today, Liddell consistently denies suggestions that she was close to Maxwell, and instead stresses her standing as a ripped-off pension scheme contributor.

The other former Maxwell man to serve as a minister in Labour's first term was Geoffrey Robinson. However much Blair and Brown would like to play the fact down, Robinson undertook a pivotal role in the early days of the New Labour project, not so much intellectually or ideologically, but simply by picking up much of the tab. In that respect, it is ironic that he was appointed to the job of Paymaster General.

Like Donoughue, Robinson was very much the product of Wilsonian corporatism. An academically gifted young man, he was personally recruited to Labour's research department in 1964 by Wilson, after an earlier national service spell in army intelligence. Four years later, he was appointed to the Government's state bank, the Industrial Reorganisation Corporation. After that was closed by the Tories, he called in favours owed to became financial controller of state-owned British Leyland at the age of just 31, and soon found himself chief executive of subsidiary Jaguar, the luxury car marque.

It was while at Jaguar that he met the improbably named Joska Bourgeois, an extremely wealthy older woman who had held the Jaguar distribution franchise in Belgium since the Second World War. There has been much speculation over whether their friendship was sexual, despite a considerable age gap between the two and despite Robinson's marriage.

Still nursing both political and business ambitions, Robinson became MP for Coventry North West in a by-election in 1976. In the years that followed, he was judged worthy only of a couple of relatively lowly front-bench positions. For Robinson, politics was about being in government rather than opposition. After 1979, his heart did not seem to be in a long drawn-out fight with the Conservatives. Instead, he spent much of his time in the 1980s studiously pursuing his business interests, accumulating a personal fortune in the process.

In 1981 he had founded Transfer Technology, manufacturer of sophisticated machine tools, and was seeking ways to grow the business. Five years later he met Maxwell at Labour's conference in Blackpool, for the first time since they had briefly bumped into each other almost two decades earlier. As it happened, one of Maxwell's companies, Hollis, was bidding for some engineering firms. Not having expertise in this area, Maxwell was seeking a non-executive chairman. Always one to extend favours to the rich and powerful, Robinson happily accepted the job.

Seven months before Maxwell's demise, Robinson was effectively handed control of the publisher's engineering interests in a complex reverse takeover deal, based around a buy-out of Hollis. Robinson ultimately emerged as as the largest shareholder in the entity that became TransTec.

But what really made Robinson a wealthy man was the death of Bourgeois in 1994. He was left a legacy of £9m. The money certainly came through at around the right time. TransTec's share price had fallen sharply, after the company was found to have used unorthodox but legitimate accountancy techniques to put an optimistic valuation on unfinished projects and to flatter its bottom line. The City demanded Robinson's head, and in November 1994 he stepped down as chief executive to become non-executive chairman. However, he remained TransTec's largest shareholder, and the company began to prosper once more, with a string of acquisitions.

On the political front, Tory hegemony was by now visibly falling apart. Robinson had made a point of cultivating such coming men as Blair, Brown and Mandelson right from the birth of the New Labour project. Given his standing as a successful businessman, his counsel was only too welcome to the modernising faction. As an added bonus, he was rich. Where there was a problem that money could be thrown at, Robinson could be depended on to write the cheque.

Soft-left magazine the *New Statesman* – under the able editorship of Steve Platt – had the temerity sometimes to run articles critical of the modernisers. No problem. Robinson bought the journal for £375,000 in February 1996 and promptly sacked non-compliant journalists.

Over dinner with Robinson three months later, Mandelson discussed his accommodation situation. Again no problem. A £373,000 loan from Robinson provided Mandelson with the means to buy a house in London's fashionable Notting Hill.

Robinson himself was the owner of numerous desirable residences in several countries, and was accordingly always good for a free holiday. That summer Gordon Brown and his brother stayed at the flat Robinson inherited from Bourgeois in Cannes, while the Blair family holidayed at his Tuscan estate in San Gimignano.

Just how far Robinson's largesse extended throughout the Labour hierarchy is one of the remaining riddles of Labour funding in the 1990s. What did he pay and when did he pay it? One key question is whether his support for Blair was limited to a free stay in Italy, or whether he donated a large sum to the Blair blind trust. Robinson claims in his memoirs that around this period he gave the party leader's private office a substantial undisclosed sum. Press reports put the figure as high as £250,000.[5]

The Labour Leader's Office Fund trustees issued a statement insisting that such a gift had not passed through this particular conduit:

In light of the inaccurate stories in the press we have checked the accounts of the Labour Leader's Office Fund and we can confirm that Geoffrey Robinson did not donate to the fund. We have only taken this exceptional step in this case because of the sustained nature of this misinformation campaign.[6]

The confusion deepened when Jonathan Powell – link man between the trustees and Blair himself – confirmed he met Robinson before the 1997 election to discuss the possibility of a donation, but added that in the event, no donation was made. Robinson complicated matters further by saying that he could not remember exactly to whom he had given the quarter of a million pounds. 'I made a contribution to Tony's office for the support work of his office. As far as I remember, I made it through the Labour Party and that is an end of it.'[7]

Yet Labour's general secretary Margaret McDonagh told the Neill Committee on party funding: 'The leader's office has never been funded by the Labour Party in its history.' The statements made by McDonagh and Robinson seem flatly to contradict one another.[8]

Despite his boasts of considerable financial backing for Blair, Robinson was somewhat closer to Brown. Robinson's penthouse suite at the Grosvenor Park Hotel was a regular plotting retreat for the shadow Chancellor and his entourage, who even became known as the Hotel Group. Robinson would frequently throw some £50 notes on the table and tell the boys to get the beers and pizzas in.

Indeed, his largesse extended to rather more than six-packs and takeaways. Robinson gave Brown's office £200,000, channelled through a vehicle called the Smith Political Economy Unit, which only existed for one year between November 1996 and October 1997. Its total income for the period was £208,500, so Robinson must have been virtually its sole benefactor.[9]

Robinson even offered to finance much of the research the Brown team needed to devise its tax policies. Even here he secured a bargain, getting Arthur Andersen to crunch the numbers on the proposed windfall tax on privatised utilities for a cut-rate price. He also persuaded merchant bank Warburgs to draw up a report on tube privatisation for just £10,000, rather less than the £100,000 it would normally have charged.[10]

Unsurprisingly, after such unstinting support, Brown made sure that Robinson got a job on his team at the Treasury following the 1997 election win. As Paymaster General, he became the man responsible for Britain's taxation policy. It was only now that his past began to catch up with him.

By December, both the Bourgeois legacy and the existence of a Channel Islands trust known as Orion, where most of Robinson's stake in TransTec was held, became public knowledge. The latter revelation was particularly embarrassing, given Labour's earlier fulminations against offshore tax havens. Matters were compounded when Terry Burns, Permanent Secretary to the Treasury, refused to put his name to a statement that he had been aware of the situation and given it clearance. Burns was adamant that he had only been told of the existence of a Robinson family trust, and not informed of its offshore status.

In January 1998, parliamentary standards commissioner Sir Gordon Downey cleared Robinson of breaking Commons rules in this instance. But this was the first in an extended series of ultimately fatal wounds.

In February, the Tories pressed a further series of charges over a number of directorships held by Robinson in the 1980s. In particular, they pointed to Pergamon accounts dating from 1990, which appeared to show that Maxwell paid Robinson £200,000 for the latter's role at Hollis Industries. No such payment was ever declared in the register of members' interests. According to Robinson, that was because he never received the money. Such details could only have been included in the Pergamon figures in error, he maintained.

Andersen conducted an independent audit of the relevant papers, which found no conclusive evidence of payment. But strong circumstantial evidence did come to light, in the form of an invoice and handwritten notes which referred to '£200,000 paid to G Robinson'. Definitively establishing the truth of the matter would require a search of some 300 boxes of documents remaining in the Pergamon archive, at a cost of perhaps £20,000.

Downey gave Robinson the benefit of the doubt, concluding that the Hollis accounts were indeed wrong and that even the invoice and notes 'did not establish a prima facie case that payment was made'. Indeed, there was a 'likelihood' that Robinson had been the victim of an accounting error, and that the money had been owed to him but had not been paid.

The cross-party – but Labour-dominated – Committee on Standards and Privileges agreed, rebuking Robinson only for his failure to register two paid directorships. Their report concluded: 'Mr Robinson did not meet all the requirements of registration. His conduct as a member of parliament does not reach the threshold which would justify the imposition of any penalty by the House.'

Blair immediately declared that the Paymaster General enjoyed his 'complete confidence'. That was hardly true. In fact, Blair tried to get rid of Robinson in the July 1998 reshuffle, and the Paymaster General was only retrieved after Brown's personal intervention. There followed a 55-second Robinson apology to the Commons over the Orion affair in November, when he assured MPs that he had never used his ministerial position to advance his private interests. Seemingly he was off the hook.

But just days later, it emerged that the DTI was investigating Robinson in connection with 13 possible breaches of company law between 1988 and

1992. Robinson was hoist by his own petard. He himself had signed Hollis accounts suggesting the £200,000 had been paid. If the money wasn't handed over, then *ipso facto* Robinson had filed inaccurate accounts.

And the head of the department looking into these allegations was none other than Mandelson, the man to whom he had privately extended a home loan of £373,000 two years before. All in all, it was just about the worst conceivable time for details of the borrowing to become public. In line with sod's law, that's just what happened. Just before Christmas, Mandelson, Robinson and Brown spin doctor Charlie Whelan all lost their jobs after the story broke.

Robinson felt especially aggrieved. As he viewed it, the situation had arisen not because of the loan per se but because of Mandelson's conflict of interest at the DTI. There followed dark suggestions in the press that Robinson possessed photographs of an unnamed Labour politician in a compromising position.

Almost exactly a year later, on the last day before Parliament closed for the Christmas 1999 recess, Mandelson's replacement Byers inserted into Hansard a written answer, revealing that the DTI's Hollis inquiry was over. Releasing such an announcement when little media coverage could have been expected suggests the timing was carefully chosen as an early example of a good day to bury inconvenient news.

Robinson had not been exonerated, but he had not been blamed either, which in the circumstances was probably as good as it gets. No further action was proposed. Moreover, as Byers made clear in a letter to a Tory frontbencher, the findings were not for publication.

There the matter might have rested. But come Christmas Eve, three days later, the stock exchange suspended TransTec. Later that day, the company went into receivership, with debts of £70m, after revelations of accounting irregularities. In particular, an £11m claim from Ford Motors for late delivery of components, made in 1997, had not appeared in its accounts. Robinson's fortune, previously estimated at £32.6m, was all but wiped out, leaving him just about down to his last lousy million. Under the Companies Act, Byers had no alternative but to appoint DTI inspectors to deliver a report on the collapse, this time for publication. Meanwhile, the West Midlands police fraud squad was also called in.

Another book, another bombshell. Investigative journalist Tom Bower's unauthorised biography of Robinson was published at the start of 2001, claiming that Robinson had actually asked for payment of the disputed £200,000 on an invoice written from his mansion in Surrey, submitted in October 1990.

Six weeks later, in December 1990, a cheque for £200,000, drawn on a Pergamon account and numbered 001751, had been paid into a London branch of NatWest bank by an unknown person. On the same day, it was transferred to a Birmingham NatWest branch where both Robinson and TransTec held their accounts. There the trail stopped dead. Bank records no longer existed, making it impossible to identify the account into which the money had been paid.

Bowers' book – serialised by the *Daily Mail* – caused further uproar after an infuriated Byers said he was considering legal action over the suggestion that he had effectively buried the DTI report on Robinson. The writ never came, although the mere threat was enough to stop WH Smith stocking the title.

Once again, Robinson's business affairs were subject to the scrutiny of the parliamentary watchdog. Elizabeth Filkin, who had replaced Downey as standards commissioner, concluded that Robinson had failed to declare an important business interest.

The Committee on Standards and Privileges heard Robinson again in April 2001. The following month it ruled that he failed to provide 'full and accurate responses' during the 1998 investigation into Hollis.[11] It also reiterated Filkin's conclusion that Robinson had been misleading in 'denying that he had agreed or solicited the £200,000'.[12]

Somewhat charitably, the committee gave him three months to prove his assertion that he had never received the money. With a general election almost certain within that period, the move was probably intended to offer Robinson the opportunity to stand down with good grace. But he chose to stand again and was duly re-elected.

Hauled once more before the Committee on Standards and Privileges in October 2001, Robinson was banned from the House of Commons for three weeks. This is one of the heaviest penalties the Commons can impose on an MP. But, given the gravity of the allegations against him, there is an argument that it was hardly condign.

Despite the suspension ruling, the committee still accepted that Robinson had not been paid the £200,000 by Maxwell, making the point that 'we do not assume payment was made to Mr Robinson'.[13]

Robinson's suspension offence was merely that he had not provided full and accurate answers to the committee's questions. In other words, he was no worse than a dissembler, an inheritor of the Alan Clark tradition of economy with the *actualité*.

Robinson is now back in business with a non-executive directorship at Smart Technology Group. The company is described as 'specialising in high technology involving materials and control processes and in traditional machine tool activities'. In addition, he is also a non-executive director at Torgram, a London waste management and consultancy company. Meanwhile, having looked into TransTec, neither the West Midlands fraud squad nor the DTI have decided to mount a prosecution.[14]

It's worth mentioning one other member of Labour's inner circle who also worked for Maxwell, although not in such elevated or lucrative capacities as Donoughue, Liddle or Robinson. Blair's press man Alastair Campbell is a former political editor of the *Daily Mirror*. Clearly he thought well of the old brute. So distraught was he at the news of Maxwell's death that he threw a punch at another political journalist who had cracked a joke about it. Presumably he no longer feels quite the same way.

NOTES

[1] On the career of Robert Maxwell, see *The Economist*, 1 November 1986; *Business Age*, April 1993

[2] *Mail on Sunday*, 21 October 1992; *Private Eye*, 9 February 1996; *Sunday Times*, 1 March 1998

[3] *Daily Mirror*, 31 March 2001; *Guardian*, 31 March 2001

[4] *Guardian*, 17 May 1997

[5] *Daily Telegraph*, 18 October 2000

[6] BBC News Online, 21 October 1999

[7] Ibid.

[8] Ibid.

[9] *Observer*, 3 January 1998

[10] Tom Bower, *The Paymaster* (London, Simon & Schuster, 2001), p.116, p.127

[11] *Financial Times*, 24 October 2001

[12] *Guardian*, 26 July 2001

[13] *Daily Telegraph*, 25 October 2001

[14] *Financial Times*, 26 February 2002

12. 'I'LL HAVE TONY TEST THE WATERS': LABOUR AND THE MEDIA

WHEN it comes to setting Labour's political agenda, the major media companies simply have more bargaining chips than any other business sector. The Government regards their support as crucial to its electoral fortunes, with editorial endorsement by a single mass-circulation national newspaper worth more than all but the largest corporate donation. Just as is the case with Labour's wider campaigning, the swing voters get singled out for special treatment.

The *Mirror* – Labour's only consistent national newspaper friend – is taken for granted, and of late has taken to criticising the party from the left. *The Guardian* generally does as it is told, but is still capable of embarrassing the Government if it is feeling stroppy on the day. At the opposite end of the spectrum, the *Daily Mail* and *Daily Telegraph* remain as staunchly Tory as ever. Simply toning down their in-born hostility is seen as something of a triumph.

Most of Labour's attention has been paid to the titles in between the two camps. Relationships with News International in particular have been transformed beyond all recognition. Yet this is still an uneasy rapport. New Labour has made important political concessions to Murdoch, many of them unimaginable even a decade ago, and even run political errands for him. But it has nevertheless drawn a line at some of the naturalised American's demands, particularly where they conflict with other political imperatives. Even though Murdoch is Britain's most important media baron, he is not so dominant that the Government can afford to forget that his rivals have their interests too.

Labour's links with Express Newspapers, previously owned by long-standing Labour supporter Lord Hollick and now by pornographer and party benefactor Richard Desmond, are also worth closer scrutiny. And, as ever, New Labour donors and favourite sons have noticeably prospered where appointments have been in the party's gift, most notably at the BBC.

Labour's media strategy is centred on the assumption that press political bias is a decisive determinant of voting patterns. This is a faulty premise. If that was the case, there would never have been a Labour government ever before. Psephology shows us that newspaper buyers in general take little notice of editorial column voting recommendations, one way or the other. A majority of *Sun* readers have always backed Labour, even when that paper was gung-ho for Thatcher. A full one-third of *Daily Telegraph* readers vote Labour. The truth is that most people choose their daily paper for many different apolitical reasons, ranging from superior sports coverage, difficult crosswords, a favourite cartoon strip or a liking for topless pin-ups. There are all sorts of other influences on political ideas, not least including the prevailing ideological climate in society.

But Labour remains haunted by the *Sun's* insistence that it alone swung the 1992 general election for John Major, illiterately proclaiming from its front page that 'It was the *Sun* wot won it'. Accordingly, endorsement from Britain's biggest circulation tabloid was a top priority in the 1997 campaign, for which Blair was ready to pay almost any price.

This represented a reversal of earlier Labour thinking. The notion of the 'Tory press' was in the 1980s – and even as late as the early 1990s – deeply embedded in the party's collective belief system. Only Maxwell's Mirror Group was more or less onside, and even that support sometimes proved a hideous embarrassment.

Rupert Murdoch – chairman and chief executive of News Corporation, in which he holds around a one-third stake – was regarded as the Great Satan. Like their proprietor, all five of the British papers he then owned were fanatically Thatcherite throughout that woman's reign. In that respect, they were no different from the vast majority of the UK national press, which regarded Labour in the Bennite years as a socialist challenge to the profit system. Relatively low-level Labour activists were routinely hounded in the most vicious and personalised ways. The 1980s Labour Party developed the analysis that, broadly speaking, three groups controlled 70 per cent of national daily circulation and 80 per cent of the Sunday market. This virtual monopoly should be broken up, by law if necessary, it argued.

Animosity against Murdoch peaked after the 1986 Wapping dispute, a carefully contrived – and highly successful – master plan to break the pervasive influence of the print unions. In collaboration with Eric Hammond, leader of the EETPU electricians' union, Murdoch engineered a strike by some 6,000 Fleet Street printers. This gave him carte blanche to sack the lot of them, and replace them with EETPU members on no-strike contracts.

The collapse of the dispute the following year was perhaps second only to the defeat of the miners as the most important setback for organised labour during the Thatcher decade, opening the way for sweeping derecognition across the newspaper industry. For years afterward, official Labour policy was to refuse interviews with all News International titles, although Blair was one of not a few Labour MPs who took little notice of the ban. As late as 1992, the Labour manifesto promised a Monopolies and

Mergers Commission inquiry into concentration of press ownership. It didn't mention Murdoch by name. But then again, it didn't have to.

Britain is only one outpost in a global media empire on which the *Sun* never sets. News Corporation, with an annual revenue of around £7bn, controls some 800 subsidiaries around the world. Around 60 of these are based in tax havens such as Bermuda, the Virgin Islands and the Cayman Islands. Through this complicated network – specifically designed efficiently to facilitate tax minimisation – Murdoch controls Twentieth Century Fox film studios, the Fox TV network in the States, the *New York Post*, 200 newspapers in Australia, satellite broadcaster BSkyB, the LA Dodgers baseball team, and book publisher HarperCollins, which in turn owns Fourth Estate.

Murdoch's main holding company in the UK is Newscorp Investments, which owns News International. In its turn, News International owns *The Times, The Sunday Times, The Sun* and the *News of the World*. It has clocked up profits of over £1.3bn since 1987. Yet it has incurred little or no tax, even picking up rebates in some years. Huge losses from the early years of BSkyB are still being used to reduce current tax exposure.

Such are the complexities that it is impossible to get to the bottom of Murdoch's taxation affairs. But on one estimate, if Newscorp Investments had only paid corporation tax at prevailing rates, it would have provided the Inland Revenue with £250m since 1990. That could have paid for seven new hospitals or 200 primary schools.[1]

After Blair took over the leadership, signs started to emerge – initially via kite-flying in the press – that both sides were softening their stance. Murdoch told German news magazine *Der Spiegel*: 'I could even imagine myself supporting the British Labour leader Tony Blair.' New Labour took the hint.

There were press leaks that Heritage spokesperson Mo Mowlam wanted Labour's media policies to be rewritten. When competition spokesperson Richard Caborn demanded that the Tories launch a monopolies probe into BSkyB, fully in line with party policy, Blair publicly humiliated him by repudiating the call. Dinner dates between Blair and Murdoch soon followed. Rapprochement reached its apex in July 1995, only months after *The Sunday Times* had smeared former Labour leader Michael Foot as a KGB agent, subsequently publishing an abject apology. Blair flew to Australia's Hayman Island at Murdoch's expense, clocking up 50 hours flying time, to address a conference of top News International managers. By this point, it was abundantly clear that the guest speaker would be Britain's next prime minister.

Blair didn't cross the globe for nothing. His speech was clearly intended to be reconciliatory. 'There have been changes on both sides. The past should be behind us. Neither of us is in the business of trading policy or editorial support. But we should know where the other is coming from,' he told the gathering.[2]

Both Blair and Murdoch deny anything as unseemly as striking a deal. But tacit understanding does seem to have been reached, at least as far as the Labour leader was concerned. Former *Sunday Times* editor Andrew Neil recalls having been told by Blair: 'How we treat Murdoch's media interests when in power will depend on how his newspapers treat the Labour Party in the run up to the election and after we are in government.'[3]

Murdoch's newspapers responded to Blair's overtures. *The Sun* started to carry pro-Labour material, while *The Times* became neutral. For his part, Blair made it clear that a future Labour government would not be bound by policies of the past. The idea of a monopolies inquiry was quietly forgotten about, while Labour even opposed Tory proposals for tougher restrictions on newspaper group control of television stations.

Compare and contrast the manifesto commitments. In 1992, Labour promised: 'We will safeguard press freedom. We will . . . establish an urgent inquiry by the Monopolies and Mergers Commission into the concentration of media ownership.'[4] By 1997, this comparable section was worded:

> The regulatory framework for media and broadcasting should reflect the realities of a far more open and competitive economy, and enormous technological advance, for example with digital television. Labour will balance sensible rules, fair regulation and national and international competition, so maintaining quality and diversity for the benefit of viewers.[5]

Such changes found favour with a range of media figures. Gerry Robinson – chairman of BSkyB as well as independent television broadcaster Granada – came out as a Labour supporter, and was paraded to the nation in a party political broadcast. Another BSkyB director, Dennis Stevenson, was appointed head of Labour's review on the use of information technology in schools.

But, even this late in the day, the *Sun*'s endorsement was still open to the highest bidder. Murdoch met Major at Chequers and offered him the paper's support in exchange for explicit rejection of British entry into the single European currency. The then Prime Minister refused to budge from his 'wait and see' stance.[6] By contrast, Blair penned a eurosceptic article for the tabloid. So it was that in 1997, *The Sun* came out for New Labour. As ever, it backed the winning side.

In office, Labour has gone to some lengths to keep Murdoch on board. Crucially, News International is still able to keep its tax bills below 2 per cent, through the use of perfectly legal tax avoidance methods. But there have been several other examples of the Government keeping its new-found friend sweet.

In 1998, the Tory-dominated House of Lords voted to outlaw the *Times*'s loss-leader cover price tactics, clearly aimed at putting the struggling *Independent* out of its misery. Introducing the bill, Lib Dem peer Lord McNally argued that Murdoch's power was 'reaching dangerous and unacceptable proportions'. Once that was Labour mainstream orthodoxy. But New Labour's response was to get the vote overturned in the Commons. It was left to the Office of Fair Trading to rebuke News International over the issue.

That same year, Murdoch wanted BSkyB to buy a controlling interest in Italian television group MediaSet, owned by his Italian counterpart Silvio Berlusconi. A bid was likely to trigger unfavourable political reaction in Italy, given Berlusconi's considerable clout as former prime minister. Murdoch was not shy about calling in his deposits in the favour bank. Neil claims that Murdoch brazenly told senior colleagues: 'I'll have Tony test the waters.'[7] Tony did just that. Murdoch asked Blair to sound out Italian Prime Minister Romano Prodi on News Corporation's chances. Blair duly made the call. Within two days, the Prime Minister rang Murdoch back to tell him that Prodi was having none of it, and was seeking an Italian purchaser. Murdoch's bid subsequently collapsed.

Relations between the two sides had become so cordial that BSkyB became the first Murdoch company known to have given financial support to Labour, with a £20,000 contribution in the form of sponsorship of a party conference youth event held in a Blackpool nightclub and hosted by celebrity DJ Chris Evans. This was not declared in the party's accounts, with Labour arguing that it was not an official Labour function, but rather a fringe meeting of sorts.[8]

But in September 1998, only weeks after the conference knees-up, BSkyB launched a £623m bid for Manchester United. This was at a time when sport, and football in particular, was considered the primary reason for people to subscribe to digital television. Murdoch happily paid astronomical sums, way beyond the reach of public service broadcasters, to acquire rights for major sporting events. Moreover, the world's top soccer side is a major stock exchange listed company in its own right, and such an acquisition would be entirely of a piece with News Corporation's ownership of top baseball, basketball and ice hockey clubs in the US.

Manchester United fans – a lobby not insignificant even in the corridors of power – were overwhelmingly against the takeover, and the move was also opposed by the Secretary of State for Culture Chris Smith. Secretary of State for Trade and Industry Peter Mandelson referred the deal to the Competition Commission, which ruled against the takeover the following year. It was not lost on *The Sun* that both Smith and Mandelson are homosexuals, and the paper retaliated brutally with a campaign against the 'gay mafia' supposedly running Britain.

By way of amends, the Communications White Paper, published in 2000, was interpreted as payback time for Mudoch. Proposals included relaxation of restrictions on cross-media ownership, which dictate that owners of national newspapers with a market share greater than 20 per cent cannot own more than a 20 per cent stake in national or regional television and radio stations. Murdoch, with a market share of one-third of national newspaper circulation, was the prime victim.

But the goodwill generated through the White Paper was largely dissipated through an Office of Fair Trading investigation into BSkyB, launched in December 2000, which argued there were 'reasonable grounds' to suspect that the satellite broadcaster was acting anti-competitively.

The probe was triggered by allegations from BSkyB's ITV-owned rival, then known as ONdigital, that the Murdoch satellite broadcaster was charging unfair wholesale rates for the use of premium sports and film channels, making it costly for it to offer them on its platform. The OFT ruled in December 2001 that BSkyB was guilty as charged. Potential fines are enormous, and could be set as high as 10 per cent of BSkyB's annual turnover for up to three years. That points to a ballpark figure of £700m. BSkyB was granted right of appeal, while ONdigital – renamed ITV Digital – has subsequently collapsed. It is uncertain how this mess will resolve itself.

Oddly enough for an Australian-born naturalised American citizen, Murdoch is strangely perturbed by the prospect of Britain joining the euro. Part of the reason for such animosity may stem from EU legislation effectively forbidding him from buying terrestrial television stations in Europe on account of his American citizenship. He may also be influenced by some of the more influential hacks on his payroll, including *Sun* political editor Trevor Kavanagh, and free-market economist and *Sunday Times* columnist Irwin Stelzer, who used to supplement his News Corporation salary with a £35,000-a-year retainer from Enron.

Such is the heat generated by the issue that a 1998 breakfast meeting between Murdoch and Blair, designed to thrash things out, finished in apparent acrimony. *The Sun* responded with a front page splash featuring a photograph of the Prime Minister, under the rhetorical headline 'Is THIS the most dangerous man in Britain', with the accompanying copy taking him to task on the euro. Such open animosity to New Labour had not emanated from Wapping in years. But the row was not deemed sufficiently serious to prevent Gordon Brown from addressing a News Corp convention at the Sun Valley ski resort in Idaho shortly afterwards.

Whatever the swings and roundabouts of the first term, the Murdoch press was solidly behind New Labour at the last election. For the first time ever, *The Times* called for a Labour vote. *The Sunday Times,* which backed Major in 1997, also came out for Blair. The tabloids maintained their pro-Labour position. Murdoch aides were quick to deny that such support was in any way a thank you for the Communications White Paper.

By now, Murdoch himself was becoming distinctly testy towards the Government, as witnessed in a BSkyB press conference in November 2001, when he both confirmed that he was to become a father again at the age of 71, and then implicitly threatened to withdraw the support of *The Times* and *The Sun* from New Labour.

'This is not a country that encourages success. It's anti-success,' he sneered. 'Our executives have to spend at least half their time dealing with lawyers and regulators and they would do a whole lot better if they didn't have to cope with this constant harassment.'

It was, he added, 'not his style' to use any pull he might just happen to have with Blair to push for a relaxation of media cross-ownership laws. Just to underline that this is indeed the case, he added: 'It would be interesting if a lot of our newspapers weren't so Labour-supporting. Then Tony Blair would not have to worry about being seen to look after his friends.'[9]

A Communications Bill was finally published in May 2002, representing probably the most significant media reform for two decades. The proposals still debar News International, or any other national newspaper publisher, from owning an ITV company. However, the way will soon be cleared for Murdoch to get a foothold in terrestrial broadcasting by buying into Channel 5 and turning it into a version of his Sky One satellite channel as a window for cross-promotion. While Channel 5 itself is still very much minority viewing, commentators immediately point to the huge symbolic significance of the move, and speculate that it could only have come about following some sort of deal between Murdoch and the Government.

Personal ties between News International and New Labour seemingly remain cordial. Murdoch still pops in to Number 10 for regular discussions. Meanwhile, his daughter, and former BSkyB boss, Elisabeth Murdoch, is a close friend of Peter Mandelson. She is also business partner of Lord Alli, an impeccably connected New Labour media player.

The son of a mechanic from British Guiana and a nurse from Trinidad, Waheed Alli instantly stands out in the House of Lords, which is hardly surprising for a relatively young and openly gay Asian multimillionaire.

Alli's route to the second chamber began with a first job in financial journalism, in which he performed so well that he secured a lucrative position as head of investment research for Save and Prosper. He went on to found Planet 24, a youth-oriented TV production company in 1992, together with personal and business partner Charlie Parsons and pop singer Bob Geldof. The company – named after the average age of its staff – brought *Big Breakfast*, *The Word* and *Survivor* to the nation's television screens. Schlock TV would in the past not have been the most obvious way to earn a peerage, but New Labour was suitably impressed, and Alli reached the Lords in 1998, aged 34.

Carlton Communications acquired Planet 24 for £15m in the following year, appointing Alli managing director of Carlton Productions. His major decision was to commission a remake of cultural landmark Birmingham motel soap *Crossroads*, which proved a flop. Alli quit Carlton the following year, after being passed over for the position he wanted in its management structure. He was soon drafted into the Millbank election team, and was already being talked up as a future minister. One of his friends noted at the time: 'You don't get a peerage for nothing. And Waheed has ambitions to have a more active role in government, so he has got to spend more time on politics.'[10]

A dependable Labour loyalist, Alli claims to have first been inspired to political involvement by Kinnock's attacks on Militant in 1985, a time when more young people were being radicalised by opposition to Thatcherism than hatred of the left. Alli later forked out £15,000 towards Frank Dobson's unsuccessful London mayoral bid in 2000, and Planet 24 has sponsored Labour research projects. However, he notes: 'I give more time than money.'[11]

While Alli is likely to prove a coming man, United Business Media chief executive Lord Hollick is one of the old stagers in Labour–business relations. Hollick got his peerage as far back as 1991, after earlier fundraising efforts that made him the closest thing Kinnock had to Michael Levy. One Labour source from this period remarked: 'If this job is about raising cash, Clive may be very good at it. He was always good at finding other people with money to spare.'[12]

Hollick's other Labour credentials include an important role in the 1992 prawn cocktail offensive, acting as treasurer for the first three years of the Institute for Public Policy Research, and a job as Margaret Beckett's special adviser at the Department of Trade and Industry after the 1997 election victory.

Hollick is never slow to point out his working-class roots as the grammar school-educated son of a French polisher from Southampton, who joined the party in his teens and went on to redbrick Nottingham University. Thereafter he worked for merchant bank Hambros, becoming its youngest-ever director, before launching his own money-broking business in the shape of MAI. By the 1990s, he was paying himself a salary of several million pounds a year, and once arranged for senior MAI employees to be paid in gold bars as a perfectly legal tax avoidance measure. Hollick has also served on the British Aerospace board. Then Foreign Secretary, Robin Cook, is said to have blamed Hollick's influence when Number 10 overruled his attempt to ban the export of 16 BAe Hawk jets to Indonesia, fearing they would be used to repressive ends.[13]

188

Other highlights of Hollick's business career include a stint on the board of Mirror Group, where he engineered the appointment of Ulster unionist hard man David Montgomery as chief executive. Mirror staff soon nicknamed Montgomery 'Rommel', on the grounds that the Second World War general Montgomery was on our side. Rommel went on to sack over 100 journalists, with the purges eventually taking in award-winning columnist Paul Foot. Hollick resigned from the board shortly afterwards in apparent opposition to the redundancies.

Hollick's switch from the City to the media began in 1994, when MAI bought Anglia Television. Two years later, the company also picked up Express Newspapers, and was renamed United News & Media. The move saw a change in political direction at the traditionally Tory daily and Sunday tabloids. Under the Hollick-inspired editorship of feminist Rosie Boycott, the *Daily Express* became for the first time in its history a Labour paper.

The year 2000 marked a pivotal point in Hollick's career. He began the millennium by proposing a merger of his ITV interests, which then included Anglia, HTV and Meridian, with Carlton Communications. The deal could have made Hollick the most powerful man in commercial television. Sensitive as ever to ownership thresholds in the sector, even where a Labour backer was involved, the Government laid down conditions that were just too tough to make the deal worthwhile. Hollick had no compunction in selling his stations to Granada just weeks later, happily enough at the top of the market.

Towards the end of the year, he sold Express Newspapers too. The Hinduja brothers – then surrounded by speculation that one of their number had effectively purchased a British passport in exchange for a £1m donation to the Millennium Dome – seemed the most likely buyers. Gopichand Hinduja even started putting it about that Blair was supporting their £100m bid for the titles.

But the Indian entrepreneurs were pipped at the post by self-professed former Tory Richard Desmond, a one-time drummer who started in business by launching a magazine for musicians. Desmond's company Northern & Shell went on to diversify into pornography before launching the stupendously successful *OK!*, which is to celebrity gossip what *The Economist* is to serious foreign affairs reportage.

Hollick's company, currently known as United Business Media, has now lost all of its most glamorous assets, and is left with an unsexy but profitable trade press, newswire and exhibitions business, a third of Channel 5, some 20 per cent of ITN and market researchers NOP. The City sees the business as something of a hotchpotch, but isn't quibbling with its success. These days Hollick even finds time for a spot of quangocracy, and has been appointed chairman of London's South Bank Centre, one of the biggest arts complexes in Europe.

Desmond's takeover of Express Newspapers proved an immediate source of controversy. Here was a man whose businesses included 38 'top-shelf' magazines, an 'adult entertainment' television channel and a number of websites purporting to show live sex and pictures of 78-year-old women in the nude.

His detractors pointed to the precedent set in 1990, when the regulatory authorities barred porn baron David Sullivan, owner of the salacious *Daily Sport*, from buying the Bristol United Press regional newspaper publisher on public interest grounds. Surely the Competition Commission would once again intervene?

Within ten minutes of wrapping up the Express deal on 22 November 2000, Desmond was telephoned by Downing Street and invited to meet the Prime Minister. The two men duly got together just before Christmas. Following conversations with Labour Party general secretary Margaret McDonagh and Lord Alli, at some point around this time Desmond offered Labour free advertising in his newspapers. But the party asked instead for the cash, promising that in return it would advertise in the Express titles.

In February 2001, Secretary of State for Trade and Industry Stephen Byers announced that he had decided not to refer Desmond's takeover deal to the Competition Commission. Within a week of the ruling, Northern & Shell handed the Labour Party £100,000, only days before the new regulations on the disclosure of corporate political donations came into force. As a result, Desmond's support did not become public until May 2002, with a disgruntled former employee suspected of leaking the news.

Both Express titles backed Labour at the last general election. Labour duly refunded most of Desmond's cash by taking out advertising. A few months later, McDonagh was named as general manager of the *Daily Express*, *Sunday Express*, *Daily Star* and *OK!*, despite having no previous publishing experience. Her appointment came shortly after a decision to lay off 140 Express employees. Fortunately for whatever remained of McDonagh's feminist consciousness, she was spared the responsibility of overseeing *Asian Babes*, *Nude Readers' Wives*, *Horny Housewives* and *Big Ones*.[14]

Known for her humourless and ruthless management style, McDonagh started political life as a Bennite, but by 1994 was deemed sufficiently trustworthy to help organise Blair's leadership campaign. As the control freak's control freak, she played a key role in both ensuring that Livingstone did not get Labour's nomination as mayor of London and that Rhodri Morgan was at first kept out of the Welsh Assembly top job, although both men eventually secured the positions they wanted. During the last election, she accused BBC, ITN and Sky of 'inciting and colluding' with anti-government protesters, cowering the broadcasters into semi-submission.

McDonagh did not intend to stay in her new role for any length of time, leaving Express Newspapers after six months to study on a business course at Harvard University in the United States.

After Desmond's support for New Labour became public knowledge – generating tremendous uproar – the erstwhile Tory justified his political conversion. He was now, he even averred, a bit of a leftie: 'Britain has never had it so good. We're all socialists. We all came from humble beginnings. We're not Lord Rothermere. We must be socialists, we're sitting here. We've done alright.'[15] That's not everyone's definition, comrade.

Meanwhile, the fall-out from the affair was the probably the final straw for Byers, still reeling from the controversies over Railtrack and the Moore/Sixsmith spin wars. Shortly after the story broke – along with word of his tangential involvement – he resigned from the Cabinet.

Broadcasting has been the career arena of choice for many New Labour business backers. Now their party has control of appointments at the state-owned British Broadcasting Corporation, and has appointed sympathisers to several key positions. After a long career in independent television that has garnered him an estimated personal fortune of £20m, Greg Dyke took over as director general of the BBC in January 2000. Dyke formally severed his Labour ties on appointment, after having given the party more than £50,000 over the previous five years. By the following year, Dyke was earning a salary of £347,000, augmented by a performance-related bonus of £91,000. Performance indicators included the downsizing the workforce, a task he has set about with gusto.[16]

Like Hollick, Dyke is another grammar-school boy. Originally a Marks & Spencer trainee and local newspaper journalist, he went on to become a mature student at York University, and stood unsuccessfully as a Labour candidate in the 1977 Greater London Council elections. By this period, he was working as a researcher at London Weekend Television, where he enjoyed rapid promotion.

Dyke was soon poached to preside over the dumbing down of the breakfast channel TV-am. Out went heavyweight current affairs coverage, in came Roland Rat. Thereafter his career took him back to LWT, where he introduced such programmes as *Blind Date* and *Beadle's About*, and rose to the rank of chief executive. Thanks to the company's executive share option scheme, Dyke became a millionaire in 1991.

He was ousted from the top job in 1994, although a £9m pay-off must surely have eased the pain. A few months later, he was one of a dozen or so senior media figures invited to a party held at the home of LWT colleague Barry Cox, where substantial donations were gathered towards Blair's campaign to become Labour leader. Dyke wrote out a cheque for £10,000, and also contributed to Jack Cunningham's Industry Forum group.

Within the year, Dyke was recruited by Pearson Television as chairman and chief executive. While in that job, he donated £25,000 to Labour's 1997 election funds. Shortly after Labour took office, he was charged with drawing up a charter setting out the rights and responsibilities of NHS patients, not a task for which he had any recognisable background.

Dyke was also involved in the controversy over BSkyB's bid for Manchester United, which he has supported all his life, perhaps oddly in light of his London origins. By now a director of the club, he even offered to resign as a mark of opposition to the offer. But this and all other outside interests were dropped on taking over at the Beeb, where he has presided over its increasing commercialisation and a reduced commitment to serious current affairs and arts programmes.

More recently, Dyke has been joined at the BBC by another of Labour's longstanding business supporters. Gavyn Davies was appointed chairman in September 2001. He has certainly caused controversy since taking up the post, especially after publicly accusing 'southern, white, middle-class, middle-aged and well-educated' viewers of a conspiracy to 'hijack' BBC output. Remarks like that hardly give the impression that the dynamic New Labour duo of Dyke and Davies are cut of Reithian cloth.

Davies previously worked as chief international economist and senior partner in the London operation of Wall Street bank Goldman Sachs on a salary of around £2m a year. In addition, he pocketed a reported £15m in August 2000, after selling 219,000 shares in his employer. The total value of his shareholding has been put at around £85m. Once a journalist asked him if he felt guilty about being extremely rich. 'I think I may have felt like that as a young kid, but I grew out of it,' came the deadpan reply.[17]

Davies was born in Rhodesia, and studied at both Oxford and Cambridge Universities before joining the Number 10 policy unit at the age of 23, working as an adviser in both the Wilson and Callaghan governments. Under Callaghan, Davies pushed a prototype 'right to buy' scheme for council tenants. That policy later became a reality under Thatcher, all but destroying social housing in Britain in the process. It was in this period that he met Sue Nye, later to become his wife. Nye now runs Gordon Brown's private office, and the couple's kids acted as bridesmaid and pageboy at Brown's wedding to Sarah Macaulay.

After Downing Street, Davies went on to make his fortune in the City. Initially he worked for Phillips and Drew, then Simon and Coates, and, from 1986 onwards, Goldman Sachs. In his own time, he continued to advise the Labour leadership as part of Kinnock's economic secretariat.

From the 1990s, he clearly aligned himself with Labour's moderniser faction, providing it with an invaluable bona fide City link. Testifying to his influence, a Labour source told a specialist City publication in 1996: 'Gavyn doesn't write policy, but he is our own City sounding board. We draft the ideas and Gavyn tells us what the effect will be on the economy and what the response will be in the markets.'[18]

Having become extremely wealthy , Davies began to devote more time to public appointments. In 1999, Labour appointed him to review BBC funding. Davies drew up plans for a huge increase in the licence fee, combined with the proposal that the state broadcaster strengthen its commercial activities. These must have met with the Government's approval, for he was appointed vice-chairman and then chairman of the BBC in short order. On taking up the latter post, he resigned from Goldman Sachs. His new salary, just £77,590, is a pittance compared to his City earnings.

Reinforcing the impression that this is something of a closed circle, Dyke's predecessor as director general at the BBC is another London Weekend Television old boy. Lord Birt was also a Labour Party member until his appointment in 1992, a matter he failed to declare to BBC governors.[19]

Today he is largely remembered at the corporation for the introduction of the new layers of bureaucracy celebrated as 'Birtism'. His tenure was also noted for a tax avoidance scheme under which the BBC's top man was technically retained as a freelance consultant, with his salary and perks paid into a private company. This even enabled him to claim a wardrobe allowance of £3,666. With much of this sum spent on Italian designer suits, the episode was naturally dubbed 'Armanigate'.

Created a peer in 2000, Birt sits as a crossbencher rather than a Labour supporter. That hasn't stopped Blair giving him an extensive policy role since he left the BBC with a six-figure early retirement pay-off.

Before the last election, Blair asked him to draw up a strategy to tackle crime, which was never published. Home Office officials let it be known they considered the document banal. Nevertheless, Birt continued to enjoy Blair's trust, and has now been appointed to Number 10's forward strategy unit, enjoined with the task of coming up with 'blues skies thinking' on vexatious questions.

Chief among these tasks is the development of transport policy, and Birt is assisted in this effort by former CBI chief Adair Turner, former United Utilities director Clive Elphick and erstwhile head of Coca-Cola UK Penny Hughes. Already there are concerns over Birt's lack of accountability, after he invoked his status as a Lord when refusing to give evidence to the Commons select committee on transport.

Birt also maintains a number of directorships that have given rise to perceived conflicts of interest. For instance, he sits as chairman of a company called Lynx New Media. Lynx is managed by the Virgin Media Group, part of the same Richard Branson empire that also includes Virgin Rail and Virgin Atlantic and thus companies with a natural interest in government transport policy.[20]

Completing New Labour's seeming inexhaustible supply of former LWT millionaire executives is Barry Cox, now deputy chairman of Channel 4. His key fundraising role in Blair's leadership campaign has already been discussed.

Cox has been appointed head of the Digital Stakeholders Group, a supervisory body for digital television. This has inevitably led to yet more accusations of cronyism on the one hand, and satellite broadcaster charges that he is biased toward terrestrial stations on the other.

But perhaps the media figure who has had the most impact on politics in formal terms is Gus Macdonald, Chancellor of the Duchy of Lancaster. The boy from the Gorbals left school at 14 for a job in the Glasgow shipyards. There he met two young trade unionists called Alex Ferguson and Billy Connolly, later to become respectively manager of Manchester United and a top comedian. Together the three activists lead an apprentices' strike, and Macdonald was recruited to the Trotskyist left.

He came to London in the mid-1960s to act as circulation manager for *Tribune*, then broke into journalism with the legendary *Sunday Times* Insight team and later *The Scotsman*. Broadcasting beckoned, and Macdonald went to work for Granada Television, producing *World in Action* and party conference coverage.

By now converted from revolutionary socialism to the free market, he joined Scottish Television as programme controller in 1985, rising to chief executive within five years. While in the top job he merged the station with Grampian and bought *The Herald* newspaper to create today's Scottish Media Group, boosting its market value from £50m to £500m. By now a pillar of Scottish business, the former shipyard militant became a director of the Bank of Scotland in 1998.

Shortly afterwards he was awarded a peerage, enabling him to serve as junior minister at Scottish Office for business and industry, even though he had not been a Labour Party member for 20 years. Indeed, Macdonald admits to having voted for all of the main parties at one time or another, presumably including the Tories. One former colleague was moved to remark: 'If Gus was a bit younger and the Scottish National Party looked like they could pull it off, I'm sure he would be a key player for them. If Thatcher had been around for another couple of years, he would have gone the whole way.'[21] Macdonald is currently Minister for the Cabinet Office and Chancellor of the Duchy of Lancaster.

The last of our Labour media supremos has promised that he will shortly be disappearing from the scene. Gerry Robinson – or Gerrard Jude Robinson as he styles himself in *Who's Who* – has pledged to retire in 2003, aged 55, and devote himself to sailing, painting and carpentry in his native Donegal.

Robinson was chairman of Granada from 1996 to 2000, and still serves as a non-executive director. He has also sat on the boards of ITN and BSkyB, and is chairman of wines and spirits group Allied Domecq. Before his very public change of heart a few years ago, Robinson was a convinced Tory. Yet a man who supported the Conservatives throughout the Thatcher years, even as they crushed the miners' strike and sought to impose the poll tax, was one of the stars of New Labour's 1997 election campaign.

In a party election broadcast shown just before the poll, Robinson is heard to boast: 'I have always voted Conservative. I've been a Conservative voter ever since I was allowed to vote.' Here he was, now backing Labour.[22]

Whichever party he chooses to support, his business career has certainly made him a wealthy man, with a £1m-plus salary and a share option award of £5.3m in 1999. The following year, he pocketed over £10m from the demerger of Granada and its Compass Hospitality catering arm. He is listed as a £5,000-plus donor to Labour in 1997, 1998 and 1999, and gave £20,000 in 2001. Since his political conversion, Robinson has been made chairman of the Arts Council, where he liaises closely with South Bank Centre chairman Hollick.

What is clear from all this is the extreme seriousness with which New Labour treats leading figures in the media. In men like Alli, Desmond, Hollick, Dyke, Davies, Robinson and Cox, it is now fair to speak of an entrenched New Labour media elite.

NOTES

[1] *Observer*, 24 February 2002

[2] *Observer*, 29 March 1998

[3] *Observer*, 30 March 1998

[4] Labour Party manifesto, 1992

[5] Labour Party manifesto, 1997

[6] *Daily Mirror*, 14 February 1998

[7] *Observer*, 29 March 1998

[8] *Observer*, 19 September 1999

[9] *Daily Telegraph*, 3 November 2001; *Guardian*, 3 November 2001

[10] *Guardian*, 15 November 2000

[11] *Daily Telegraph*, 4 February 2000

[12] *Observer*, 17 February 2002

[13] Andrew Rawnsley, *Servants of the People* (London, Penguin, 2000), pp.170–1

[14] *Daily Telegraph*, 12 October 2001

[15] *Daily Telegraph*, 14 May 2002

[16] *Daily Telegraph*, 5 July 2001; *Daily Telegraph*, 14 July 2000

[17] *Daily Telegraph*, 16 March 2002

[18] Cited in Robin Ramsay, *The Rise of New Labour*, p.94

[19] *Sunday Times*, 6 June 1999

[20] *Observer*, 3 February 2002

[21] *Sunday Times*, 12 December 1999; *Independent on Sunday*, 2 January 1993

[22] www.psr.keele.ac.uk/area/uk/pebs/pblab97.htm as of 16 November 2001

13. 'HOUSTON, WE HAVE A PROBLEM': LABOUR AND THE ENVIRONMENT

ENRON'S sudden collapse in late 2001 – the largest and most spectacular corporate failure in US history – probably damaged Labour more than any business scandal since Maxwell. Enrongate hit home not because of the size of the bung, which the company could have paid out of its petty cash box, but the sheer scale of the company's misdeeds, and its explicit admission that the money it gave the party was seen as the price of access to the top.[1]

Enron's support for Labour reportedly totalled just £38,000. In this era of £1m-plus political donations, that is not qualitatively more than the £25,000 it gave the Tories, and a pittance compared to the massive donations doled out across the Atlantic to Democrats and Republicans alike.

Enron's US lobbying expenditure in 2001 came to £3.2m. Campaign contributions went to 71 senators and 188 members of the House of Representatives, including 53 out of 58 members of the House energy and commerce committee. Keeping links to both main British parties open was simply an insignificant each-way bet in comparison.

It's not even as if Labour was unaware that Enron was a potential liability. The company had long been perceived as a nasty piece of work and critics of Labour's corporate links consistently pointed to its unsavoury track record in the Third World.

It is the only company – as opposed to government – ever to be the subject of an Amnesty International report. Villagers at Dhabol, near Bombay in India, were brutally beaten up by police and Enron security staff, simply for protesting against pollution and excess water use caused by an Enron power plant project. Demonstrators' homes were broken into, and protesters warned they would be in the line of fire if they continued to oppose the scheme. Thousands were jailed for their legitimate protest.

The plant was later closed after its sole client – the Maharashtra State Electricity Board – refused to pay bills of $45m, arguing that Enron was ripping it off by charging four times more than domestic producers.[2]

When violence failed to win the day, Enron used its political clout to lay down the law to one of the largest countries on earth. Chief executive Kenneth Lay insisted that India could face US sanctions unless it recompensed Enron for the $1bn cost incurred in building the plant. Given Lay's ties to President Bush, India knew he wasn't bluffing.

Enron's connections to the man in the White House date back to its origins in the merger of two gas pipeline businesses in Houston in 1985. The company was savvy enough to take full advantage of the privatisation of state and city utilities and the deregulation of energy prices, and soon realised the advantages of keeping its fingers in the political pie. Enron carefully cultivated those who could smooth the path to its corporate goals. As a Texas-based concern, its lobbying naturally started in the Lone Star state.

Lay became a personal friend of governor George W. Bush. The two men were on better than first name terms. Dubya routinely referred to his buddy by the nickname 'Kenny Boy'. Cementing that friendship, Enron became the largest donor to Bush's victorious presidential campaign, giving $825,000. At least 30 senior Bush administration officials and ambassadors held Enron stock, and access to the US government was readily available to the company.

By now Enron had hit the corporate big time, after it diversified into trading energy derivatives in the realisation that there was more money to be had in making markets than in actually generating power. Energy derivatives are so-called because they 'derive' from the underlying value of a yet-to-be-produced unit of electricity or a future barrel of oil. For a small deposit, the owner of a derivative buys the right – but not the obligation – to buy or sell the underlying asset at a future date, at a specified price.

Derivatives were originally designed as a hedge against adverse market movements. But because the right deal can land huge profits for a small outlay, most transactions are now speculative. That suited Enron's purposes admirably. It went on to trade derivatives based on fibre-optic cable capacity, newsprint, advertising space and everything but the kitchen sink.

The rise of the Internet came as a huge boost, allowing Enron to make many of its trades online. *Fortune* magazine hailed it as America's most innovative company, the perfect weightless business model for the new economy. It rapidly became the largest company of its kind, and, by 2000, the seventh-largest in America, with a market capitalisation of over $100bn.

It had long been established in Britain. In 1989, Conservative Secretary of State for Energy John Wakeham gave Enron's Teesside Power subsidiary a £700m contract to build the world's largest combined heat and power plant at Grangetown near Middlesbrough, as part of Britain's electricity privatisation programme.

Grangetown's subsequent safety record caused concern even before Enron's financial troubles. In August 2001, three employees were killed after a transformer exploded. Three years earlier, it had been fined £10,000 by the Health and Safety Executive, after a worker received 62 per cent body burns when liquid naptha leaked from an untightened pipe. Yet Grangetown did not recognise trade unions, leaving them unable to play the vital role in workplace safety they undertake elsewhere in the power industry.[3]

But for Wakeham and Enron, this was the start of a beautiful friendship. After leaving government, Wakeham became a non-executive director, serving on the audit and compliance committee. He earned £80,000 a year, with consultancy fees of £4,000 a month on top. Given that Wakeham has a qualified chartered accountant qualification, it should not have been too much to expect that his audit role should have given him some sort of handle on Enron's book-keeping.

Wakeham pleads both ignorance and innocence. But Enron's collapse forced his resignation from his major role in public life. As chairman of the Press Complaints Commission, the accountant incapable of supervising his own company's accounts was charged with supervising Britain's media. Yet for several months after his departure, he stayed on the payroll, picking up his £156,000 salary without even having to put in the two mornings a week he previously worked to earn it.

Under New Labour, Enron's expansion in the UK accelerated. In 1998, the company – by now sponsoring Labour events – sought government permission to buy Wessex Water, which it regarded as a first step into the international water privatisation market. The deal got the go-ahead from Secretary of State for Trade and Industry Peter Mandelson, without the widely anticipated reference to the Monopolies and Mergers Commission. Under Enron's control, Wessex's pollution record saw it fined on several occasions for the discharge of sewage into rivers and streams.

The following year, Industry minister Helen Liddell gave Enron permission to build a gas-fired power plant on the Isle of Grain in Kent. In so doing, she overturned Labour's previous moratorium on gas-fired power stations, designed to protect the coal industry by reversing the Conservative 'dash for gas'. Her decision was endorsed by Mandelson's successor, Stephen Byers. True, the Department of Trade and Industry was subject to considerable pressure as the Clinton administration pressed Enron's case. Enron had also hired leading lobbyists – and Labour donors – GJW. Among the employees working on the account was Karl Milner, former aide to Chancellor Gordon Brown and bit player in the cash for access affair.

Enron secured at least seven meetings with government ministers and advisers in this period. The $64,000 question – or at least the £38,000 question – is whether the donations made a difference. Enron itself certainly thought so. Ralph Hodge, head of the company in Britain and recipient of a CBE in the 2001 new year honours, explained: 'I do not think we would have been successful at getting [to] the table without donations . . . It is clear that in the current climate, sponsorship and donations are the most efficient ways of getting access.'[4] A Labour-connected lobbyist added: 'Enron had a reputation for being aggressive, even more than most American corporations, in demanding meetings once they'd paid their money for sponsorships.'[5]

Even after Enron had secured a political decision clearly detrimental to the coal industry, it still sought to snap up one of Britain's few remaining deep mines. As late as autumn 2001, it was in the running to buy Hatfield colliery near Doncaster, scene of the film *Brassed Off*, which had gone into liquidation with the loss of 220 jobs.

But now the fates were to intervene. Enron executives had formed a series of partnerships between its directors and business associates, nominally independent but under Enron's de facto control. These off balance sheet vehicles facilitated concealment of massive debts. Registered offshore, they also enabled the company to avoid US taxes almost completely. Creative accountancy enabled them to record non-existent profits that totalled – or more pointedly, didn't total – at least $1bn between July 2000 and October 2001 alone. To take one example, Enron and video store chain Blockbuster set up a perfectly proper pilot scheme to experiment with video on demand to 1,000 homes. Enron sold its future earnings from the project to a bank for $115m, and booked that sum as a profit.

The Enron scam worked well enough while the company's share price rode high. Lay routinely used online chats with the workforce to insist that shares were a bargain, urging them to talk up the company to their family and friends. Many of the workforce ploughed their pension plans and savings into their employer's stock. On Wall Street, Citigroup made a similar case to a more financially sophisticated audience.

But come the dot com bust, Enron stood revealed as a virtual company making only virtual profits. Meltdown started in November 2001, as its plunging share price generated bid speculation. Both BP and Shell considered an offer, but were deterred by the sheer level of Enron's debts. Italy's Enel and Germany's Eon – then in the process of acquiring Powergen – were also interested.

Enron was forced to restate its accounts, revealing the falsified profit figures for all to see. Managers, with the help of accountants Arthur Andersen, began deleting e-mails and running incriminating documents through shredding machines. By December, Enron filed for bankruptcy with debts of £55bn. Most of its 25,000 employees were out of a job. Their shares – priced $90 each only a year before – were now all but worthless. British banks including Barclays, the Royal Bank of Scotland and Abbey National were stung for £600m. Yet a couple of dozen senior executives, well aware that the company was going under, cashed in 17.3 million shares before things fell apart. Kenny Boy himself was one of the most prolific sellers, pocketing $101m.

'HOUSTON, WE HAVE A PROBLEM': LABOUR AND THE ENVIRONMENT

In the British public's mind, New Labour was guilty by association. Moreover, Arthur Andersen's winning ways with waste paper made Enron a double whammy. Andersen and former sister firm Accenture – known until 1999 as Andersen Consulting – both had close ties with Britain's governing party.

The Tories had stripped Arthur Andersen of the right to receive government contracts in 1982, after it failed to prevent fraud at Northern Ireland-based car maker DeLorean, resulting in the loss of massive amounts of public money. Andersen had even then mastered the knack of doing whatever it takes to keep a client happy. Three years later, the British government sued the firm for £200m. The action dragged on for years, excluding the company from all the lucrative privatisation work of the Thatcher period.

Still out in the cold by the mid-1990s, both wings of Andersen actively courted the opposition. In 1993, Andersen Consulting offered its services to an internal Labour commission on social justice. The following year, the commission's deputy chair Patricia Hewitt left her job as Kinnock's press officer to become Andersen Consulting's director of research. Three years later, the firm arranged a seminar for Labour backbenchers on how to handle being a minister. Meanwhile, Arthur Andersen provided Gordon Brown with substantial cut-price help in devising his policies on the windfall tax, capital gains tax and advanced corporation tax.

After Labour's 1997 election win, the legal action was rapidly settled, following the Treasury solicitor's proposals for mediation. Andersen paid just £21m, only one-tenth of what the Conservatives had demanded. It went on to advise the Government on numerous matters, including the London Underground sell-off, Railtrack, the Millennium Dome, Education Action Zones, the Jubilee Line extension, British Nuclear Fuels, the air traffic control privatisation and many other deals.

Two senior Andersen staffers, Chris Wales and Chris Osborne, became advisers to Brown and Robinson at the Treasury. The firm also proved helpful to beleaguered Paymaster General Geoffrey Robinson. As liquidator of Robert Maxwell's private companies, Andersen controlled many of the papers relating to the £200,000 payment allegedly made by Maxwell to Robinson, but prevented parliamentary investigators from seeing them.

Hewitt, meanwhile, had got herself elected MP for Leicester West, and was rapidly promoted to Economic Secretary to the Treasury, then e-business minister. After the 2001 victory, she became Secretary of State for Trade and Industry, giving the firm a former employee in high places.

But the backlash from Enron has left Andersen no longer in a position to call-in any outstanding favours. Following the defection of a string of major clients, Andersen is in the process of being dismembered, with practices in various countries sold off to the highest bidder. It has since emerged that

Andersen had also audited the accounts of US telecoms major WorldCom, which by mid-2002 was found to have systematically overstated its profits by billions of dollars.

The Enron affair underlines that Labour in office has proved no more green than red. Short-term relationships with energy companies are placed ahead of broader environmental imperatives that would require some sort of limitation of their activities. In particular, British Petroleum appears to enjoy something close to favourite company status.

Following its acquisitions of Amoco in 1999 and Atlantic Richfield and Burmah Castrol the following year, BP is now the world's third-largest private sector oil group. It has always been a very political concern, with the worldwide scope of its business naturally facilitating close ties to some sections of the Foreign Office. But, like all oil multinationals, its activities in countries from Colombia to Azerbaijan have generated extensive criticism from both greens and human rights campaigners.

BP has of late expended much time and effort trying to convince sceptics of its right-on credentials, very publicly proclaiming its intention to hire more gay employees. An entire advertising campaign centred on the notion that the nasty old oil giant is now an environmentally friendly energy producer that is somehow 'Beyond Petroleum'. But BP's close ties with New Labour have given rise to an alternative version: Blair Petroleum. The crossover in personnel terms indicates just how much influence it exercises on government energy policy.

Labour's desire to bring BP on board is best illustrated by the case of Lord Simon of Highbury, who accepted a peerage immediately after the 1997 election, enabling him to take up a dual role as both Minister for Competitiveness in Europe and Minister for Trade. Blair gushed: 'The post I have created for him is vital to the future success of our country. It will cover the whole competitiveness agenda in Europe, pushing forward our objectives of completing the single market and spreading flexible labour markets throughout Europe.'[6]

In keeping with convention, Simon resigned all directorships before commencing ministerial office. In his case, this meant not only stepping down as chairman of BP, which had paid him £1.2m in salary and shares the year before, but also leaving directorships at Deutsche Bank, Rio Tinto and Allianz AG. His earnings from such positions had left him sufficiently wealthy to decline a ministerial salary.

Simon was nevertheless entitled to hang on to various shareholdings, including his £2.25m stake in BP, which went into a trust. But he failed to declare his interest in the company in the House of Lords register of interests, despite a ministerial brief clearly impacting on the oil industry. The Tories – in a surprising display of parliamentary tactical competence –

were able relentlessly to push the point home. Simon was forced to sell up, donating the £360,000 by which the shares had appreciated since Labour took office to charity. The Government announced that Simon would not henceforth be involved with any matter that could conceivably affect BP.

Partly as a result of this row, partly out of his personal frustration at lack of progress towards a single currency, Simon stepped down from the Government after just two years. He keeps some sort of foothold in politics as an adviser to the Cabinet Office, when not otherwise engaged on the European advisory board of Morgan Stanley Dean Witter and as an advisory director of Unilever.

While hardly a New Labour business success story, the Simon saga is just one of numerous interfaces between the company and the party. Many BP executives hold public appointments. The best known is probably Bryan Sanderson, former BP Amoco managing director and now chairman of BUPA and non-executive director at Corus, the privatised British Steel. Sanderson, who picked up a CBE in 1999, sits as chairman of the Learning Skills Council, and serves on the Industrial Development Advisory Board, a DTI competitiveness taskforce, and a company law review steering group. From 1997 to 1998, Sanderson was also a member of the Labour Party's advisory group on industrial competition policy. He also joins David Watson, BP group treasurer, on the UK round table on sustainable development.

Links don't end there. Rodney Chase, BP managing director of exploration, sits on an advisory committee for business and the environment, alongside BP colleague Dr John Harford. Alan Jones, general manager of BP Exploration, is a member of the oil and gas industry taskforce, while BP Amoco company secretary Judith Hanratty is on the board of the Competition Commission. The company's head of chemicals, Byron Groat, has been helping the DTI on competitiveness issues.

Chairman John Browne was awarded a peerage to add to his knighthood after doing his level best to help the government during the fuel crisis of 2000. His remuneration package has now hit £7m a year, after picking up a 58 per cent rise in 2001.

The ties go both ways. Leading Labour moderniser, pollster Philip Gould, undertakes research and conducts focus groups for BP, in much the same way as he does for the party. Meanwhile, two Labour peers – Lord Gordon and Lady Smith, widow of former leader John Smith – sit on BP's Scottish advisory board.

Other important figures in the BP/New Labour nexus are Nick Butler and Anji Hunter. Butler is BP's group policy advisor, and one-time Labour parliamentary candidate, close to both Mandelson and Jonathan Powell. While routinely tipped for a government job, such an appointment has yet to materialise. The most popular explanation is that Butler doesn't fancy the cut in salary.

Recent BP recruit Hunter is a friend of Blair's from school days, who went on to become his private secretary. For years she played one of the most influential roles in his private office, controlling who got access to the Prime Minister and for exactly how long. When she first mulled a switch to the private sector, Blair was so concerned to keep her that he promoted her to director of government operations, on a salary of £120,000. But in late 2001, and amid suggestions that she had fallen out with Alastair Campbell, Hunter left anyway, accepting a job as BP's director of communications. Her contacts book alone could well prove worth her £200,000-a-year pay cheque.

Much criticism of BP's closeness to government ensued. The company appears to have been stung by the backlash, and in March 2002, following the Mittal and Enron affairs, announced that it was to halt all political donations worldwide. BP has not made any donations in Britain for at least a decade, although it gave £600,000 to US politicians in 2001. It will continue other corporate lobbying activities.

Another big disappointment for greens is the Government's stance on genetically modified foods. Massive consumer resistance has so far been the main obstacle to their widespread introduction: the public simply does not wish to buy them. Yet there is an obvious intention to force them down British throats. So much for consumer sovereignty. The GM testing programme is rapidly being expanded, with 44 new trials announced in January 2002. Many will be planted so close to existing crops that cross-contamination is virtually guaranteed.[7]

Officially, Tony Blair maintains that that while he is not a proponent of genetic modification, such crops should nevertheless be evaluated scientifically. In practice, he has consistently rejected calls for limitations on their use, hitting out against media 'scaremongering' and 'nonsense about Frankenstein foods'.[8]

Yet anything Labour has to say on the issue is automatically compromised by the Government's links to the GM industry, symbolised by just one man. Ministerial responsibility for genetically modified crops has been given to the party's largest financial backer, despite his business interests in GM crops. David Sainsbury – an Old Etonian, although that fact is omitted from *Who's Who* – has given Labour over £9m in recent years. He can afford it, of course. Sainsbury is Britain's third-richest man, worth around £3bn.

This is someone clearly used to bankrolling politicians. He was a major financial supporter of the SDP in the early 1980s, remaining a trustee until 1990. He did not vote at all in 1992, and, as late as 1995, his support for Labour was decidedly lukewarm. The family firm, J. Sainsbury plc, which owns the Sainsbury's supermarket chain, issued a statement that its boss had 'expressed his personal opinion that if he votes at the next general election, it is likely it would be for the Labour Party'.[9]

Just three years later, the 'don't know' floating voter was both a Labour peer and Science minister in a Labour government. With an unearned income estimated at £35m or more a year, he was, like Lord Simon, happy enough to do the job gratis. Sainsbury sees no problem with enormous generosity to Labour on the one hand and his unelected office on the other. He simply argues that he is 'proud to support the Labour Party financially alongside the many other people who contribute to it', presumably as he was once proud to support the SDP.[10]

Although Sainsbury stood down as Sainsbury's chief executive on appointment, his role in government naturally turned the spotlight on the company's activities. Each planning decision for out-of-town supermarkets that went Sainsbury's way attracted notice, especially after Blair stressed his sympathies for such schemes.

But most controversial of all is Sainsbury's continued ownership of two genetics companies, Diatech and Innotech Investments. While his shares were placed in the same trust as his supermarket stake when he became a minister, he still benefits from any profits they make.

In addition, Lord Sainsbury funds GM research at the Sainsbury Laboratory in Norwich by around £3m a year, channelling the money through his Gatsby Charitable Foundation. It is also backed by the state. In the last year of the Major administration, it was given £300,000. Since Sainsbury became Science minister in July 1998, government support has risen to £1.2m a year, a 300 per cent increase.

As if the Science minister's personal imprimateur for GM foods was not enough, lobbyists are engaged to make sure New Labour hears what the industry has to say. One of those charged with getting the message across has been David Hill, former Labour chief spokesperson turned director of lobbyist Bell Pottinger, who has worked closely with GM food giant Monsanto on media presentation. Monsanto representatives have met Secretary of State for Agriculture Jack Cunningham, his deputy Jeff Rooker and Environment minister Michael Meacher. Bell Pottinger denies that Hill set up these occasions. Monsanto director of public affairs Ann Foster revealingly comments: 'He doesn't do political work for us. If I want to see a minister I just do it myself.'[11]

All told, some 16 GM food firms met civil service officials or ministers from the environment and agriculture departments on 81 occasions between May 1997 and February 1999. Top of the list was Zeneca, with 31 meetings, followed by Hill's clients Monsanto with 22.[12]

Another important player in the GM world is Swiss chemical giant Novartis, which is developing genetically modified maize. The firm's British offshoot, Novartis Pharmaceuticals UK, spent an undisclosed sum sponsoring a seminar for newly elected Labour MPs after the 1997 election, earning it a place on the £5,000-plus sponsors list for that year. Novartis also retains its former employee, Labour MP Nick Palmer, as a parliamentary adviser.[13]

The Government's analysis of wider environmental issues, in so far as it has one, seems to be based on the premise that the market forces that caused most of the problems can somehow be harnessed to correct them.

Blair speeches on environmental concerns have been notably few, perhaps indicative of the lack of priority they are accorded. Even when they do occur, they are frequently delivered on the platforms of corporate front groups that exist primarily to paint multinationals green.

A case in point is his October 2000 presentation to an audience of members of the Confederation of British Industry and the Green Alliance, his first on the environment since taking office three years earlier. Revealingly, the speech was entitled 'Richer and Greener'. Blair stressed that safeguarding the environment was now a world market worth £345bn, as large as pharmaceuticals or aerospace.[14]

Of course, the Green Alliance is not a body to which the ordinary environmental activist can sign up. Membership is restricted to companies, which pay £2,500 for the privilege. The 'greens' we are talking about here include Thames Water, fined many times for breaches of pollution controls; oil majors Shell and BP Amoco; Glaxo SmithKline; and National Power.

The Prime Minister's more recent public utterances have carried the same richer and greener message. 'Green technologies are on the verge of becoming one of the next waves in the knowledge economy revolution,' Blair told the Worldwide Fund for Nature in 2001. The global market for environmental goods and services could be worth £440bn a year by 2010, he went on. 'I want Britain to be a leading player in this revolution.'[15] Don't worry about global warming then. Just think of it as a business opportunity.

NOTES
[1] For a perceptive left-wing account of the Enron affair, see Lynn Walsh's article 'The Enron Affair' in *Socialism Today* magazine, March 2002
[2] *Financial Times*, 24 August 2001
[3] *Private Eye*, 24 August 2001
[4] *Daily Mail*, 29 January 2002
[5] *Guardian*, 28 January 2002
[6] *Financial Times*, 8 May 1997
[7] *Guardian*, 5 February 2002
[8] *Guardian*, 25 September 1999
[9] *Guardian*, 19 June 1995
[10] *Guardian*, 9 September 1999
[11] *Daily Mail*, 13 February 1999

[12] Ibid.
[13] *Daily Mail,* 6 February 1999
[14] *Daily Telegraph,* 25 October 2000
[15] *Guardian,* 7 March 2002

14. 'MORE PRO-BUSINESS THAN EVER BEFORE': LABOUR'S SECOND TERM

EVEN if the date of the poll had to be put back a month or so on account of the foot-and-mouth pandemic, 2001 was always going to be an election year. And even before the official campaign began, New Labour was doing its best to stress its pro-capitalist credentials.

The theme was uncompromisingly hammered home in an interview Blair gave to *Forbes Global*, a right-wing American business magazine that advertises itself under the pithy but accurate slogan 'capitalist tool'. Billionaire owner Steve Forbes is a former hard-right Republican presidential hopeful. Blair's explicit message was that the main problem with Thatcherism was that it had not done enough to foster private enterprise, an argument seemingly on a par with the notion that Pol Pot was just too damn soft on the urban petty bourgeoisie.

The Prime Minister told the publication: 'Basically, the 1980s produced in the Thatcherite reforms of that period a more flexible labour market in the trade union reform [*sic*], a commitment to enterprise that we have kept.' The key theme of Labour's second term would be:

> creating the right enterprise culture in Britain, which we still haven't driven all the way down in our country, by any means at all. I want to see far more emphasis on entrepreneurship in schools, far closer links between universities and business. I want to see us develop a far greater entrepreneurial culture. We have only just gone beneath the surface of this so far.[1]

The text was reinforced by Gordon Brown during a meeting in Manchester at the start of his pre-budget consultation process, when he proclaimed: 'Our aim is to create the stronger enterprise culture that America enjoys.'[2]

Formal overtures to business leaders began in earnest in February, with what was billed as a 'pre-election summit' at Chequers, the state-owned country house. Top business figures in attendance included BT chairman Sir Iain Vallance, Terry Leahy of Tesco, Glaxo SmithKline's Sir Richard Sykes, Pearson's Marjorie Scardino, BSkyB chief executive Tony Ball, Bass chairman Sir Ian Prosser, Unilever boss and euro campaigner Niall FitzGerald, Ford

Europe chairman Nick Scheele and Marconi's Lord Simpson. Also on the guest list was Vodaphone chief executive Chris Gent, former chairman of the Young Conservatives and still a Tory as far as anybody is aware.

Reportedly, the main theme of the gathering was competitiveness, with agenda items covering the euro, regulation and taxes. But Blair and Brown's real purpose was primarily to reassure their guests that whatever flights of rhetoric Labour would shortly be forced to resort to in order to placate the core vote, it was still listening to business concerns.[3]

Prawn cocktail offensive take three was to be led by e-commerce minister Patricia Hewitt, former director of research at Andersen Consulting, who was already lined up as the next Secretary of State for Trade and Industry. Her efforts were assisted by Lord Hollick and Lord Sainsbury, Labour's top two fully on-board business stars. The programme was largely organised by Roger Sharp, head of Labour's business liaison unit and a recent signing from the pro-euro Business in Europe campaign.[4]

Hewitt and Co successfully secured some new – if relatively minor league – business endorsements. These included Adam Singer, chief executive of cable TV group Telewest, and Russell Chambers, managing director of online investment bank Wit Soundview Europe. But Labour was insistent that this time it was simply setting out its stall to business, with fundraising not even on the agenda. 'It has nothing to do with getting donations,' an anonymous party official told the *Financial Times*.[5]

Finally came the launch of the campaign proper. Business featured heavily from the outset. Blair's first official campaign engagement was a meeting with businessmen in Coventry, accompanied by Stephen Alambritis of the Federation of Small Businesses.

The next task was to organise one of those obligatory round robin letters signed by business chiefs that have been a curious feature of recent British elections. The tactic was first tried by the Tories in 1997, when the *Daily Mail* ran a front-page splash based on a missive signed by 38 people – hyped up as 'a remarkable array of top businessmen', with the solitary token woman not deemed worth a mention – arguing that a Labour government would damage Britain's prosperity. In an exercise patently got up by Conservative Central Office, signatories were exclusively known Tories, including Chris Gent, Unipart's John Neill, Sir Stanley Kalms of Dixons, and Neville Simms of Tarmac.

According to the charge sheet, Labour had not yet got its head round the success of privatised industry, offered 'obsessive support' to the EU social chapter and the minimum wage, still believed in regulation and intervention, and did not know how to keep unemployment down. Given that the dole queue stretched way beyond three million in the early 1980s, keeping people in work could hardly be considered a Tory speciality either.[6]

This shot was clearly judged successful, and repeated during the 2001 campaign on a larger scale. This time 145 business worthies signed up for a similar pro-Tory letter, placed on this occasion in the *Daily Telegraph*. Labour tried a similar stunt in Rupert Murdoch's *Times*, but could only muster 58 business supporters. Moreover, as the Conservatives triumphantly pointed out, their signatories generally hailed from rather larger concerns than Labour's.[7]

The Tory petition was organised by Sir Clive Thompson, a past president of the CBI best known for his extreme disdain for trade unionism, once likening dealing with organised labour to 'pest control'. Other star names included Lord Bell, Rupert Hambro, Lord Harris, Lord Hanson, Sir Stanley Kalms, Sir Michael Richardson, Eddy Shah, Lord Sheppard, and Lord Young. With the exception of *Lock, Stock and Two Smoking Barrels* producer Matthew Vaughn, it was otherwise pretty much a case of round up the usual Thatcherite suspects.

This time the gripes concentrated on increased taxes and greater regulation in a second Labour term, which would 'pose a significant risk to Britain's future prosperity'. Moreover, the reforms of the Thatcher and Major years were increasingly being taken for granted, the public was warned. 'Britain's reputation of having an attractive regime, intelligent regulation and a flexible labour market is still under threat,' it was alleged, despite Blair's assurances to the contrary in *Forbes Global*.[8]

But conspicuously missing from the Tory missive were Gent and Sir John Browne of BP, heads of two of the biggest businesses in Europe. Both had been neutralised by New Labour.

Labour's response saw business leaders back the proposition that:

> Labour has done much to create the stable business environment that British companies and overseas investors need. Inflation has been kept low, unemployment and interest rates have fallen and economic growth has averaged 2.7 per cent. We believe that business should support the party that since May 1997 has done so much to promote stable economic growth and a renewed spirit of enterprise in the British people.

This letter was put together by Sir Terence Conran, and also centred on established supporters and donors. Among the signatories, which included seven executives from FTSE 100 companies, were Lord Haskins, Lord Hollick, Lord Patel, Alec Reed, Bryan Sanderson, Sir Trevor Chinn, Chai Patel, Gerry Robinson, Gulam Noon, Adam Singer, John Napier of Kelda Group, David Potter of Psion, Moni Varma of Veetee Rice and serial director Allan Leighton. Other names included Chris Powell, head of Labour's former advertising firm and brother of Blair's chief of staff Jonathan, and Sandy Leitch of Zurich Financial, a financial supporter of New Labour.[9]

Brown expressed himself 'grateful' for the signatories' support, adding that the letter was 'a sign of the relationship which this New Labour government is forging with business'.[10]

As with the Tories, some former backers were conspicuous by their absence. Body Shop's Anita Roddick, a 1997 supporter, did not renew her endorsement, disquieted over the Government's record on environmental issues. Another surprising omission was Unilever's Niall FitzGerald, a leading single currency enthusiast.

Labour's next move was to publish a special manifesto for small businesses, promising companies the chance to scrutinise new regulations that affect them. Under proposals masterminded by Hewitt, Lord Haskins' better regulation taskforce was to be strengthened by secondments from the private sector, including small businesses. More dealings with Government would be possible online, VAT would be simplified, and more details on early growth funding made available.[11]

Towards the end of May, Labour published a second manifesto for business before a selected audience of 100 corporate leaders, under the title 'The Best Place to do Business'. It's official, then. Britain now equals business heaven. Even the venue for the launch was symbolic, taking place in the London offices of US-owned financial newswire service Bloomberg.

That company's founder, Michael Bloomberg, shortly afterwards became mayor of New York on a Republican ticket. Although a lifelong Democrat, the billionaire had apparently found it easier to win the Republican nomination, and wasn't going to let a little thing like party affiliation get in his way. His massive campaign spend simply swept the opposition aside. Incidentally, Bloomberg – the UK company as opposed to the man himself – is a financial backer of New Labour.

In surroundings designed to symbolise the fast pace of life in the City, Blair proclaimed his desire for a 'deeper and intensified' relationship with business.[12] Policies on offer that day included deregulation, fewer restrictions on mergers, speeding up planning inquires and lesser penalties for bankruptcy. While the manifesto was broadly welcomed by business, the CBI tartly pointed out that it contained little that was not already known party policy, and that the whole launch was little more than a presentational stunt.

Business premises featured elsewhere in the campaign trail, too. Little more than a week before the election, Blair and Stephen Byers visited the British headquarters of Microsoft – surely the world's most powerful corporation – just before it was due to launch a new software package.

The Prime Minister and his wife were pictured being given a demonstration of the system in front of a giant screen counting down the days, hours, minutes and seconds to the release. Television viewers saw Tony and Cherie beautifully framed by the Microsoft logo. Asked if the company would find the publicity beneficial, a Microsoft press officer enthusiastically gushed: 'Yes, two days before the launch, it's tremendous.'[13]

As a significant supplier to the public sector, Microsoft has solid commercial reasons for wanting to stay on good terms with the Government. Within months of Blair's visit, it signed a £50m deal to licence its operating software to the NHS. Microsoft supremo Bill Gates – the world's richest man – has also discussed with Secretary of State for Health Alan Milburn the supply of software for a NHS 'university' online.

To make up for losing the war of round robins, Labour was clearly victorious in the battle of the 2001 CBI dinner. Indeed, the event, held at London's Grosvenor House Hotel, made history in its own small way. Presumably for the first time ever, not one Conservative frontbencher accepted the CBI's invitation to attend. Hague, Portillo and even Tory trade and industry spokesperson David Heathcoat-Amory pleaded other engagements. By contrast, Brown, Byers and four other Labour ministers didn't need asking twice. 'I have been pleased with the working relationship the government has had with the CBI,' proclaimed CBI director-general Digby Jones. 'They have shown they want to talk to us because they want to know what business is thinking.'[14]

Even Tory open letter organiser Sir Clive Thompson, CBI vice-president, was forced to admit: 'This is not a government of the centre-left, it is a government of the centre-right. So it is understandable that a number of people should be backing it.'[15]

On 7 June Labour was returned to office for a second time. Somehow it had lost three million voters between 1997 and 2001. Labour was elected with the support of 42 per cent of those who did vote, and just 25 per cent of those entitled to vote. Add to the equation the many people – mainly young, poor, and/or black – who don't see the point of being on the electoral register, and the Government can claim active endorsement from perhaps one in five of those it governs. That is a frightening statistic for democracy.

Yet the agenda for the second term is just as unrelentingly skewed in favour of private enterprise as it was for the first. Brown, still seen in some quarters as a closet Old Labourite, summed up the party's current ideology with the argument that 'the Labour Party is more pro-business, pro-wealth creation, pro-competition than ever before'.[16]

One of the forms that being more pro-business than ever before is likely to take is being more pro-privatisation than ever before. Intellectual justification has been provided by the Institute of Public Policy Research's commission on the role of private firms in public services over the next 20 years. The findings – published just after the election – called for a dramatic extension of contracting out in the public sector work over the next two decades, extending the method to take in clinical health services, schools management and most aspects of local government.[17]

213

The private sector should no longer be confined to the provision of capital under the PFI, since 'the crucial ingredient the private sector possesses and the public sector needs is management'. Given such recent triumphs of unfettered private sector managerial nous as Railtrack, Equitable Life and Marconi, the proposition is at least debatable. Instead, the Government is enjoined 'to reject the defeatist strand of thought which maintains that all new forms of private involvement in the delivery of public services should be put on hold'.[18]

The commission recommends that the Government allow private sector bids for a £1bn contract to replace some 3,000 general practitioners' premises and coordinate GP support services such as payroll, administration and IT. In the longer term, the private sector is envisaged as provider of health and community services for primary care trusts, on a contract basis. Voluntary and private management of state schools is not seen as an emergency measure, but an option open to all schools. School governing bodies should be entitled to hire privately run management services. Local authorities should be set targets for the proportion of services contracted in, while consortia of private prison operators should be encouraged.

Obviously the recommendations of the report – some already in the process of being implemented – offer business opportunities of considerable magnitude for many companies. So it is interesting to note who paid for much of the research, which cost as much as £200,000.

Backers included consultants KPMG, which has advised private sector clients on over 50 health service contracts; Norwich Union, which offers private health insurance and owns the privatised fund providing loans to doctors for surgery improvements; British Telecom, which sells IT consultancy services; and Serco, with over 400 public sector contracts. All four, in other words, have a direct financial stake in seeing New Labour open up as many public services as possible to for-profit private sector input.[19]

Further business input was guaranteed by commission chairman Martin Taylor, also chairman of WH Smith and adviser to Goldman Sachs. Another interesting participant was David Denison of ICL, the British wing of Fujitsu, who is charged with developing the company's relationships with local government. Denison represents the CBI on the Department of the Environment's local government procurement steering group.

How far the commission represented a disinterested search for policy-making truth, rather than a celebration of de facto convergence of interest between policy anoraks and major businesses dependent on lucrative public sector contracts must therefore be open to question.

The same questions can be asked about another favourite New Labour think tank, Demos, which has taken funding from British Gas, Cable and Wireless, NatWest, Shell, Northern Foods and Tesco.[20]

Blair's second term has already seen probably the most stunning confirmation yet of private enterprise's failure to deliver public services, in the shape of the Railtrack collapse. The experience calls into question much of what New Labour is trying to do with the public services as a whole, not least the entire rationale behind the creation of complex internal markets in entities it makes sense to run as a coordinated whole.

Railtrack's responsibilities included ensuring the maintenance of Britain's railway infrastructure, but the company did not actually do that work itself. Instead, it relied on around a dozen prime contractors, who in turn pushed the work out to an astonishing 2,000 subcontractors, creating the ridiculous degree of fragmentation so accurately parodied in Ken Loach's film *The Navigators*. In many cases, the prime contractors are exactly the same companies that are taking over London Underground.[21]

Railtrack defined its core competence as management, and farmed out everything else. By putting everything out to tender, costs can of course be ground down relentlessly. But the cohesion naturally inherent in an integrated single business cannot be replicated in such a complex network of contractual arrangements.

Railtrack, of course, emerged from the privatisation of British Rail. Labour was initially completely against the sell-off. Transport spokesperson Frank Dobson told the 1994 Labour conference: 'The next Labour government will reverse the break-up and privatisation of Britain's railways. We will bring the rail system back into public ownership and control.'[22] Had Labour maintained that renationalisation stance, City confidence would have been so undermined that the privatisation could never have taken place.

But the nearer it came to the election, the more the pledges were watered down. This provided the Conservatives with the political breathing space to go ahead with its criminal disposal of British Railways in 1996, at around a quarter of its real value. Dobson's pledges were simply ignored by 'the next Labour government', which instead continued to throw public money at the company.

In the five years that followed, Railtrack's directors pocketed more than £10m and shareholders more than £700m, while operating costs were largely met by the taxpayer. Yet even as the profits rolled in, the company failed to meet the targets for investment and for reducing delays. Maintenance expenses were reduced to a grudgingly spent minimum, rather than be allowed to detract from the bottom line by a penny more than necessary. The string of rail accidents that followed were instrumental in turning public opinion against a company widely believed to put profits before safety.

Seven died in the Southall crash in September 1997, followed by 31 at Paddington in October 1999 and four at Hatfield in October 2000. Cost-cutting and mismanagement were factors in all three cases. Even as this book was being written there was further carnage, with seven fatalities at Potters Bar in May 2002.

At the time, Hatfield proved the final straw. This time there was no way driver error could be blamed. Four people lost their lives because Railtrack had failed to ensure the replacement of a broken rail, despite having been aware of the need to do so nine months before.

Emergency speed restrictions were imposed across Britain as checks were carried out across all 11,000 miles of railway track, resulting in massive delays to services. The operation was supposed to have taken three months. It was more like six before timetables were anywhere near back to normal.

One consequence was the eventual resignation of Railtrack chairman Gerald Corbett, recruited from distillers Diageo to inject retail savvy into the rail infrastructure company. How a background in the booze business qualified him for his Railtrack role is somewhat hard to fathom.

Other consequences were financial. Railtrack's share price plummeted, and by May 2001, previously dependable profits were transformed into a thumping £534m loss. By the autumn, it had run up debts of £3.5bn, with a cash shortfall of as much again expected in the medium term.

The obvious answer would have been renationalisation, a move for which a series of opinion polls consistently indicated massive public support. Instead, civil servants secretly began working on ways to put the company into administration. Although the move had been in the offing as early as June, Railtrack was not told until the first Friday in October.

Late in the afternoon, after the Stock Exchange had closed for the week, Railtrack's new chairman John Robinson was summoned to meet Secretary of State for Transport Stephen Byers, who told him no more government cash would be forthcoming. This reversed earlier assurances that a £1.5bn payment due in 2006 would be brought forward as a means of helping overcome the Hatfield disruption. On Sunday, Byers petitioned a High Court judge to put the company into 'railway administration' under the 1993 Railways Act, which was granted by Mr Justice Gavin Lightman.

Shares were suspended at 280p on Monday, and accountancy major Ernst & Young was called in to run the show. The Government pledged to honour all trade creditors and bank lenders, collectively owed £6.5bn in the last published accounts. Only shareholders were to lose out. Byers stated categorically: 'I can say for certain that there will be no taxpayers' money made available to support shareholders.'[23]

Astonishingly, the Government did not have any detailed proposals for a replacement for Railtrack in place before pulling the plug, and instead unveiled vague plans for a not-for-profit company unofficially dubbed Newtrack. This would be financed by government subsidies and charges to operators for use of its track. It was to have no equity shareholders, and therefore pay no dividends. Any profits were to be ploughed back into the business. Partnerships UK – the merchant bank with a 49 per cent state shareholding – was to oversee the scheme.

Railtrack shareholders – led by large institutional investors including Fidelity Investments, Deutsche Asset Management, Invesco/Perpetual, Legg Mason, Marathon and Morley – were up in arms, branding the administration old-style socialist expropriation. The City covertly threatened to withhold finance for future PPP and PFI schemes, unless rewarded with substantial extra premia to compensate for political risk. Around two-dozen fund managers, including Morley's Gerald Holtham, founder of the IPPR and one of Labour's key City contacts, even organised an open letter of protest to the Chancellor. Given the City's time-honoured preference for sorting such matters out behind closed doors, this was strong stuff.

Three months after the administration order, the Department of Transport announced that £67.5bn was to be spent on the rail network over the coming decade. Of this sum, £34bn would come from private investors and £33.5bn from the Government. It was only on closer analysis that the headline-grabbing news was revealed as a statistical fix. Some £7.5bn of the public money needed to secure private funding had been double counted to boost the total.[24]

In March 2002, Byers announced that Newtrack – now officially christened Network Rail – would buy Railtrack out of administration for £500m, including £300m of taxpayers' money. The bid would see shareholders receive 250p a share, just 30p less than the price prevailing at administration. So much for his earlier categorical assurances that no public money would be available for such purposes. The move was, explained the head of UK equities at UBS Asset Management, 'a victory for City pressure'.[25] Network Rail will be chaired by former Ford UK chairman Ian McAllister, with Adrian Montague of Partnerships UK serving as his deputy. Meanwhile, the rump of Railtrack – now predominantly a property business – has relisted on the London stock exchange.

Apart from the railways, the other main industrial policy controversy so far in the second term has been the once and future Post Office, currently in the process of changing its name back to the Royal Mail after squandering £2m on a harebrained plan to brand itself as Consignia. Towards the end of 2001, Consignia revealed that it was losing £1m a day, and argued it needed to make 30,000 staff redundant to get back on an even keel.

In a matter of months, the picture was even bleaker. Postal services regulator Postcomm announced early in 2002 that it was opening up the postal market to greater competition. So far deregulation is limited to bulk mail-outs of 4,000 letters or more, although these already account for almost half of all letters posted. Other deliveries will be subject to competition over the next few years, with all restrictions set to end in 2006. The end result could be the collapse of a universal service at a low uniform price, as private operators cherry pick the more lucrative parts of the business and ignore unprofitable but socially desirable services.

Managing the Consignia crisis is chairman Allan Leighton, an individual member of the Labour Party. The former chief executive of Asda quit the supermarket business – now owned by WalMart of the US – as part of a deliberate strategy of taking on a portfolio of non-executive posts. Leighton is busily engaged with around a dozen part-time jobs at any one time, including roles as chairman of British Home Stores, Lastminute.com, and Wilson Connolly; deputy chairman of Leeds Sporting plc; and directorships at Dyson, George Weston Inc, Scottish Power and Murdoch's BSkyB.

His position at Consignia officially occupies him for just two days a week, and pays a notably restrained £20,000 a year plus perks, although Leighton stands to pocket ten times that amount in bonuses, providing he meets a series of performance targets. He has probably gone some way towards that goal with one of his first acts after assuming the chairmanship, which was to announce 15,000 job losses, mostly at Parcelforce, and his intention to close 3,000 urban post offices, equivalent to one-third of the urban network.

Consignia may not be long for the public sector. Sell-off discussions have already been held with Dutch company TPG, but broke down because Leighton felt that the £5bn or so on offer did not amount to a fair valuation.[26] A number of other companies, including Hays, Securicor, Labour donor UPS, Deutsche Post and TNT, are also likely to be interested in buying all or part of Consignia.

The pivotal issue in British politics over the coming period, and probably the biggest single decision of the Blair premiership, will be the decision on whether or not Britain joins the euro. Business is seriously divided on the issue, as are all major parties, not least Labour.

Despite Blair's earlier flirtations with euroscepticism in the Murdoch press, the Prime Minister undoubtedly does want to sign up for the single currency. But electoral considerations, combined with opposition from Brown and a significant number of MPs, make it impossible for him simply to say so outright.

The cracks are currently wallpapered over by a nominal set of five conditions that have to be met before Britain is ready to join, as part of a strategy dubbed 'prepare and decide'. All of them are suitably difficult to measure, and therefore easy to fudge. Ever the pragmatist, Blair is also accused of wanting a 'sixth test', namely the likelihood of a comfortable majority in any referendum on the issue, perhaps as much as two-thirds.

Yet the inescapable fact is that the EU remains Britain's largest trading partner. Sooner or later, Blair will have to come off the fence and start an all-out campaign for euro membership. He will certainly be mindful of the short, sharp campaign under the Wilson government that transformed a majority against joining what was then the Common Market into a majority for membership. In the run-up to the last general election, Blair hinted strongly at the likelihood of a referendum on the euro within two years.

Roger Liddle, the Blair advisor on Europe embroiled in the cash for access affair, reportedly told a private dinner for a small group of European socialist party leaders that early 2003 has been pencilled in for the event, giving plenty of preparation time before the 2004 euro-elections. This kind of timescale is underlined by Whitehall documents that have made their way into the press, giving 1 May 2003 as polling day for 2005 entry.[27]

Broadly speaking, multinational businesses increasingly favour membership and are lining up behind Labour as the party perceived as most favourable to their cause, while opponents are coalescing around the Conservatives.

One recent poll of directors of Britain's 500 largest companies found 59 per cent in favour of the euro. The larger the company, the more likely it is to back the single currency.[28] There is little trace of patriotic sentiment in any of this. One senior businessman argues:

> Business does not see a role for the sort of Little England the Tories seem attached to. Some businessmen may go home and put on Union Jack waistcoats for all I know. But they see their businesses operating in a global environment, and the Tories' nationalist approach has nothing to offer them.[29]

There are already fears that Britain is losing out on inward investment, with Japanese, US and other investors now preferring to locate within the eurozone. Meanwhile, many UK domestic retailers are accepting the new currency over the counter as a matter of course, while home-buyers are already benefiting from mortgages at lower euro interest rates.

Prominent business advocates of joining the euro include Unilever chairman Niall FitzGerald, an Irish citizen and one-time Communist who co-chaired the 2002 Davos economic summit. His honorary knighthood in the 2002 New Year honours list is widely seen as Blair's endorsement for his work with pro-euro lobby group Britain in Europe. FitzGerald has called on the Government to hold a referendum as soon as possible, backing his demand with some not so subtle threats.

Not holding a referendum, he argued, 'would force [Unilever] to examine very carefully whether the UK continued to be the place in which to locate manufacturing for the 50 per cent of our market which is in Europe . . . and whether this was the appropriate place for the headquarters of an international company.'[30]

Britain in Europe is formally a cross-party campaign supported by Liberal Democrat leader Charles Kennedy and such leading Tories as Michael Heseltine. But its advisory council takes in a whole slew of top Labour-connected business figures, including Lords Hollick, Simon, Haskins, Puttnam and Trotman, as well as such Labour-aligned lobbyists as Colin Byrne, Mike Craven and Paul Adamson. Campaign director Simon Buckby is a former researcher for John Prescott. Throw in numerous Labour MPs and MEPs, and there is little doubt where its centre of political gravity lies.

Incidentally, Labour appears to have earmarked a key business liaison role in any future euro referendum campaign for Anthony Nelson, one of its star recent signings. Nelson was a Tory MP for 23 years, eventually rising to the rank of Treasury minister. He stood down in 1997 to pursue a City career. As vice-chairman of Citigroup Bank, Nelson dramatically defected to Labour towards the end of the 2001 campaign.

In contrast, the Business for Sterling anti-euro campaign is very much led by the remnants of the old Thatcherite right of the business world, making it somewhat unattractive from a New Labour perspective. According to one unpublished Labour document, its application for exhibition space at Labour's 2000 conference was rejected, explicitly on the grounds that it is 'an adjunct to the Tory party'.[31]

Signatories of its launch document include Tim Melville-Ross of Institute of Directors fame, and Stan Hardy, formerly an official of the Economic League, an organisation that maintained a commercially available blacklist of trade union activists. Others are major donors to the Tory Party, including Sir Anthony Bamford of JCB, Sir Richard George of Weetabix and party treasurer Sir Stanley Kalms. The late Sir Emmanuel Kaye – a contributor to Blair's blind trust – also signed the appeal.

Where now for British politics? For the best part of a decade, New Labour has deliberately positioned itself on the radical-right cutting edge of European social democracy. The process of delabourisation, while not yet complete, has clearly gone a long way. The second term will decide the fate of the party.

But, little more than a year after securing re-election, Labour was looking in worse condition that at any time since it entered office. There was mounting backbench disquiet at the Prime Minister's alliance with the leaders of right-wing parties elsewhere in Europe, and the prospect of British backing for a US invasion of Iraq that few other countries will support. There were even rumours of a stalking-horse leadership challenge, while the Conservatives were narrowing the gap in the polls. All of a sudden, Blair wasn't looking quite so bulletproof. Maybe British politics is about to get a little more interesting.

NOTES

[1] http://www.forbes.com/2002/02/14/tonyblair1_print.html

[2] *Financial Times*, 30 January 2001

[3] *Financial Times*, 16 February 2001

[4] *Financial Times*, 12 March 2001

[5] Ibid.

[6] *Daily Mail*, 25 April 1997

[7] *Daily Telegraph*, 21 May 2001

[8] Ibid.

[9] *Times*, 14 May 2001

[10] http://news.bbc.co.uk/vote2001/hi/english/newsid_1329000/1329419.stm

[11] *Financial Times*, 15 May 2001

[12] *Financial Times*, 30 May 2001

[13] *Daily Telegraph*, 30 May 2001

[14] *Financial Times*, 23 May 2001

[15] Ibid.

[16] *Financial Times*, 28 March 2002

[17] *Guardian*, 16 May 2001

[18] Ibid.

[19] *Guardian*, 1 June 2001; *Observer* 10 June 2001

[20] *Financial Times*, 3 April 2002

[21] See the analysis by Peter Martin in the *Financial Times*, 9 October 2001. Martin notes: 'Getting this web of relationships to work properly was a daunting task. Gaps in communication, and the consequent "blame culture" are thought to be important causes of the track problems that led to the Hatfield crash which undermined Railtrack's credibility.'

[22] Cited in *Tribune*, 3 February 1995

[23] Cited in *Guardian*, 3 April 2002

[24] *Financial Times*, 19 January 2002

[25] *Financial Times*, 25 March 2002

[26] *Tribune*, 5 April 2002

[27] *Daily Telegraph*, 25 October 2001; *Daily Mirror*, 26 February 2002

[28] *Financial Times*, 30 August 2000

[29] *Financial Times*, 23 May 2001

[30] *Financial Times*, 12 June 2001

[31] January 2000 Labour NEC finance committee minutes, Labour document NEC 28/3/00

15. CONCLUSION: NOT QUITE THE BUSINESS

NEW Labour is institutionally corrupt, in the same sense that the Metropolitan Police is institutionally racist. That is not an easy or a comforting thing to say, but after a thorough examination of the evidence, no other conclusion can logically be reached. It's not enough to take each individual scandal outlined in this book in isolation, point to the various inquiries that have exonerated the individuals involved, and argue that no Labour politician has ever faced criminal charges in any of these cases.

Even for those of a disposition sufficiently charitable to accept every tortuous explanation proffered by every Labour politician suspected of fingers-in-the-till behaviour – and some of them frankly strain credulity – a clear pattern emerges. New Labour is a repeat offender, to the extent that several senior figures deserve to be electronically tagged before being allowed to leave their well-appointed abodes of an evening. The Prime Minister professes to believe that public servants have left scars on his back. It is businessmen, however, that have left stains on his reputation.

'Tory sleaze' – and don't those words bring the early 1990s flooding back into your mind? – was always going to be a tough act to follow. But somehow New Labour has done just that. Before the 1997 election, only 19 per cent of poll respondents described Labour as sleazy, compared to 63 per cent who saw the Conservatives in those terms. By February 2002, Labour was firmly on top. Some 60 per cent found it 'sleazy and disreputable', while only 41 per cent had reached the same conclusions about Iain Duncan Smith's lot. Almost four out of five of those polled thought that Blair gave special help to business donors. Even if there was no basis in fact for this belief – and you've just read a book outlining ample basis in fact – the very perception makes the point.

Given the current open market in political funding, both major parties are widely viewed as a pair of rigged fruit machines that pay out every time. Being in office, New Labour currently offers bigger prizes for a line of cherries.

Rightist commentators routinely used to refer to Labour being 'in hock to its trade union paymasters'. Fewer voices are these days being raised to suggest that it might now properly be described as in hock to former second-hand car salesmen with an interest in advertising cigarettes.

Obviously it is up to the political left to make this case, because the right is too incriminated to do so with any credibility.

There has been much debate in the left press over whether or not Labour can now be described as in any sense a workers' party. The answer is probably still 'yes' . . . but only just. Political and financial links with the trade unions, while much attenuated, remain in place.

Moreover, despite its best efforts, Labour is not *the* party of business. Neither are the Conservatives any more. But both can fairly claim to be parties of business. Britain now has a system not dissimilar from the US, where government alternates between two safe pairs of hands, one of them marginally more union-friendly.

Much as it craves the love of a good businesswoman, New Labour's problem is this. The Tories have networks within the establishment that date back centuries. Labour still has no real organic links with the ruling class. After starting almost from scratch, even after a decade its business base is still relatively limited. Accordingly, most of the controversial donations have come not from the FTSE 100 crowd, but from the sort of business wide boys still anxious enough about their social position to pay to shore it up. In many cases, they have a definite policy agenda.

In an attempt to extricate itself from repeated controversy, in May 2002 Labour established a committee of party worthies to vet all donations of over £5,000. Major donors will be asked to put it in writing that they are not seeking personal or commercial advantage, and are 'broadly committed' to the party's aims and values. All contacts between donors and party staff and fundraisers are to be recorded.

Yet the composition of the committee is such that it can hardly be described as an independent watchdog. Members include Lord Levy and Baroness Jay, erstwhile trustee of Blair's blind trust. How much impact it will have in practice remains to be seen.

Another remedy currently under discussion is state funding for political parties, something that already exists to a surprising degree. The argument for extending it further is deeply unattractive. The cure is worse than the disease.

For a start, state funding could only address the problem of sleaze if all other donations were banned. Otherwise it would simply represent a handy little top-up. In practice, this would be tantamount to state licensing of the existing political parties, based on past electoral performance. Legitimate newcomers would be severely disadvantaged. And not only would it take companies out of politics, it would take trade unions out of politics as well.

Worst of all, state funding offends against basic democratic principles. In a democracy, political parties are voluntary organisations. If people want to support them, they do. If they don't want to, they don't. That is how it should be. There can be no justification for forcing taxpayers to pay for parties they are either indifferent towards or even heartily despise.

Likewise there can be no justification for banning individuals from writing out cheques to parties whose policies they believe in, although an argument might usefully be had on whether there ought to be an upper limit. Let all parties raise their cash in relatively small doses from their genuine supporters.

It's high time to democratise institutional political funding. Several trade unions are reviewing previous automatic support for Labour, and considering balloting their memberships on where political fund money should go. Let them do so. Let companies be required to ballot shareholders before making political donations too.

There should also be new legal penalties for abuse of political position. At the moment, the worst punishment that can be inflicted on an errant MP is temporary suspension from Parliament, while ministers might suffer loss of cabinet status. In both cases they still keep a job and a salary many people would kill for, frequently providing a launch pad to haul in six-figure sums. Who knows? A spell in the remand wing of a PFI jail might even give some parliamentarians grounds to reconsider prison privatisation.

But, from my point of view, the best answer of all would be the rise in England and Wales of a new socialist political force along the lines of the left and red-green parties that are now a fixture in most European polities, exemplified by the alternative the Scots already have in the form of the Scottish Socialist Party. Peter Mandelson might think that we're all Thatcherites now. A lot of us still ain't.

APPENDIX 1 – CORPORATE DONATIONS TO THE LABOUR PARTY

Figures from Labour Party annual reports, Election Commission returns and the annual survey of political donations compiled by the Labour Research Department (LRD), unless qualifed as 'reported'. These are based on claims made in mainstream national newspapers. Some details of businesses are taken from the Red Star Research website.

Where money was donated as cash it is listed as 'donation'. Otherwise it is listed as 'sponsorship' or 'dinner tickets' as appropriate.

ADSHEL: Bus shelter advertising multinational. £5,000+ sponsorship 1998
ACCENTURE (Previously ANDERSEN CONSULTING): Unspecified services in kind 1999
APCO (UK): £6,000 donation 2001
ATCO LTD: Unknown amount, reported 1997
AWAYVALE: Vehicle for stage producer Trevor Nunn. £5,000+ donation 1997
BAE SYSTEMS: The arms manufacturer formerly known as British Aerospace. Paid £12m to sponsor Mind Zone section of the Dome. £5,000+ sponsorship 1998; £5,000+ sponsorship 1999; £5,000+ sponsorship 2000
BALLATHIE ESTATES: £25,000 donation in two instalments to Scottish Labour 2001
BELL POTTINGER: Public relations company co-founded by Tory PR man Tim Bell. £5,000+ sponsorship 1999
BERGMANS: Newcastle-based PR firm which has employed former Labour staffers. Specialises in arms manufacturers, working for Boeing, GKN, GEC, Thomson and others. £5,000+ sponsorship 1997
BG (Previously BRITISH GAS): Privatised gas supplier British Gas. £5,000+ 1996 (reportedly about £6,000 for dinner tickets); £5,000+ sponsorship 1998; £5,000+ sponsorship 1999; £5,000+ sponsorship 2000
BIRMINGHAM INTERNATIONAL AIRPORT PLC: £5,000+ sponsorship 2000
BLOOMBERG: Financial information firm owned by Republican mayor of New York Michael Bloomberg. £17,625 donation 2001; £11,548 sponsorship in two instalments, also 2001
BOOTS: Staunchly non-union retail chemist chain. £5,000+ sponsorship 1998
BRITISH AIRWAYS: Privatised airline. £1,450 donation 2001
BRITISH AMERICAN FINANCIAL SERVICES: Financial services operation hived off from cigarette giant BAT. Controls Allied Dunbar, 'named and shamed' for mis-selling pensions. £5,000+ sponsorship 1997
BRITISH BROADCASTING CORPORATION: £5,000+ sponsorship 2000
BRITISH MIDLAND: Airline group. £5,000+ sponsorship 1999

226

BRUNSWICK GROUP: Financial PR. £5,000+ dinner tickets 1998; £5,000+ dinner tickets 1999; £5,000+ dinner tickets 2000; £9,000 donation 2001

BSKYB: Murdoch-owned satellite broadcaster. £5,000+ sponsorship 1999 of Labour youth event, reportedly £20,000, only weeks after launching bid for Manchester United; £5,000+ sponsorship 2000

BT: Privatised telecoms company. £5,000+ sponsorship 1997

BUTLER KELLY: £5,000+ sponsorship 1999

CABLE COMMUNICATIONS ASSOCIATION: Members include Eurobell, Cable & Wireless, Atlantic, NTL and Telewest. Table at £500-a-plate dinner 1996; £5,000+ sponsorship 1997; £5,000+ sponsorship 1998; £5,000+ sponsorship 1999; £5,000+ sponsorship 2000

CALEDONIAN MINING: Gave £270,000 to Tories between 1982 and 1994. £5,000+ donation 1997 (£20,000 LRD)

CAPARO GROUP: Steel and engineering group chaired by Labour peer Lord Paul. £40,000 donation 1995 (LRD); £109,000 donation 1996 (LRD); £5,000+ donation 1997 (£76,000 LRD); £5,000+ donation 1998; £5,000+ donation 2000. Reportedly gave £47,000 donation to John Smith blind trust 1996. Has also made donations to the Conservatives, according to LRD.

CAPITAL & PROVIDENT: £5,000+ donation 2000

CARLTON TELEVISION: £5,000+ sponsorship 2000

CASTLE POINT HEATING AND GAS: £5,000 donation to Castle Point constituency party 2001; £1,500 donation to Southend West constituency party 2001

CBA ENTERPRISES: £2,500 donation to Tatton constituency party 2001

CENTRAL MIDLANDS ESTATES: £900 quarterly rental for premises to Stafford constituency party 2001

CENTURION PRESS: Printing company that undertakes extensive work for Labour and the trade unions. £5,000+ sponsorship 1997. Peerage for chairman Lord Evans 1998

CHRYSALIS GROUP: Media. £5,000+ dinner tickets 2000

CITIGATE PUBLIC AFFAIRS: Blair peer Lord Faulkner is director of parent company Incepta Group. £5,000+ dinner tickets 1999; £5,000+ dinner tickets 2000

CITIGATE WESTMINSTER: Political PR outfit, one of top three for public sector concerns. £5,000+ sponsorship 1997; £2,500 1998 (LRD), with £5,000+ sponsorship 1998; £5,000 donation 1999 (LRD); £16,161 donation in two instalments 2001

CITYGROVE LEISURE: London-based property developers, with interests in retail and entertainment complexes and casinos. £5,000+ donation 1998; £5,000+ donation 1999

CLAYTON, DUBILIER & RICE LTD: Large US investment company. Head of European operations Christopher Mackenzie is also individual donor (see entry). £5,000+ sponsorship 1999

COMPAQ: Computer hardware manufacturers. £7,500 donation 2001

CONNEX RAIL: Operator of 'misery line' from Tilbury to Fenchurch Street, owned by French utility major Vivendi. £5,000+ sponsorship 1999

CONNEX TRANSPORT UK: £5,000+ sponsorship 2000

CO-OPERATIVE WHOLESALE LTD: £5,000+ donation 1997; £5,000+ sponsorship 1998

CO-OPERATIVE WHOLESALE SOCIETY: £5,000+ donation 1996; £5,000+ sponsorship 1997; £5,000+ sponsorship 1999; £5,000+ sponsorship 2000

CORMAC HOLLINGSWORTH: Bond trader. £2,000 donation 2001

CRAG GROUP: £5,000+ sponsorship 1997; £5,000+ dinner tickets 1998; £5,000+ dinner tickets 1999; £5,000+ dinner tickets 2000

CREATE LTD: £5,000+ sponsorship 1997

CREATION RECORDS: Oasis' label. £5,000+ donation 1997 (£24,838 LRD)

CURFIN INVESTMENTS: Motor dealer. £1,000 donation 1992–3 (LRD)

CURRIE GROUP: Motor dealership headed by Abe Jaffe. £5,000+ donation 1996; £5,000+ donation 1997

DAILY MAIL AND GENERAL TRUST: Reported £500 donation 1998

DAILY RECORD AND SUNDAY MAIL: Scottish tabloid arm of Trinity Mirror newspaper group. £5,000+ sponsorship 1997; £5,000+ sponsorship 1998

DE BRUS MARKETING SERVICES: £3,000 donation to Warwick & Leamington constituency party 2001

DELOITTE & TOUCHE: Accountants with several major government contracts. £5,000+ sponsorship 1998

DESIGN COUNCIL: £5,000+ sponsorship 2000

DIXONS: Electrical group chaired by Sir Stanley Kalms, treasurer of the Tory party. £5,000+ dinner tickets 2000; £5,000+ dinner tickets 2001

DELTA CLOUD LTD: £2,000 to Barnsley East constituency party 2001

DESIGN COUNCIL: £5,000+ sponsorship 1999

DLA CORPORATE ADVISORY LTD: £5,554 donation in two instalments 2001

DLA PARTNERS: £11,050 donation 2001

DLA UPSTREAM: PR company. £5,000+ sponsorship 1999; £5,000+ dinner tickets 2000

EASTERN GROUP: The privatised Eastern Electricity. At the time of the first donation headed by Thatcherite Lord Hanson. £5,000+ donation 1996; £5,000+ donation 1999

EDELMAN PUBLIC RELATIONS WORLDWIDE: £5,000+ dinner tickets 2000

ELECTION.COM: £5,000+ sponsorship 2000

ELSTEAD HOTEL (BOURNEMOUTH) LTD: £5,000+ dinner tickets 1998

ENERGY AND MARITIME TRAINING AUTHORITY: £5,000+ sponsorship 1999; £5,875 donation 2001; £1,550 donation to Lincoln constituency party 2001; £6,800 donation 2001

ENFIELD TURKISH GROUP: £1,306 donation to Enfield North constituency party 2001

ENGINEERING COUNCIL: £5,000+ sponsorship 1997

ENRON EUROPE: Subsidiary of collapsed US-owned energy company. Chairman Ralph Hodge got CBE 2001. £5,000+ sponsorship (£12,500 backing for gala dinner at Hilton, according to Friends of the Earth) 1997; £5,000+ sponsorship 1998; £5,000+ dinner tickets 1999, booking whole table at £500-a-plate dinner; £5,000+ dinner tickets 2000. Overall support reportedly totalled £38,000

ERNST & YOUNG: World's second-largest management consultancy. Unspecified services in kind 1998; unspecified services in kind 1999

ESSON PROPERTIES: £5,000 donation to Scottish Labour 2001

EVANS HUNT SCOTT: Telephone fundraiser that has worked for the Labour Party. Press reports of £5,000+ donation 1996 denied by the company

EXPRESS: Daily newspaper, at the time part of Lord Hollick's United News & Media. £5,000+ sponsorship 1998

FA WORLD CUP 2006 BID: £5,000+ sponsorship 1997

FAMILY ASSURANCE: Largest tax-exempt friendly society in the UK. £5,000+ sponsorship 1998

FINSBURY LTD: PR firm. £5,000+ dinner tickets 1998; £5,000+ dinner tickets 1999; £5,000+ dinner tickets 2000

FIRST CONSULTING GROUP: Management consultants to 22 of the top 25 UK pharmaceuticals companies. £5,000+ sponsorship 1998

FIRST SOFTWARE UK LTD: Supplier of software to local authorities. £5,000+ sponsorship 1999

FREESERVE: Internet service provider. Unspecified services in kind 1999

FREIGHTLINER LTD: Largest UK intermodal rail and road haulage operator. £5,000+ sponsorship 1998

FREUD COMMUNICATIONS: Owned by Matthew Freud, personal friend of Mandelson. The company undertook Dome PR work. £5,000+ sponsorship 1997

GIBRALTAR, GOVERNMENT OF: £5,000+ dinner tickets 2000

GJW: Lobbyists, with clients including BAA and Scottish Power. £5,000+ sponsorship 1997; £5,000+ dinner tickets 1998; £5,000+ dinner tickets 1999; £5,000+ dinner tickets 2000

GLC LTD: City firm managing investment futures. £30,000 1995; £5,000+ donation 1997 (£30,000 LRD)

GLENYORK LTD: North London engineering company run by Uri David. £5,000+ 1997; £5,000+ dinner tickets 1998 (jointly with David) £5,000+ dinner tickets 1999

GMI HOLDINGS: £5,000 donation to Copeland constituency party 2001; further £2,000 donation 2001

GNER: £5,000+ sponsorship 2000

GPC: Lobbyists, with clients including Powergen, British Telecom, BG. £5,000+ dinner tickets 1998

GRANADA TELEVISION: Independent television company. See entry for Robinson, Gerry. £5,000+ sponsorship 1998

GRANDFIELD PUBLIC AFFAIRS: £5,000+ dinner tickets 1998

GREATER LONDON ENTERPRISE: Co-operative industries. £5,000 + donation 1996; £5,000+ donation 1997

GREEK CYPRIOT BROTHERHOOD: £5,000+ donation 1997

H.H. ASSOCIATES: £5,000+ dinner tickets 2000

HIGHGATE BEDS: £2,000 donation to Dewsbury constituency party 2001

HOUSE MAGAZINE: £5,000+ sponsorship 2000

IAN GREER ASSOCIATES: Lobbying company at centre of Tory cash for questions scandal in early 1990s. £5,000+ donation 1996

INDEPENDENT NEWS AND MEDIA: Daily newspaper owned by Irish billionaire Tony O'Reilly. £5,000+ sponsorship 1999; £5,000+ sponsorship 2000; £25,000 sponsorship 2001, when the company also provided £18,800 sponsorship to the Conservatives and £6,600 to the Liberal Democrats

ISPAT INTERNATIONAL (UK): British arm of Lakshmi Mittal's worldwide steel empire. £5,000+ donation 1997

J&P UK: £5,000+ dinner tickets 2000

JACOBS & TURNER: Clothing company controlled by Kushi family. £1200 1997 (LRD)

JAMES FISHER & SONS: Barrow-based shipmanagers that operate nuclear fuel carriers for British Nuclear Fuels Ltd. Headed by David Cobb, who was president of the Chamber of Shipping at the time when the industry secured important tax breaks. Cobb got CBE 1999. £1,500 donation 1998 (LRD); £1,500 donation 1999 (LRD)

J. BARBOUR & SONS: Wax jacket manufacturer. £1,000 donation 1999 (LRD)

JUST2CLICKS.COM: £5,000+ dinner tickets 2000; £5,000+ sponsorship 2000

KINGFISHER GROUP: Owner of Woolworth, B&Q, Comet, Superdrug. Headed by Geoff Kalms, a leading Conservative financial supporter. Reportedly spent £17,000 on Labour sponsorship, dinner tickets and provision of equipment 1994; £5,000+ donation 1996; £5,000+ dinner tickets 1999

KPMG: Accountants and management consultants. Unspecified services in kind 1999. Undertook study recommending that membership services be contracted out 1999

LABOUR FRONT BENCH RESEARCH FUND BOARD: £26,863 donation to Parliamentary Labour Party 2001

LANCASHIRE ENTERPRISES: Management and property services company with local and central government contracts. Provided employee David Taylor as adviser to Prescott 1997. £5,000+ sponsorship 1997

LAW BUSINESS RESEARCH LTD: £1,500 donation to Bristol East constituency party 2001

LAWSON LUCAS MENDELSOHN: Lobbyists, with clients including News International and Tesco. £5,000+ dinner tickets 1998

LEO ABSE & COHEN: £2,100 donation to Wales Labour 2001

LEOPOLD JOSEPH: Private bank providing offshore banking and trust services, based in London, Guernsey and the Bahamas. £1,000 donation 1998 (LRD)

LINDLEY CATERING INVESTMENTS LTD: Stadium caterers to many top football clubs, owned by individual donor Peter Coates (see entry). £5,000+ donation 1998; £5,000+ donation 2000; £25,000 donation 2001

LITTLEWOODS: Pools company. £1,200 donation 1992–93 (LRD), also giving larger sums to Tories and Liberals. £5,000+ donation 1996

LONDON EXPORT LTD: Managing director Stephen Perry reported individual donor (see entry). £5,000+ donation 1997

LOTUS: Unspecified services in kind 1998; unspecified services in kind 1999, believed to be e-mail software and services

MANCHESTER AIRPORT PLC: Expansion work on its second runway claimed 1,000 acres of greenbelt land, sparking major environmental protest. £5,000+ sponsorship 1998; £5,000+ sponsorship 1999 (sponsored conference gala dinner for £20,000); £5,000+ sponsorship 2000

MANRO HAYDAN TRADING AND MANROS LTD: £5,000+ sponsorship 1997

McDONALD'S: Fast food chain. £5,000+ sponsorship 1999; £5,000+ sponsorship 2000; reported £15,000 drinks reception at conference 2001

McNIFF CIVIL ENGINEERING: £5,000+ sponsorship 1999

MECONIC: Speciality metals group, LRD report £1,000 donation to Labour mid-1990s

MERRILL LYNCH EUROPE: European end of US merchant bank. £5,000+ dinner tickets 1998

MFI FURNITURE: £5,000+ dinner tickets 2000

MOTOROLA: Representative attended £350-a-ticket corporate day at Labour conference 1994

NATIONAL EXPRESS: Coach operator. £5,000+ dinner tickets 2000

NATIONAL FEDERATION OF SELF-EMPLOYED AND SMALL BUSINESSES: £400 donation to Dunfermline East constituency party, Gordon Brown's constituency 2001; further £1,000 in raffle prize football shirts and tickets 2001

NATIONAL POWER: Privatised electricity generator. £5,000+ sponsorship 2000

NATIONWIDE: Building society. £5,000+ sponsorship 2000

NORTHERN & SHELL: Owners of Express Newspapers, OK! magazine, 38 top-shelf titles, a pornographic television station and adult websites. Controlled by Richard Desmond, a former Conservative donor. £100,000 donation a week after DTI cleared Express takeover

NORTHUMBRIAN WATER: £5,000+ donation 1996, reportedly sponsoring champagne reception at Labour conference in Blackpool; £5,000+ sponsorship 1998

NOVARTIS: UK subsidiary of Swiss-based company which is Europe's largest pharmaceuticals concern, and a leading manufacturer of GM sugar beet and maize, as well as organophosphate dips. £5,000+ sponsorship 1997 (reportedly 'thousands of pounds' on seminar for newly elected MPs)

NTL CABLETEL: Reported sponsors of Blair's welfare reform roadshow 1998

ONE 2 ONE: Mobile phone company owned by Deutsche Telekom. £5,000+ sponsorship 1999

ORACLE: Unspecified services in kind 1998; Unspecified services in kind 1999. Reportedly built Labour website and provided server

ORANGE: Telecoms. £5,000+ sponsorship 2000

ORTIVUS UK LTD: £5,875 donation 2001

PARTNERSHIP IN ACTION: £1,175 donation to Kilmarnock & Loudoun constituency party 2001

PEARSON GROUP: Publishers of the Financial Times, television interests. First public company to make a substantial donation to Labour with 1995 gift of £25,000. Knighthoods for chairman Dennis Stevenson and former chief executive Frank Barlow in the 1998 New Year Honours list

PEEL HOLDINGS PLC: £5,287 donation 2001

PEOPLES LTD: Car dealers. See also entry for Gilda, Brian. Unspecified services in kind 1999; £2,000 transport support in kind to Scottish Labour 2001

PFIZER: Pharmaceutical giant, manufacturer of Viagra. £5,000+ sponsorship 1999

PHILIP MORRIS: Tobacco manufacturers. Sponsored Labour's first ever 'corporate day' 1994. Sponsored after-dinner port and cognac at £500-a-plate dinner

POLITICAL ANIMAL LOBBY: British-based arm of the US International Fund for Animal Welfare, an animal rights campaign, led by Angela Beveridge, sister of Labour MP Tony Banks. £1m donation 1995; £5,000+ donation 1996; £5,000+ donation 1998; £5,000+ dinner tickets 1999; £5,000+ dinner tickets 2000; £30,000 donation 2001; £47,582 donation in two instalments 2001. One of the £5,000+ donations reportedly £100,000

LABOUR PARTY PLC

PRICEWATERHOUSECOOPERS: £22,958 support in kind 2001

QSP LTD: Web hosting. £8,000 2001

RAILTRACK: Privatised railway infrastructure operator. £5,000+ sponsorship 1998

RANGER OIL (UK): Parent company based in Canada. Former Conservative sports minister Colin Moynihan sits on board. £5,000+ donation 1997 (£5,000 LRD)

RAPIER MARKETING LTD: £5,000+ dinner tickets 1998

RAYTHEON SYSTEMS: One of the world's big three arms manufacturers, supplying such repressive regimes as Saudi Arabia and Indonesia. £800m MoD contract for the supply of battlefield radar spy-plane system 1998. £5,000+ sponsorship 1997

RICHALIS: Software company. £8,000 donation to Gosport constituency party in two instalments 2001

RUOBAL PROPERTIES LTD: Landlords. £2,000 donation to Hitchin & Harpenden constituency party 2001; £2,000 to North East Hertfordshire constituency party 2001

SAFEWAYS: Supermarket chain. £5,000+ sponsorship 1997; reportedly supported *New Statesman* party at Labour conference 1998

J SAINSBURY'S PLC: Supermarket chain. Former major shareholder Lord Sainsbury is Labour's biggest individual backer. £5,000+ sponsorship 1997

SANDERSON KNIGHT PROPERTIES: Property developer. £1,500 donation to North Shropshire constituency party 2001

SCOTTISH POWER: Multi-utility company. Chief executive Sir Ian Robinson is chairman of Scottish New Deal taskforce. £5,000+ sponsorship 1997; £5,000+ sponsorship 1998; £1,500 sponsorship to Scottish Labour 2001

SEA CONTAINERS: Hotels, hovercraft, luxury trains, shipping containers. £5,000+ dinner tickets 2000

SEEBOARD: Privatised electricity supplier in the south-east. £5,000+ sponsorship 1999; £5,000+ sponsorship 2000; £8,700 2001, also gave to Tories

SEMA: IT services. £5,000+ sponsorship 2000

SEVERN TRENT: Privatised water group. £5,000+ sponsorship 1999

SLP INVESTMENTS: London-based property developers. Managing director Stephen Perry reported individual donor. Company also gives to pro-Europe pressure groups. £5,000+ donation 1998; £5,000+ donation 1999; £5,000+ donation 2000 (£25,000 LRD)

SOMERFIELD: Supermarket chain £5,000+ sponsorship 1998, reportedly £38,500 to have name on conference security passes that year

SOMERS HANDLING PLC: £5,000+ donation 1997 (£5,000 LRD)

SPRINTINCA: Catering group. £20,000 donation 1999 (LRD)

SUN LIFE & PROVINCIAL HOLDINGS: Part of French-owned insurers AXA Group. £10,000 donation 1995 (LRD); £20,000 donation 1996 (LRD); £5,000+ donation 1997; £5,000+ donation 1998

SWISS LIFE (UK): Insurance. £5,000+ dinner tickets 1999

TATE & LYLE: Sugar company with decades-long track record of support for right-wing causes, including the Economic League, which blacklisted union activists. £7,500 donation 1995

TESCO: Largest UK supermarket chain. Backed Millennium Dome with reported £12m. Representative attended £350-a-ticket corporate day at Labour conference 1994; £5,000+ sponsorship 1997; £5,000+ sponsorship 1998; £5,000+ dinner tickets 1999; £5,000+ sponsorship 1999

TEXACAN TROUSERS: £2,000 donation to Blackburn constituency party 2001

THOMAS COOK: Travel agents, now German-owned. £5,000+ sponsorship 1998 (reportedly footed £25,000 champagne bill for £200-a-head gala dinner at that year's conference)

THOMPSONS SOLICITORS: Law firm representing many trade unions. £5,000+ donation 1996; £5,000+ sponsorship 1997; £5,000+ donation 1998; £5,000+ dinner tickets 1999; £5,000+ dinner tickets 2000; £15,400 donation in three instalments 2001

THOMSON-CSF RACAL: £5,000+ sponsorship 2000

THOMSON LITHO: See entry for Thomson, Matt under individual donors

TITAN TRAVEL: Travel company. £5,000+ donation 1996

TRINITY MIRROR (formerly MIRROR GROUP): Publishers of *Daily* and *Sunday Mirror*, provincial newspapers. Gave £21,000 to fund research assistant for then shadow Northern Ireland secretary Mo Mowlam in mid-1990s. £5,000+ donation 1996; £5,000+ sponsorship 1997; £5,000+ sponsorship 1998; £5,000+ sponsorship 1999; £5,000+ sponsorship 2000; £5,000 donation to Welsh Labour Party 2001

TU FUND MANAGERS LTD: Trade union investment company. £20,000 donation 1995; £5,000+ donation 1996; £5,000+ sponsorship 1997. LRD lists donations of £1,904 in 1997 and £12,000 in 1998

UNITE INTEGRATED SOLUTIONS: £14,100 donation 2001

UK DEFENCE FORUM: £5,000+ sponsorship 1997

UPS (UK) LTD: British operation of US parcel delivery company, interested in Post Office privatisation. £5,000+ sponsorship 1998; £5,000+ sponsorship 1999; £5,000+ sponsorship 2000; £17,625 donation 2001

VAUXHALL MOTORS: UK subsidiary of General Motors. Chairman Nick Reilly is a leading New Labour quangocrat awarded CBE in 2000. £5,000+ sponsorship 1999; £5,000+ sponsorship 2000; £7,050 donation 2001

VISION POSTERS: Midlands-based manufacturers of illuminated billboards, provides advertising space for Labour. £5,000+ donation 1998

WALES AND WEST PASSENGER TRAINS: £1,500 donation to Wales Labour 2001

WESTMERE LTD: £2,000 donation to South Thanet constituency party 2001

WIGGINS GROUP: Commercial and residential property developers. Own Manston Airport in Kent. £5,000+ sponsorship 1998; £8,000 2001

WILLIS CORROON: Holding and investment company. £5,000+ donation 1996. Earlier incarnation Willis Faber was a major donor to the Tories in the Thatcher period

WINTERTHUR GROUP SERVICES: Swiss-owned insurer. £5,000+ dinner tickets 2000

WISE TRADING LTD: £1,500 donation to Ealing Southall constituency party 2001

YORKSHIRE TELEVISION: ITV company. £5,000+ sponsorship 1997; £5,000+ sponsorship 1999; £5,000+ sponsorship 2000

ZURICH FINANCIAL SERVICES (UKISA) LTD: Headed by Sandy Leitch, head of the New Deal taskforce. £5,000+ dinner tickets 1999; £5,000+ sponsorship 1999; £5,000+ dinner tickets 2000

APPENDIX 2 – INDIVIDUAL DONATIONS
TO THE LABOUR PARTY

Figures from Labour Party annual reports, Election Commission returns and the annual survey of political donations compiled by the Labour Research Department (LRD), unless qualifed as 'reported'. These are based on claims made in mainstream national newspapers. Some details of donors' business interests are taken from the Red Star Research website.

ABBS, BRIAN: Author. £1,931.17 donation 2001; £300 donation 2001

ADAMSON, PAUL: Founder of Brussels-based lobbyists Adamson BSMG, now part of Shandwick. Clients included McDonnell Douglas, SmithKline Beecham, Shell, Glaxo Wellcome. £5,000+ donation 1999, reportedly £10,000

AISBITT, JON: Co-chairman of Goldman Sachs Australia. £5,000+ donation 1997; £5,000+ donation 1999

ALLEN, J.J.: £8,150 donation 2001

ALLI, LORD: £15,000 donation to Dobson London mayor bid 2000

ALLIANCE, SIR DAVID: Iranian-born chairman of Coates Viyella textiles. Chairman of N. Brown mail order group. Personal wealth reportedly £250m. £5,000+ dinner tickets 1998

ALTARAS, JONATHAN: Celebrity agent. £1,500 donation to Islington South constituency party 2001

APOSTOLOU, DEMETRIOS: Director of electrical equipment retailers. £5,000+ donation 1999

ARCHER, VERA: £100,000 donation 2001

ARNOLD, STANLEY: £31,000 donation 2001; further £37,128 donation 2001

ASHBY, ROBIN: PR executive. Unknown amount, reported 1997

ASTAIRE, JARVIS: Millionaire boxing promoter and former deputy chairman of Wembley plc. £5,000+ donation 1997

ATTENBOROUGH, LORD: Film-maker. Unknown amount, reported 1997

BANNATYNE, DUNCAN: £5,000+ donation 2000

BARBOUR, MARGARET: £5,000+ donation 2000

BARCLAY, STEPHEN: Chairman of Talisman House plc, holding company for financial services concerns. £5,000+ donation 1997; £5,000+ donation 1998

BARKER, D.: £1,750 donation to Loughborough constituency party 2001

BEDDINGTON, PROFESSOR JOHN: £5,000+ donation 2000

BELL, FIONA: Actress. £7,000 donation 2001; further £3,366 donation 2001

BERNSTEIN, LORD: Former chairman of Granada Television. Peerage 2000. Reportedly donated to Blair blind trust 1996. £5,000+ donation 1997; £5,000+

donation 1999; £5,000 donation 2000

BERRILL, SIR KENNETH: Former chairman of Securities and Investments Board and Robert Horne Group. Member of 1000 Club of high-value donors under Kinnock, has attended £500-a-plate dinners

BHATTACHARYYA, PROFESSOR SUSHANTHA KUMAR: Professor of Manufacturing, University of Warwick. Member of competitiveness working party and West Midlands regional competitiveness working party. £5,000+ donation 1998; £5,000+ donation 1999; £5,000+ donation 2000

BOTTRIELL, BILL: Director of staffing and software company. £2,000 donation to Battersea constituency party 2001; £5,000+ donation 2000

BOURNE, C.: £5,000+ donation 2000

BOURNE, ROBERT: Director of over 50 companies, mostly in property sector. Nominal head of unsuccessful Legacy consortium bid for Dome. Married to donor Sally Greene. Reportedly gave at least £40,000 to Tories under Thatcher. £5,000+ donation 1998; £5,000+ donation 1999; £5,000+ donation 2000. Donations reportedly total £100,000. Has given money to Islington South constituency party

BOYLE, JIMMY & SARAH: £5,000+ donation 1997. Jimmy Boyle – former Glasgow gangster turned sculptor and drugs rehabilitation project worker – also gave £5,000+ donation 1999. Jimmy Boyle alone £5,500 donation 2001

BOYLE, JOHN: Founder of Direct Holidays, sold to Airtours for £81m in 1998, with Boyle pocketing £41m. Chairman of Motherwell FC. £5,000+ donation 1999 (reportedly £20,000)

BRAGG, LORD: Television presenter and former controller of arts at LWT. £5,000+ donation 1997 (reportedly £25,000); peerage 1998; attended £500-a-plate dinner 1999; £5,000+ donation 1999

BROWN, DAVID CBE: Founder of Artix Ltd, heavy dump truck manufacturer. Managing director of Multidrive Ltd. Chairman of Motorola. Chairman of University for Industry advisory group. £5,000+ donation 1997; £5,000+ donation 1999

BROWN, LUCY: £5,000+ donation 1997 (legacy)

BUTTELL, N.: £5,000+ donation 1999 (legacy)

BUTTERFIELD, LESLIE: Chairman of Partners BDDH, one of the top 30 advertising agencies. Clients include Mercedes, *The Guardian*, BT, Sainsbury's. £5,000+ donation 1997; £5,000+ donation 1998; £5,000+ donation 1999

CASSIDY, MICHAEL: Former chairman of the Corporation of London policy committee. Attended £350-a-ticket corporate day at Labour conference 1994

CHARLTON, J.: £5,000+ donation 1999 (legacy)

CHINN, SIR TREVOR: Chairman of Lex Services, Britain's biggest motor dealers. Reportedly donated 'about £5,000' to Blair blind trust 1996. Vice-chairman of Commission for Integrated Transport and also on Cleaner Vehicles taskforce. Lex was subsequently awarded a £500m PFI contract to provide civilian vehicles to the army

CLARKE, BRIAN: Boss of Pandrol UK, manufacturer of rail fastenings used on 220 railways worldwide. £5,000+ donation 1997

CLAYTON-JONES, D.: £2,000 donation to Welsh Labour Party 2001

COATES, PETER: Former chairman Stoke City FC. Owns Labour corporate donor Lindley Catering Investments (see entry) which has contracts at many major football grounds, and Provincial Racing, a chain of betting shops. £5,000+ donation 1997

COHEN, SIR RONALD: Founder and chairman of Apax Partners, a private equity company with interests in PFI schemes. Vice-chairman of EASDAQ, the European stock exchange. Chairman of government Tech Stars taskforce (formally known as the Steering Group on Barriers to Growth of Emerging/Growth Technology firms) and Social Investment taskforce, serves on DTI UK competitiveness committee. £5,000+ donation 1997 (reportedly £100,000); knighthood 2000; £100,000 donation 2001

COLLINSON, LEONARD: Chairman of Newsco Publications. £5,000+ donation 1999; £6,600 donation 2001

COOK, THOMAS: £10,000 donation 2001

COOKE, LIONEL MEMORIAL FUND: Fund chaired by former SDP peer Lord Diamond, which acted as SDP conduit in the 1980s. £5,000+ donation 1998; £5,000+ donation 1999; £5,000+ donation 2000; £20,000 donation 2001

COOPER, T.: £3,822 donation to Doncaster Central constituency party 2001

COSTELLO, J.: £5,000+ donation 1997 (legacy)

CRAWFORD, GORDON: £5,000+ donation 2000

CRICKMER, I.: £5,000+ donation 1999

CUSACK, SINEAD & JEREMY IRONS: Actors. £5,000+ donation 1997

D'ARCY, DOUG: Former managing director of Chrysalis Music. £5,000+ donation 1997

DAVID, URI: See entry for Glenyork Ltd

DAYELL, KATHLEEN: £5,000 donation to Linlithgow constituency party 2001

DEMPSEY, BRIAN: Property developer removed from board of Celtic FC 1990, after trying to get club to move to a ground in which he had an interest. More recently involved in takeover bids for both Celtic and Clydebank FC. £5,000+ donation 1997

DENNIS, FELIX: Former Oz obscenity trial defendant. Founder of Dennis Publishing, publisher of *Maxim*. Personal wealth reportedly £200–250m. £5,000+ donation 1997; £5,000+ donation 1998; £5,000+ donation 1999 (reportedly two donations each of £83,333); £5,000+ donation 2000

DEVEREUX, ROBERT: Brother-in-law of Richard Branson and former boss of Virgin Cinemas. Reported donations of £100,000 in 1997, when Virgin Cinemas was awaiting planning permission on multiplex development in Hampshire. More recently director of the Gleneagles Group and Scottish Mutual Assurance Society. £5,000+ donation listed 1997. £5,000+ donation 1998. Personal wealth reportedly £35m.

DIAMOND, LORD: Former Labour Chief Secretary to the Treasury, defected to SDP where he led the party in the Lords before returning to Labour. Chairman of Lionel Cooke Memorial Fund, which funded the SDP for nine years in the 1980s (see separate entry). Reportedly gave unspecified amount according to leaked document 1999; reportedly pledged £80,000 1999

DICKSON, JIM: £1,500 donation to Old Bexley and Sidcup constituency party 2001

DRAYSON, DR PAUL: Multimillionaire chief executive of PowderJect. Estimated family fortune £100m. Gave £50,000 to election campaign 2001; gave a further £50,000 as company was negotiating a £32m vaccines contract with NHS

DUNCAN, JAMES G.: £5,000+ donation 1999

DYKE, GREG: Director general of the BBC, cutting formal ties with the party on appointment. Former Thames Television and Pearson boss, chairman of Channel 5 and Manchester United director. Quango job as chairman of NHS charter taskforce. Personal wealth £14m. £5,000 donation to Mo Mowlam blind trust 1994; unknown donation to Jack Cunningham 1996; 'substantial five-figure sum' reported 1996; £5,000+ donation 1997 (reportedly 'five-figure sum'); £5,000+ donation 1998

EARL, ROBERT: British-born but Florida-based restaurateur behind Planet Hollywood burger chain. £5,000+ donation 1997 (reportedly £1m to replace funds lost in returning £1m cheque to Bernie Ecclestone)

ECCLESTONE, BERNIE: Formula One racing entrepreneur. £5,000+ donation 1997. This £1m donation was subsequently returned after the controversy over alleged policy concession on tobacco advertising

EGAN, JOHN: Chief executive of privatised airports group BAA. Attended £350-a-ticket corporate day at Labour conference 1994

ELTON, BEN: 1980s alternative comedian, now novelist and playwright collaborator of Andrew Lloyd Webber. £5,000+ donation 1997

EMERY, MARTIN: Sugar trader. £5,000+ donation 1996

ENNIS, HAROLD OBE: Directorships include Northern Ireland packaging manufacturer Boxmore International, pharmaceutical company Galen Holdings and Irish property company Dunloe Ewart. £5,000+ donation 1997; £3,000 donation 2001

EVANS, CHRIS: Owner of Virgin Radio. Fell out with Labour in 2000 over London mayor contest, pledging £200,000 to dissident Ken Livingstone. Has since reportedly pledged £1m to New Labour

EVANS, DR CHRIS: Founder and chairman of Merlin Scientific Services plc. Well-connected in biotechnology circles, sitting on several government taskforces and Lord Sainsbury's research team on biotechnology clusters. Knighthood 2001 New Year Honours list. Personal wealth £100m. £5,000+ donation 1998; £5,000+ donation 1999

EVANS OF WATFORD, LORD: Head of Centurion Press, a printer that undertakes extensive work for Labour and the unions. Blair peerage 1998. Member of 1000 Club, but annual donations under £5,000

EYTON, AUDREY: Author of the F-Plan diet. £5,000+ donation 1998; £5,000+ donation 1999

FALLON, PAUL: £5,000 donation to Rushcliffe constituency party 2001; £1,500 second-hand computer equipment to Rushcliffe constituency party 2001

FAULKNER, LORD: Former managing director of lobbyist Westminster Communications. Blair peerage 1999. £5,000+ donation 1996, reportedly £10,000. 1000 Club member

FERGUSON, ALEX CBE: Manager of Manchester United. £5,000+ donation 1997

FOLLETT, BARBARA: Member of Parliament. £3,000 use of premises to Stevenage constituency party 2001; £4,000 donation to Stevenage constituency party 2001; further £3,000 donation to Stevenage constituency party 2001

FRAENKEL, ERNST: Director of the Institute for Contemporary History. £5,000+ donation 1996

FRANKEL, GERALD: Chairman of British Office Technology Manufacturers' Alliance.

Attended £500-a-plate dinner 1991. Chairman of Labour's Industry Forum

FRAYN, MICHAEL: Author. £5,000+ donation 2000; £10,000 donation 2001

FRIEND, ADRIAN: Interim European director of Trust-e, internet privacy licensing company. Reported £100,000 pledge 1999; £5,000+ donation 2000

GABRIEL, PETER: Genesis progressive rock singer. £5,000+ donation 1997, through his company Peter Gabriel Ltd. Subsequently won 'five-figure' contract to promote Dome

GALLAGHER, TONY: Birmingham-based owner of AC Gallagher Holdings, parent company of Gallagher Developments and J.J. Gallagher. Reported £100,000 pledge 1999. Tony and Rita Gallagher £9,9998.98 donation to Scottish Labour 2001

GAVRON, LORD: Former chairman of printing group St Ives. Former chairman Guardian Media Group. Personal wealth reportedly £50m. Peerage 1999. Expressed admiration for Thatcher, courted by SDP. Reportedly gave £100,000 to Labour under Kinnock, but became unhappy at plans to reverse Tory anti-union laws under Smith. Reportedly donated 'at least £35,000' to Blair blind trust 1996; £5,000+ donation 1996 (reportedly £100,000); £5,000+ donation 1999, reportedly £500,000 in the same month as he became a peer.

GILDA, BRIAN – PEOPLES LTD: Individual and corporate donations not separated in annual report. £5,000+ sponsorship 1997

GILMAN, PETER: Construction businessman. Former director of Leeds FC, who made £5.5m on sale of his interests in the club. Chairman of Thorpe Park (Leeds) Ltd, which owns a major business park outside the Yorkshire city, aimed at the call centre sector. £5,000+ donation 1998

GOLDMAN, CYNTHIA: £5,000+ donation 2000

GOLDMAN, DAVID OBE: Died 1999. Computer software developer, chairman BATM Communications. Attended £500-a-ticket dinner 1996; £5,000+ donation 1997. Gave £1m to the Government's literacy programme for schools, but denied press reports he had pledged £1m to the Labour Party 1999

GOLDSMITH, LORD: Friend of Cabinet Office minister Lord Falconer. Former chairman of the Bar Council, chairman Financial Reporting Review Panel. Peerage 1999. £5,000+ donation 1996, reportedly £6,000

GORDON OF STRATHBLANE, LORD: Head of Scottish Radio Holdings. As journalist, was political editor of STV. Reported donor prior to peerage 1997

GOUDIE, BARONESS: Former public affairs director for the World Wildlife Fund, and before that, organiser of Labour Solidarity, the secretive early 1980s Labour right-wing caucus. Steering committee of the 1000 Club. Reported donor prior to peerage 1998

GOULD, PHILIP: Pollster; advertising director, Labour Shadow Communications Group. £5,000+ donation 1996

GRANTCHESTER, LORD (aka SUENSON-TAYLOR, JOHN): Millionaire dairy farmer. £5,000+ donation 1999

GREEN, MARTIN: £5,000+ donation 1996

GREEN, P.B.: Peter [Brian] Green, secretive Bermuda-based businessman who married Mary-Jean Mitchell, one of the world's richest heiresses. £5,000+ donation 1996; £5,000+ donation 1997

GREENE, SALLY: Theatre impresario and former actress, married to donor Robert Bourne. Managing director Old Vic. £5,000+ donation 1998; £5,000+ donation

1999; £5,000+ donation 2000. Donations reportedly total £100,000

HAMLYN, LORD: Publishing entrepreneur, now deceased. Peerage 1998. Personal wealth variously estimated at £215–325m. £100,000 donation (at least) specifically to develop Labour arts policy 1990; £5,000+ donation 1995; £500,000 donation to finance Road to the Manifesto policy document, listed as £5,000+ 1996; £5,000+ donation 1997; £5,000+ donation 1998; £5,000+ donation 2000, probably the £2m donation revealed in 2001.

HANDOVER, RICHARD: Chief executive WH Smith. Attended £500-a-plate dinner 1998

HARDING, MATTHEW: Head of insurance broker Benfield and vice-chairman of Chelsea FC who died in helicopter crash 1996. £5,000+ donation 1996, reportedly £500,000 and pledge of further £500,000

HARDING, RUTH: £5,000+ donation 1999. Ms Harding is widow of Matthew Harding, and this donation is thought to have been a substantial amount from his estate, probably £500,000 to make good his pledge. Now remarried and known as Ruth Gist, she undertakes charity work with Cherie Blair. £5,000+ donation 2000; £6,000 donation 2001

HARPER, PETER: Director of Hanson, the aggressive 1980s asset strippers. Attended £350-a-ticket corporate day at Labour conference 1994; attended £500-a-ticket dinner 1996

HART, GARRY: Former partner at City law firm Herbert Smith, appointed special adviser to Lord Irvine, prompting a row over cronyism in 1998. Godfather to one of the Blair children. £5,000+ donation 1997

HASKEL, LORD: Labour Finance and Industry Group stalwart and Lords frontbencher. £5,000+ donation 2000. £6,000 donation 2001

HASKINS, LORD: Chairman of Northern Foods, whose subsidiary Convenience Foods Ltd is a repeat pollution offender. Peerage 1998. Multiple quango appointments. Has reportedly given at least £5,000 a year since 1992 and £14,000 in election year 1997. £5,000+ donation 1996; £5,000+ donation 1997; £5,000+ donation 1998; £5,000+ donation 1999; £5,000+ donation 2000; £10,000 donation 2001

HATTER, SIR MAURICE: Chairman of IMO Precision Controls. Personal wealth £50m. Conservatives allege donations to blind trusts. Reportedly pledged £1m to party in 1999. Admitted previous £5,000 to party and £1m to government literacy and numeracy programme for schools. Knighthood later that year. £5,000+ donation 2000

HAUGHEY, WILLIAM: Chief executive of City Refrigeration, Britain's largest specialist refrigeration management company. One of ten Scottish businessmen to write a letter of support for Labour to *Scotland on Sunday* in 1999. £5,000+ donation 1999; £5,000+ sponsorship 1999; £5,000+ donation 2000

HAWTIN, DR U.G.: £5,000+ donation 1998 (legacy); £5,000+ donation 1999 (legacy)

HODGE, MARGARET: Member of Parliament. £1,032 donation 2001

HOLLAND, IAN: £5,000+ donation 1996

HOLLICK, LORD: Erstwhile money broker, now head of United News & Media. Strong Labour business backer since Kinnock era. £5,000+ donation 1997 (reportedly 'between £25,000 and £50,000')

HOLLINGSWORTH, CORMAC: £2,000 donation to Battersea constituency party 2001

HOWARD-SPINK, GEOFF: Advertising agent. £5,000+ donation 1997

HUCKNALL, MICK: Lead singer of Simply Red. Personal wealth £40m. £5,000+ donation 1997 (reportedly £50,000); £5,000+ donation 1999 (reportedly £25,000); £5,000+ donation 2000

HULME, JANET: Wife of founder of Computer Centre. £5,000+ donation 1997

HUNT, RICHARD: £2,000 donation to Colne Valley constituency party 2001

HUNTER, TOM: Scottish businessman who made £252m from sale of Sports Division in 1998. £5,000+ donation 2000; £100,000 donation 2001

HURLSTON, MALCOLM: £5,000+ dinner tickets 1998

HYAMS, NORMAN: Property developer. £5,000+ donation 1997

IRONS, JEREMY: Oscar-winning actor. £5,000+ donation 1996. See also entry for Cusack, Sinead & Jeremy Irons. Subsequently won 'five-figure' contract to promote Dome through New Millennium Experience Company

IZZARD, EDDIE: Comedian. £5,000+ donation 1997; £10,000 donation 2001

JARVIS, BRUCE: £5,000+ donation 1998; £5,000+ donation 2000

JARVIS, GORDON R.: Chairman of the Laban Centre for Music and Dance. £5,000+ donation 1997

JEFFREY, GERALDINE & PHILIP: Founders of the Fads DIY chain. £5,000+ donation 1996, reportedly £300,000 for the rapid rebuttal computer system; Geraldine Jeffrey £10,000 donation 2001; £2,000 donation to Hammersmith & Fulham constituency party 2001

JOFFE, LORD: Former deputy chairman of Allied Dunbar. Served on the Royal Commission on long-term care for the elderly. £5,000+ donation 1997; peerage 1999; £5,000+ donation 2000; £10,000 donation 2001

JOHNSON, DEREK: Chairman of Johnson Stevens Agencies shipping agents. Admitted pledging £100,000 donation 1999 but said he had 'yet to cough up'. £5,000+ donation 2000

JONES, GRAHAM: £5,050 donation 2001

KAYE, SIR EMMANUEL: Made fortune with industrial truck company. Former Tory donor. Reportedly donated to Blair blind trust 1996; also reportedly donated £50,000 to Brown's blind trust. Died 1999

KAYE, ISAAC: Deputy chief executive of Ivax Corporation, Florida-based health company. Reportedly past assistance to South Africa's pro-apartheid National Party. £5,000+ donation 1997; £5,000+ dinner tickets 1998; £5,000+ donation 1999, reportedly £100,000; £10,000 donation to Frank Dobson mayor of London campaign 2000; £5,000+ donation 2000

KERR, J.: £5,000+ donation 1997

KYTE, DAVID: Chairman of Kyte Group, largest independent clearer on the London International Financial Futures Exchange. £5,000+ donation 1998

LAWSON, J.: £5,000+ donation 1998

LAWSON, NEAL: Lobbyist with Lowe Bell, later founded cash for access scandal firm LLM. Attended £500-a-plate dinner 1996

LEACH, CLIVE CBE: Chairman of Yorkshire Enterprise Ltd and Leeds Health Authority. £5,000+ donation 1998; £5,000+ donation 1999

LEVY, LORD: Music business entrepreneur and now special envoy to the Middle East. Key Labour fundraiser, reported to have gathered donations of more than £7m prior to 1997 election, although never listed as a donor himself

LOWE, FRANK: Founder and chairman of Lowe Group advertising agencies. £5,000+ donation 1997; £5,000+ donation 1998; £5,000+ donation 1999; £5,000+ donation 2000

MACKENZIE, CHRISTOPHER: Head of European operations for Clayton Dubilier & Rice, a large American investment firm (see entry under corporate donors). £5,000+ sponsorship 1997; £5,000+ dinner tickets 1998; £5,000+ donation 1999; £5,000+ donation 2000

MACKINTOSH, SIR CAMERON: Theatrical producer owning four West End theatres and running three more. Personal wealth reportedly £400m. £5,000+ donation 1997

MALINIAK, G.: £5,000+ donation 1998

MARKS, ALEXANDRA: Partner at law firm Linklaters, with major PFI interests. £1,300 donation to Islington South constituency party 2001

MAXTON, JOHN: £1,025 donation to Cathcart constituency party 2001

McGEE, ALAN: Founder of Creation Records. Attended £500-a-plate dinner 1999; £5,000+ donation 1999. Personal wealth reportedly £25m

McINESPIE, JOHN: Lawyer. £5,000+ dinner tickets 1998; £5,000+ dinner tickets 1999; £5,000+ dinner tickets 2000; £6,634 donation 2001

McISAAC, SHONA: Member of Parliament. £1,003.62 donation 2001

MILLETT, ALAN: Reported £2,500 donation 1999

MILLWARD, MAURICE: Former chairman of Millward Brown. £5,000+ donation 1997; £1,500 donation to Warwick & Leamington Spa constituency party 2001

MITCHELL, LORD: Chairman of Syscap plc. £5,000+ donation 2000; £25,000 donation 2001

MITTAL, LAKSHMI: Indian-born UK-based steel maganate, whose company Ispat International is a corporate donor. £125,000 donation 2001

MITTAL, USHA: Wife of Ispat International's Lakshmi Mittal. Reported £5,000 donation to Keith Vaz's election expenses 1997

MOGFORD, MR & MRS JEREMY: Jeremy Mogford founded Brown's restaurant chain, which he sold to Bass for £35m in 1998. £5,000+ donation 1997. Gave £100,000 according to leaked document 1999

MONTAGUE, MICHAEL: Chairman of Montague Multinational, tourist and hotel group. £5,000+ donation 1996

MORGAN, JOAN: £5,000+ donation 1996; £4,000 donation in two instalments 2001; £300 donation 2001

MORGAN, PETER: £5,000+ donation 1997 (legacy)

MURDOCH, ELISABETH: Daughter of media baron Rupert Murdoch and former BSkyB executive. Attended £500-a-ticket dinner 1998

MURRAY, ROBERT: Chairman of Sunderland FC and non-executive director of engineering group Chairman Sterling Capital, Sovereign Capital Corporation and Omega International. Personal wealth reportedly £30m. £5,000+ donation 1998; £5,000+ donation 1999

NOON, GULAM: Head of Indian food manufacturer involved in trade union recognition dispute at his west London factory in the late nineties. Thought to have donated to all major parties. Personal wealth variously estimated £10–40m. £5,000+ donation 1999 (reportedly £100,000); £100,000 donation in two instalments 2001. Knighthood 2002

NORTON, JON: Merchant banker and partner of Mo Mowlam. Attended £500-a-plate dinner in early 1990s

O'FARRELL, JOHN: Author. £2,000 donation to Maidenhead constituency party 2001

ONDAATJE, CHRISTOPHER: Made fortune by establishing investment companies in Canada. £2m donation revealed 2001; additional £100,000 donation 2001; £1,200 donation to Islington South constituency party 2001; £1,500 donation 2001; £1,000 donation 2001

ONDAATJE, PHILIP: £5,000+ donation 2000

PATEL, A.: £1,500 donation to Batley & Spen constituency party 2001

PATEL, DR CHAI: Chief executive of private healthcare group Westminster Healthcare. £5,000+ donation 1999

PAUL, LORD: Chairman of steel group Caparo, a corporate donor. Sits on competitiveness working party and West Midlands' regional competitive working party. £5,000+ donation 1996. Attended £500-a-ticket dinner 1996, the year of his peerage; £10,000 donation 2001

PEEL, CHARLES: Old Etonian descendent of police force founder, a self-professed 'capitalist' backing Blair because of Labour's support for small businesses, in which his stockbroking business Peel Hunt specialises. Made £45m when Peel Hunt was sold to a Belgian bank in 2000. 'I'm not a socialist for the last 40 years or anything like that,' he explained. 'I've had a bit of luck. I've got to give some credit to the government at the time.' Reported £50,000 donation 2001

PERRY, STEPHEN: Managing director of SLP Investments and London Export Ltd, both corporate donors (see entries). Reported £25,000 donation 1999

PHILIPS, PETER: £5,000+ sponsorship 1997; £5,000+ sponsorship 1998

PHILLIPPS, G.: £5,000+ donation 1997

POOLE, G.: £5,000+ donation 1997 (legacy)

POTTER, DR DAVID: Chairman of hand-held computer company Psion. £90,000 donation 2001

PRENTICE, GORDON: Member of Parliament. £1,227 donation to Pendle constituency party 2001

PURI, NATHU RAM: Owner of engineering, packaging, textiles and plastics companies, leading supplier of cigarette paper. Puri's company Melton Medes is one of Britain's 100 largest private companies. Personal wealth £90m. £5,000+ donation 1997. Largest single donor to Kenneth Clarke's Tory leadership campaign, giving £25,000 donation in 2001

PURVIS, A.: £5,000+ donation 1997 (legacy)

PUTTNAM, LORD CBE: Film director and former SDP backer. Quango jobs as head of National Endowment for Science, Technology and the Arts, Creative Industries taskforce and School Standards taskforce. Chair of General Teaching Council, despite zero educational experience. £5,000+ donation 1996 (reportedly £25,000); £5,000+ donation 1997. 1000 Club member

RAMZAN, MOHAMED: £2,000 donation to Glasgow Govan constituency party 2001

REAY, MS P.: £5,000+ donation 1999 (legacy)

REED, PROFESSOR ALEC CBE: Chairman of Reed Executive, a holding company that owns Reed Employment, one of Britain's biggest recruitment agencies. Family fortune estimated at £50m. £5,000+ donation 1996 (reportedly £100,000); £5,000+ donation 1997; £5,000+ donation 1998; £5,000+ donation 1999; £10,000 donation 2001

REED, HANNAH: £1,080 donation 2001

REID, JOHN: Former manager of pop pianist Elton John, making $245m in process. £5,000+ donation 1998; £5,000+ donation 2000

RENDELL, BARONESS: Crime novelist. Peerage after election 1997. £5,000+ donation 1997 (reportedly 'about £10,000'); £5,000+ donation 1998; £5,000+ donation 2000

REYNOLDS, JOHN: Co-head of European utilities at Credit Suisse First Boston. £4,000 donation to Brent North constituency party 2001

RICHMOND, A.: £5,000+ donation 1998 (legacy)

ROBINSON, GEOFFREY: Member of Parliament, former Paymaster General until falling victim to the Mandelson loan affair. £5,000+ donation 1996; £5,000+ sponsorship 1997. Reports that he gave the Blair blind trust £250,000 were denied by the party; £200,000 to Brown funding vehicle 1996

ROBINSON, GERRY: Chairman of Granada Group, which has interests in television, catering, hotels (see entry for Granada Television). Appeared in Labour election broadcast 1997. Quango job as head of Arts Council. Salary exceeded £1m in 1999, when he pocketed £5.3m in share options. £5,000+ donation 1997; £5,000+ 1998; £5,000+ donation 1999; £5,000+ donation 2000; £20,000 donation 2001

ROBINSON, S.: £2,167 to Central Suffolk & North Ipswich constituency party 2001

ROSE, JOHN: Chief executive Rolls-Royce. Attended £500-a-plate dinner 1998

ROWBOTTOM, DR J.: £5,000+ donation 1999 (legacy)

SAINSBURY, LORD: Labour's largest single backer, with known donations now exceeding £9m. Chairman of supermarket chain Sainsbury. Peerage 1997, Science minister 1998. Reportedly gave £5,000 to fund Blair's bid for party leadership in 1994. £2m donation 1996; £1m donation 1997; £2m donation 1999; £2m donation January 2001; £2m donation December 2001

SCOTT, J.: £5,000+ donation 1999

SCRIVENER, ANTHONY QC: Leading barrister. £5,000+ donation 1997

SHALSON, PETER: £5,000+ donation 2000

SHEPHERD, BARRY: Managing director of Shepherd Offshore. Attended £500-a-ticket dinner 1996

SHERIDAN, JANE: £5,000+ donation 1996

SHERIDAN, JENNY: £5,000+ donation 1999

SHOTTON, MARION: £5,000+ donation 1997 (legacy)

SILVER, LESLIE: Founder of Yorkshire paint manufacturer Kalon and former chairman of Leeds United FC. £5,000+ donation 1996 (reportedly £25,000)

SKELLY, IAN: Founder of car dealers Ian Skelly Group. £5,000+ donation 1999

SMITH, ANDREW: £1,000 donation 2001, ruled impermissible

SNAPE, K.: £5,000+ donation 1997 (legacy)

SNOWIE, EUAN: Director of 22 companies. Main interest is the Snowie Group, a Scottish haulier that earned £27m disposing of animal carcasses during the foot-and-mouth crisis. £5,000 donation to Scottish Labour 2001

SOPHOCLIDES, HARIS: Owner J&P Ltd, one of the largest property and construction firms in the Middle East, building hotels, airports, hospitals and military bases worldwide. President of Greek Cypriot Brotherhood (see entry under corporate donors). £5,000+ dinner tickets 1999

STANSFIELD, LISA: Pop singer. £5,000+ donation 1997

STERNBERG, MICHAEL: £5,000+ donation 2000

STERNBERG, SIR SIGMUND: Property developer and Lloyd's underwriter, chairman of Martin Slowe Estates. £5,000+ donation 1996; £5,000+ donation 1997; £5,000+ dinner tickets 1998; £5,000+ donation 2000; £100,000 donation 2001

STEVENS, DOUGLAS: £2,800 in 'services purchased' for Woodspring constituency party 2001

STONE, CAROLE: Former television journalist and prominent London socialite. £5,000+ dinner tickets 1999. Appointed trustee of the Wallace Collection after donation

STRINGER, HOWARD: Chief executive Sony America. £5,000+ donation 1997

SUGAR, ALAN: Founder and chairman of Amstrad, the consumer electronics major. Executive chairman of computer company Learning Technology, formerly Viglen. Chairman of Tottenham Hotspur FC. Self-professed 'tremendous supporter of Margaret Thatcher', he publicly backed John Major in 1992. Personal wealth reportedly £585m. £5,000+ donation 1997; £200,000 donation in election campaign 2001

SUKHBINDER, S.W. SANDHA: £10,000 donation in two instalments 2001

SULIAMAN, T.: £2,300 donation to Huntingdon constituency party 2001

SULLMAN, RUSSELL: East London dentist. £1,500 donation to East Ham constituency party 2001

SWIFT, DAVID: £5,000+ donation 1996

TABATZNIK, TONY: Chairman of Generics (UK), a pharmaceutical firm. Family fortune £260m. £5,000+ donation 1997 (reportedly £25,000)

TAN, SALLY: £10,000 donation 2001

TAVENER, CHRIS: Partner at City law firm Herbert Smith (see entry for Hart, Garry). £5,000+ donation 1997

TAYLOR, LORD: £2,000 to Blackburn constituency party, Jack Straw's constituency 2001

TAYLOR, MRS I.: £5,000+ donation 1999 (legacy)

TENNANT, NEIL: Lead singer of the Pet Shop Boys. £5,000+ donation 1997; £5,000+ donation 1998; £5,000+ donation 1999; £5,000+ donation 2000

THOMAS, LORD: Chairman of Co-op Bank. Donations under £5,000

THOMPSON, PETER: Hong Kong-based chairman of the Hong Kong Port and Maritime Board. £5,000+ donation 1997; £5,000+ donation 1998; £5,000+ donation 1999; £5,000+ donation 2000; £20,000 donation 2001

THOMSON, MATT – THOMSON LITHO: Matt Thomson is chairman of the company, Scotland's largest private printing firm. Individual and corporate donations not separated. £5,000+ donation 1997; £5,000+ sponsorship 1997

TIMMS, STEPHEN: Member of Parliament. £4,000 donation to East Ham constituency party 2001

TINSLEY, HENRY: Tinsley Foods Ltd. £5,000+ donation 1999; £5,000+ donation 2000

TOULMIN, DR GEORGE: £5,000+ donation 1996; £5,000+ donation 1998

TOWNSEND, DOROTHY: £14,451 donation 2001

TOWNSEND, GERTRUDE: £14,333.34 donation 2001

TOWNSEND, PETE: Guitarist with The Who. £5,000+ donation 1997

TOWNSLEY, BARRY: Head of private stockbroking firm, sold to Insinger de Beaufort for £10m in 1999. £5,000+ donation 1998; £5,000+ donation 2000

TREVES, VANNI: Chairman of Equitable Life and Channel 4. £1,600 donation to

Islington South constituency party 2001

VARMA, MONI: Veetee Rice. £5,000+ donation 1999; £10,000 donation 2001

WANN, ROBERT: Former Leicester councillor and chairman of Leicester police authority. £5,000+ donation 1999; £5,000 donation to Leicester West constituency party, Patricia Hewitt's constituency 2001

WATERSTONE, TIM: Founder of eponymous bookstore chain, chairman of HMV record store group. £5,000+ donation 1997; attended £500-a-plate dinner 1999. £12,000 donation 2001

WATT, MICHAEL: Head of Octagon CSI Broadcasting, which produces and distributes sports television, especially satellite racing coverage to bookmakers. A New Zealander. Personal wealth reportedly £35m. £5,000+ donation 1997; £5,000+ donation 1998

WEBB, MARTIN: £1,500 donation to Brighton Kemptown constituency party 2001

WESTWATER, STUART: £5,000+ donation 1996

WHITE, PHYLLIS: £5,000+ donation 1997 (legacy)

WHITTAKER, HAROLD: £3,000 donation to Bury South constituency party 2001

WICKREMERATNE, SUNIL: £6,000 donation 2001

WILLIAMS, DR ALAN: £2,017 donation 2001

WILLIAMS, KINGSLEY: £5,000+ donation 1997

WILLIAMS, RICHARD: Managing director of corporate donor Richalis. £8,000 donation 2001

WILSON, RICHARD: Actor who played Victor Meldrew in *One Foot in the Grave*. £5,000+ donation 1997. £5,000 donation to Hampstead and Highgate constituency party 2001

WOODGATE, CHRIS: Hi-tech entrepreneur. £5,000+ donation 1998

WOODWORD, MRS C.D.: £10,000 donation to Association of Labour Councillors 2001

WRIGHT, CHRIS: Chairman of Chrysalis records and books and Queens Park Rangers FC. Personal wealth £155m. Reported £100,000 pledge 1999

WRIGHT, GILES: £5,000+ donation 1997; £5,000+ donation 2000; £2,000 donation to Holborn and St Pancras constituency party, Frank Dobson's constituency 2001

YALLOP, DAVID: Millionaire author and journalist. £2,000 donation to Sittingbourne and Sheppey constituency party 2001

GLOSSARY

AEEU: Amalgamated Engineering and Electrical Union, now part of Amicus
BBC: British Broadcasting Corporation
CBI: Confederation of British Industry
CCTV: closed circuit television
DETR: Department of the Environment, Transport and the Regions
DTI: Department of Trade and Industry
EADS: European Aeronautic Defence and Space Company, arms manufacturer
ECGD: Export Credits Guarantee Department
EEC: European Economic Community, forerunner to the European Union
ERM: Exchange Rate Mechanism
EU: European Union
FC: Football Club
FIA: Fédération Internationale de l'Automobile, governing body of Formula One racing
GMB: General, Municipal, Boilermakers trade union
GP: general practitioner
GPC: Canadian-owned international lobbying company with UK subsidiary
HBOS: bank created on merger of Halifax and Bank of Scotland
HSE: Health and Safety Executive
IoD: Institute of Directors
IT: information technology
ITN: Independent Television News
JCB: J.C. Bamford, manufacturer of excavating machines
LEFTA: Labour Economics, Finance and Taxation Association, now part of the Labour Finance and Industry Group
LFIG: Labour Finance and Industry Group
MoD: Ministry of Defence
NATO: North Atlantic Treaty Organisation
NATS: National Air Traffic Services
NLGN: New Local Government Network
NOP: National Opinion Poll, leading pollsters
PFI: Private Finance Initiative
PIN: Personal Identification Number
PPP: Public-Private Partnership

246

RCA: Radio Corporation of America, US broadcaster

SDP: Social Democratic Party

SLEC: Bernie Ecclestone's holding company, derived from the name of his wife, Slavica Ecclestone

TfL: Transport for London, executive arm of the Greater London Authority with responsibility for public transport in the capital

TGWU: Transport and General Workers' Union

UCATT: Union of Construction, Allied Trades and Technicians

UEFA: Union of European Football Associations

INDEX